December 2007

To Andrea and Rich,

Who carry on the
tradition of your parents in
giving greatly to others
and who are the California
branch of a family that means
so much to Martha and
me.

Mark

The Headmaster's Run

Mark H. Mullin

ROWMAN & LITTLEFIELD EDUCATION
Lanham • New York • Toronto • Plymouth, UK

Published in the United States of America
by Rowman & Littlefield Education
A Division of Rowman & Littlefield Publishers, Inc.
A wholly owned subsidiary of The Rowman & Littlefield Publishing Group, Inc.
4501 Forbes Boulevard, Suite 200, Lanham, Maryland 20706
www.rowmaneducation.com

Estover Road
Plymouth PL6 7PY
United Kingdom

British Library Cataloguing in Publication Information Available

Library of Congress Cataloging-in-Publication Data

Mullin, Mark H., 1940–
  The headmaster's run / Mark H. Mullin.
    p. cm.
  ISBN-13: 978-1-57886-654-0 (hardback : alk. paper)
  ISBN-10: 1-57886-654-5 (hardback : alk. paper)
  1. Mullin, Mark H., 1940– 2. School principals—United States—Biography. I. Title.
  LA2317.M845A3 2008
  371.2'012092—dc22
  [B]   2007018755

♾™ The paper used in this publication meets the minimum requirements of
American National Standard for Information Sciences—Permanence of
Paper for Printed Library Materials, ANSI/NISO Z39.48-1992.
Manufactured in the United States of America.

For Martha
and our children,
Cara, Sean, and Kevin

Contents

The Runner

THE WEST DOORS

The great pulpit of the Washington National Cathedral is magnificent and imposing. It is made of stone and covered with intricate and beautiful carvings. The central carving shows a major victory for freedom against despotic authority, the signing of the Magna Carta. The pulpit places the preacher high above the congregation.

From the great pulpit, a preacher can look westward down the nave to the high rose window that is more than a football field away. When the afternoon sun hits that enormous window, it begins to glow like a beautiful kaleidoscope. Between the pulpit and the rose window, graceful stone pillars reach toward the ceiling that is one and a half times higher than that of Westminster Abbey. The flag of every state in the Union hangs high above the nave. In one of the stained glass windows on the south side of the nave, there is a small piece of the moon. It was presented to the Cathedral by Michael Collins, St. Albans Class of 1948, who was orbiting the moon in Apollo 11 when man first walked upon it. The delicately carved wood of the rood screen forms a backdrop to the preacher. At the east end of the Cathedral, the high altar and the reredos, with its twenty-four statues of saints, are visible. But the eye is drawn to the larger-than-life statue of Christ in Majesty.

When they stand in that pulpit, preachers are humbled, knowing they stand where great preachers have stood before them. Billy Graham and Desmond Tutu have both preached here. Martin Luther King Jr. preached from this pulpit on the Sunday before he was murdered in Memphis.

On the afternoon of June 7, 1997, I climbed the steps into the great pulpit of Washington National Cathedral. I stood for a moment looking out. Behind me sat the Governing Board of St. Albans School. With them were members of the Class of 1947, returned for their fiftieth reunion. Directly in front and below me sat the men and women of the faculty. They were a talented and dedicated group. Many were close friends of mine. We had rejoiced together at the accomplishments of students and worried together about those with problems. We had laughed at the unique things that happen in a school. We had worked together to try to make St. Albans as great as possible. I was proud to be their headmaster.

I was also a priest. In front of me sat a teacher whose wedding I had performed, another whose brother I had buried, another whose daughter I had baptized. We had all mourned together on six separate occasions at the deaths of current colleagues. These were people with whom I had shared so many joys and so many sorrows for twenty years.

Opposite the faculty, and to my right, sat the members of the St. Albans Class of 1997. In their blue blazers and white trousers they were an attractive group of young men. They were a special class for me. While none of them had been born when I became headmaster of St. Albans, I had known many of them since they entered St. Albans when they were nine years old. In that first year they had gathered in this same place for the funeral of a classmate, Adrien Lescaze. He died as a passenger in an automobile accident. One member of the graduating class was my son Kevin.

Directly in front of me, in the first row of the congregation, Martha, my wife, sat looking up at me. She was usually not anxious before I spoke in public. But this time she was. On either side of her sat our two older children, Cara and Sean. Years before, they had each received their secondary school diplomas in this Cathedral.

It was the usual practice at St. Albans to have a parent speak at commencement. With Kevin, our youngest child, graduating, I was pleased to be the speaker. I had been proud when my own father had spoken at my high school graduation thirty-nine years earlier.

I knew that St. Albans had had many famous commencement speakers. Among the parents who had spoken during my time as headmaster were the Reverend Jesse Jackson, J. Willard Marriott, Vice-President Walter Mondale, Roger Mudd, and Senator John D. Rockefeller. Even though these men were much more prominent than I am, I knew that there would be particular interest in my speech this year. During the spring, St. Albans had experienced much controversy and pain because some members of the Governing Board wanted me to step down as headmaster. Many people connected with the school wanted me to stay. Everyone wondered what I would say on this most public of occasions. Many wondered if I would refer to the controversy.

I spoke only of the accomplishments of the Class of 1997, what sort of young men they were now, and what sort of adults they would be in the future. Speaking as both a faculty member and a parent, my message was, "You have become what we wanted you to become." I ended the speech by saying, "You know me well enough to know that you would not leave here without an old Irish blessing."

> May the blessings of light be with you,
> Light inside and light outside.
> May the sunlight shine upon you
> Till it makes your heart glow like a great peat fire
> And the stranger may come and warm himself beside it.
>
> May the blessings of the rain,
> The sweet soft rain, be with you,
> So that the little flowers spring up beside your path
> And shed their fragrance in the air.
>
> May the blessings of the earth,
> The good rich earth be with you.
> May the earth be soft beneath you,
> When you lie upon it
> Tired at the end of the day.
> And at the last,
> May the earth rest easy over you,
> So that your soul may be out from under it quickly,
> And up, and off, and on its way to God.

When it came time for the presentation of diplomas, I was touched by the large number of new graduates who hugged me as soon as they had their diplomas.

At a St. Albans commencement, the new graduates lead the recession to the rear of the Cathedral. They have been seated alphabetically, so they leave in that order. Then the faculty, fifty-year alumni, and the Governing Board walk out. The bishop and the headmaster are the last to leave. There is also an unofficial tradition that when the new graduates get halfway down the long nave aisle, they give a shout, break ranks, and run the rest of the way.

On Commencement Day, 1997, something happened that had not happened before. I was certainly not prepared for it. As the recession began, the first two graduates came to where I was standing. They took me by either arm and led me to the front of the recessional line. We started to walk. I caught Martha's eyes in the front row. When we were halfway down the nave, the new graduates shouted and began to run. I was in clerical vestments but thought to myself, "Go with your students." I began to run. I ran with my students down the aisle and out the west doors of the Cathedral.

CRIMSON AND BLUE

When I ran out of the Washington National Cathedral it was not the first time I had a highly emotional experience while running. For nine years as a young man I ran the mile in competition. It was always emotional.

Walk to the starting line. Turn around and face back up the track. Take a dozen or so fast strides to get the heart beating rapidly one more time and to be sure the leg muscles are warm. Listen to the pleasant crunch your spikes make as they pierce the tightly packed cinders. Enjoy the sensation of having your body respond exactly as you want it to. Ease off the pace. Turn around and walk slowly halfway back to the starting line. Jog slowly in place as you wait for the starter to call you to the line. Experience the variety of emotions that surge through a runner's being just before a race.

You are nervous. You have to be nervous before this race today. The competition is good. The runner in blue has beaten you indoors. You have never run against him outdoors. He's the one to beat. However, two other guys are almost as good as you are. Any one of these three could make things really rough for you today. For sure, they all want to beat you. You would not be so nervous if someone in the race were clearly better than you. Then you could go for the upset but not feel bad if you lost. If everyone in the race were at a lower level, you would have to worry about being upset yourself. However, you would know that if you ran well, you would probably win. But today you have to worry about three guys, any one of whom could win. And that makes you nervous. And maybe there is someone else that you don't know about among the twenty runners. Maybe he'll come out of nowhere and surprise everyone.

You can be confident. You've trained extremely hard for this. All summer you went for long runs on lonely country roads near your home in western Illinois to build endurance. During the fall, you ran cross-country. You raced up and down hills over five-mile courses. That had to strengthen you. In the winter you tore around those short eleven-laps-to-the-mile tracks with the banked curves. Now you are on a big four-laps-to-the-mile track and can really stretch out. For a week of spring vacation you had three workouts a day. Early morning was for stretching and resistance work in waist-deep water. In the late mornings, you raced your teammates over a ten-mile dirt road. As soon as you finished that long run, you did wind sprints. In the afternoon, when you were already exhausted, it was time for speed work on the track. Then came the spring track season. Sundays and Fridays were days of rest. Mondays through Thursdays the work began with vigorous calisthenics. Your coach called them the Filthy Four. Your stomach looks like a washboard: taut, rippled, and hard. Your arms are thin but tough. Your legs are ready for any command. After calisthenics came running. Mondays you ran eight miles along the Charles River, from Harvard Stadium to the Boston Pops band shell and back. These were not the pleasant runs of last summer. These were hard work, pushing yourself to improve the pace. When you got back to the track, you had to run ten 100-yard wind sprints. Tuesdays were the worst days. Run a quarter-mile at race pace. Jog for 110 yards. Run another quarter-mile at pace. Jog 110 yards. Keep that up until you have done twelve of them (three miles at one-mile pace). The last two or three hurt so much you did not know if you could finish. Wednesdays there would be three half-miles at faster than race pace. Thursday you would run 660 yards (a lap and a half) as fast as you could, then more wind sprints. If there was a meet on Saturday you took Friday off. Saturday was the day for meets. You would run a mile against competition and be totally exhausted. An hour and a half later you would be back on the track to race again. This time it would be a two-mile race. This much work produced changes in your body. You are very thin. Your pulse is only 61 percent of that of a normal person. That means that your circulatory system is amazingly efficient. When you are really exhausted you still get so much more blood and oxygen moved around your body. That much work also produces a toughened mental state in you. You have pushed yourself so hard; you have felt such exhaustion that you are ready to do it again in this race. You feel confident even in your nervousness.

You feel gratitude. You are grateful that you are a good enough runner to be representing Harvard in the Ivy League Championship meet being held at the University of Pennsylvania's Franklin Field. As a college junior in 1961 you do not realize that, years from now, whenever you go from Washington to New York on the train you will look out the west window of the train, see the Franklin Field Stadium, and remember what happened here this day. You are grateful that your event is the mile run. It is an event that has always attracted attention. Spectators appreciate it. It is long enough that positioning and strategy matter tremendously. The lead may change several times in one race. Yet it is short enough to hold a spectator's interest. You feel that the mile has a purity and symmetry about it that other events lack. In a mile, competitors run four laps around the track, starting and finishing at the same spot on the track. The Olympic equivalent, the 1,500 meters, never starts and finishes in the same place. If you can run each of these four laps in a hair under sixty seconds, you will have joined an elite club that had no members just eight years before.

You feel the emotion of fear—fear of the pain that will come. Pain you have felt before so you know how awful it is: the pain of legs pleading to stop, yet being urged to run faster; the pain of muscles in the arms and stomach aching in protest; and, worst of all, the pain in the lungs, almost like drowning because you cannot pull in enough oxygen. Unlike most other pain, this pain is self-inflicted and can be stopped any time you are willing to step off the track or even slow the pace. Therefore, the fear is not like other fears. It is not the fear of the unknown. You know what the pain will be like. There is the fear of pain. There is the fear of not being able to self-inflict enough pain. And there is the fear of stopping the pain before the finish line.

Finally, there is the emotion of expectation. The pain is not endured for its own sake. It is endured because it is necessary if you are to run a fast mile. In the same way cold and exhaustion are necessary to climb a high mountain. The expectation, the hope, that today you may do something really well, better than you have ever done it before, is one of the emotions that swirl though a runner before an important race. There is the knowledge of the satisfaction that can come when you run the good race.

Even though all these emotions are competing for mastery of your spirit, your mind tries to ignore them. You are focusing totally on the race, preparing yourself to make a maximum effort. You are unaware of the people in the stands and the athletes on the infield. Even though you are surrounded by hundreds of people, you are alone. While you focus on the effort ahead, you repeat, almost as a mantra, the words of the team trainer, James Fair, "Relax, fella, relax."

The starter calls you to the line. You turn to the runner next to you and shake hands, saying, "Good luck."

"On your marks." You put your right foot one inch behind the line. Your left foot is eighteen inches behind it.

"Get set." You crouch slightly, staring down the track.

The starter's pistol fires. You move forward with short steps. Excitement surges through you as your pent-up emotions are expressed in physical activity. Your bare arm bumps the bare arm of the runner next to you, but not hard enough to throw either of you off stride. Fifteen yards into the race, you see an opening to your left. A quick acceleration allows you to slip into second place next to the curb. You slow your pace to avoid hitting the heels of the front-runner, then stretch out to a comfortable stride. A runner comes up beside you on the outside. You are boxed in, but it is too early in the race to matter. You think to yourself that you must never be in this position at the end of a race. The pace is good. You are moving right along, but for the moment all feels comfortable. As you go into the first curve, the runner on your right drops back, trying to avoid the extra yardage of running in the second lane.

Heading down the backstretch for the first time the white shirt in front of you is moving well. You think the pace is good. You have run so many quarter-miles in practice that your body knows the difference between running a lap in sixty seconds and running it in sixty-two seconds. That is only a 3 percent change in pace, but you can tell the difference. However, knowing pace in practice is different than knowing it in a race. The excitement of a race tends to make you go faster. And it is harder to judge pace when you are running behind a runner whom you have not followed before. But the pace feels right, and you are in good position. So you stay there and stride along. This is an enjoyable part of the race. You have run so many interval laps in practice at this pace that doing the first one of the race is not a strain. You do not have to push the pace; you just follow the white shirt in front of you. What a wonderful feeling to have control over your body so that it moves over the track exactly as you want it to. Of course, what a ballet dancer does is more graceful and has the beauty of music. You think to yourself, however, that the feeling of having command of your body must be much the same.

Around the second turn you go; then you are down the homestretch past the starting line. An official holds up the number "3" and yells, "Three laps to go."

Someone else is reading times from a stopwatch. "Sixty, sixty-one, sixty-two." The pace is where you want it. You have judged correctly. You are running twenty-two feet every second. That is five times faster than the average person walks. Around the next curve and down the backstretch a second time you feel good. You are running at a good speed but are not tired. You know that you are building up an oxygen debt and that lactic acid is accumulating in your muscles. But you also know that you have reserves of strength, and you will be able to accelerate when the time comes. But will you be able to accelerate as much as your opponents will? That is the question that will be answered in the next two and a half minutes. You know the blue shirt runner is strong. And there may be somebody else waiting to steal this race.

Going into the second turn of the second lap, you are almost joyful. You have the pleasure a child feels from running. The sense of motion and the sense of freedom from the usual constraints of location and gravity are unreal. You feel almost like you are floating over the track. Yet you know that the feeling will not last long and the push of tremendous effort is about to come.

As you run down the homestretch for a second time, you hear shouting and cheering. You are not aware of any particular individual because you are concentrating on staying attached to the man in front of you. You do not even hear the official yell, "Two laps to go." Yet, you do hear the timekeeper reading off the time. The pace is okay. Then you notice a slight hunching of the shoulders above the white shirt in front of you. It is too small a motion to be visible from the stands, but you see it. Two seconds later the front-runner readjusts his stride. Now you know for sure. He is tiring, having to push his body harder to maintain the pace. You know that you will soon have to pass him. Or should you let someone else pass you both so another runner will set the pace on the third lap? No! Before that happens the pace will have slowed. You don't want that. If you slow, it will be harder to get going again. And if you slow, those behind you will get closer to you. You must pass him soon. There isn't much time to pass before the curve. But if you wait until after the curve the pace may have slowed. If you can pass him just before the curve, whoever is behind you will either have to pass on the curve and run extra yards or stay behind the white shirt. Then you can open up some distance. *Go! Go!* You accelerate. The white shirt senses you come alongside of him. He tries to pick up the pace, but you get around him and are able to reach the inside lane just ten yards into the curve.

Now is the time to put the pressure on. You can open a lead while the other runners deal with that white shirt you just passed. Even if they later close the lead, they'll pay dearly for it. *Let's go! Let's go!* It is too early for an all out drive. There are still almost 800 yards to the finish, but you've got to keep the pace moving. You urge your body forward. Now it does not respond as easily. You have run over half a mile at a fast pace. You are beginning to feel it. You have to push the pace along. Now it is an effort not a joy.

The third time down the backstretch it is quiet away from the crowd. You cannot hear anyone right at your heels. You are sure, however, that they are not too far back. They are too good to be far behind. *Push the pace! Push the pace!* It's work now. You can't get enough oxygen to clear all the lactic acid from your muscles. You are tired and you still have a lap and a half to go. *Come on! Come on!*

You round the curve and head down the homestretch. The next time you do this will be the end of the race. Just before you get to the line, an official shoots the pistol. One lap to go. You hear the timer reciting the time every second. Oh! You didn't run the third lap quite as fast as you wanted. You've let the pace drop. *Pick it up! Pick it up!* Your legs do not want to respond. Your breathing is heavy. You hear the noise of the crowd increase. Is something going on behind you? Is someone moving up on you? *Don't look back! Don't look back!* It could be fatal.

Around the next-to-last curve you fight your body to keep a strong pace. You are tired. The pain is really beginning. Your breathing sounds like a locomotive as you try to pull in more oxygen. But you are not getting enough. You know that soon you will have to run even faster for the final sprint. You want to ease off a little to give yourself a rest before that sprint, but you must not slow now. *Keep pushing! Keep pushing!*

As you leave the next-to-last curve and enter the backstretch, you hear spikes crunching cinders behind you. You try to pick up the pace, but the blue shirt is already on your shoulder. You push yourself to go faster, but he moves up even with you. You must not let him get past you before the last curve. If you can keep him beside you until the curve, he will either have to run a wider curve or drop back behind you. Now your body responds almost automatically. The two of you match strides, side-by-side, stride-by-stride. You will not let him pass you before the curve even if you collapse when you get there. It is still fifty yards to the curve. Stride-for-stride, evenly matched, the two of you, one in crimson, one in blue, race down the backstretch. Curiously, even though you have increased the pace you are not feeling the pain. Your whole being is so focused on reaching the curve even with the blue shirt that you are oblivious to lungs and legs. *You must not let him pass you! You must not let him pass you!*

You reach the final curve still matching strides. The blue shirt drops in behind you. Did he do it to avoid running extra yards, or has the effort of catching up to you and racing down the backstretch finished him? You'll know as you come off the curve. Now you are aware of the terrible gasping of your lungs. Every breath is an effort. You are drowning. Your legs are screaming in protest. You have to force each step. But you must keep the pace going.

As you leave the curve, you sense someone coming around you. You don't actually hear him; the crowd is making too much noise. But you know the blue shirt is trying again. There are still forty yards to the finish line. You have the sensation of throwing your whole body down the track toward the line. Now all other thoughts are gone. All your willpower commands your legs to keep moving. They have no strength of their own, but your mind makes them push forward.

When you are fifteen yards from the finish line, you see the string that has been stretched across the track over the finish line. You realize that no one is beside you. *You are going to win! You are going to win!* During the last two seconds of the race your mind is numb, but you keep going. You reach up and grasp the string with your two hands. It is finished.

Your momentum carries you ten yards beyond the finish line. You collapse into the arms of your friend, the Nigerian long jumper, who always waits to catch you. Your legs buckle, but with his help you are able to stand weakly. Your lungs continue to gulp in air, like those of a man who has been underwater too long. Another teammate rushes up and throws his arms around you. You feel no excitement about winning, just relief that it is over. The fear is over. The pain and exhaustion begin to subside. Gradually, you realize that they were worth it because you have run well. Your chest stops heaving, your breathing slows, your legs recover. Someone tells you your time: 4:07.1. You have just run a mile faster than any student at an Ivy League university has ever run. Immense gratitude sweeps through your tired body.

A few yards away you see the blue-shirted runner. He is bending over, hands on his knees. As you walk over to him, he straightens up. You shake his hand, and say, "Good race." You know that seven days later you will have to race him again.

• 2 •

The Professor's Son

GHOST DANCERS

I attended college and graduate school in the East and spent all but four years of my professional life there. Some people assumed that I was an Easterner. The reality is that I spent the first eighteen years of my life in Illinois. Both of my parents were born west of the Mississippi River. For three generations my ancestors were part of what we know as "The Wild West."

Joshua Drake was my great-great-grandfather. He left his wife and family in the East and headed out in the 1849 Gold Rush. He kept a handwritten diary. It begins in May 1849, in western Missouri. The diary tells of his trip by wagon train up the Platte River, across the Rockies and into California. Several things struck me about his account of the summer of 1849. First, it is clear that I carry his DNA. He is a terrible speller. Second, he makes no mention of fearing attacks by American Indians. There is concern about petty theft but no sense of real danger from the tribes on whose territories the gold-seekers were trespassing. Third, he makes frequent mention of people being "killed by accidental gun fire." When I first read this, I thought it was a euphemism for murder. Later, as I read other books about the Gold Rush, I learned that many of the forty-niners were Easterners inexperienced in handling firearms. Accidental shootings of other forty-niners or even themselves were not uncommon. The greatest threat seems to have been cholera. On many days he reports several deaths from this disease.

His last entry gives us a clear sense of frontier justice. The wagon train had reached Sacramento. Drake reports, "There was a shooting on the main street at 10:00 A.M. A jury was hastily formed, and Bill Vinson was hanged at noon." No appeals courts or stays of execution there.

Joshua Drake and another man built a general store in Sacramento. He decided to go back East and bring his family to California. As a number of people did in those days, he got a ship from California to Panama. He crossed the Isthmus by mule train and took another ship to the eastern United States. He carried with him a nugget of gold to show the Easterners that there really was gold in California.

Drake collected his family and got them as far as Missouri where the wagon trains started. Then word reached him that his store in Sacramento had burned down. Drake said, "To hell with it. Let's settle here."

The family stayed in Missouri. Some years later his son went to California. He discovered that the store had not burned. The partner had sent a fake message. Joshua Drake remained in Missouri. The gold nugget was passed down through the generations to make wedding rings. The rings that Martha and I wear were made from the last of that 1849 gold nugget.

Joshua Drake had a daughter named Charlotte. She married Captain William Norville. He had served as a cavalry officer in the Union Army during the Civil War. We have a quartermaster's receipt issued to Captain Norville in 1864 for the return of "one cavalry horse. Condition—Good." William Norville went into business with his father-in-law in Missouri.

Charlotte and William Norville's daughter, also named Charlotte, told her family that she had fallen in love with a teacher named J. Peter Mullin. Norville, an Episcopalian, said he did not mind her marrying a Roman Catholic, but he was not happy that Peter was a Democrat.

About the time Peter Mullin and Charlotte Norville married, the Ghost Dance religion swept through the remaining unconquered American Indian tribes in North America. It reached its greatest intensity among the Sioux in the Dakotas. Borrowing the concept of the Messiah from the Christian missionaries, the Ghost Dancers believed that dancing would bring the coming of an American Indian Messiah. The term Ghost Dance came from the white leather shirts the dancers wore. When word got out that the Ghost Dancers in the Dakotas were expecting a Messiah who would not only restore the vast herds of buffalo but would also clear the land of those of European descent, the whites in the area became increasingly nervous. They demanded federal troops for protection. Emissaries were also sent to try to keep the tribes peaceful. Captain Norville was asked to go to the Dakotas in 1890.

In his book, *Life of Sitting Bull*, published in 1891, W. Fletcher Johnson wrote, "Rumors went out that the Two Kettle Sioux were joining the hostiles, and Captain Norville hurried to their settlement on Bad River to see about it. They positively denied to him that they were disloyal."

At the end of 1890, an attempt was made to arrest Sitting Bull. Shots were fired, and Sitting Bull was killed. Ten days later the massacre at Wounded Knee was the last major battle in the long struggle between American Indians and those of European descent. I am pleased that my great-grandfather, William Norville, helped keep the Two Kettle Sioux from being among those massacred. Of course, one of my favorite movies is *Dances with Wolves* in which a former Civil War cavalry officer befriends Plains Indians.

J. Peter Mullin, son-in-law of Captain William Norville, was born on a farm in Iowa. His mother, Esther, was born in Ireland, and his father, James, was first-generation Irish American. James and Esther Mullin never saw a movie or a television. It would be unimaginable to them that, in 2006, on the History Channel's movie *Paddy Whacked: The Irish Mob*, their great-great grandson, Kevin Mullin, would play an Irish farmer during the Potato Famine who brings his family to New York. In one scene, Kevin's character was supposed to attack a British soldier. The director asked Kevin if he was ready.

"Am I ready?" answered Kevin. "My people have been waiting two hundred years to do this."

There were so many Irish settlers in the area that the town nearest to the Mullin Iowa farm renamed itself Parnell, after the Irish parliamentarian. Esther and James Mullin had twelve children, seven of whom became teachers. One of them, my great-uncle Mark, became the first principal of the Parnell High School. I am named for him, a high school principal.

Two years after Wounded Knee, Peter and Charlotte had a son whom they named Robert Norville Mullin. They were living in Kearney, Nebraska, while Peter was teaching at what would become a branch of the University of Nebraska. The rough Nebraska winters were hard on Charlotte, and she developed tuberculosis. Her condition worsened, and during a bad December Peter decided that he had to get his wife to California where he had siblings. This was in the late 1890s. The train had to stop often to take on more fuel and water. On New Year's Day it stopped in El Paso, Texas. It was a warm sunny day. Charlotte got off the train to stretch her legs and get some sun.

"Oh, Peter. I am so tired of traveling and it is so warm here. Let's not go all the way to California. Let's stay here. Please."

Within a few years, Peter was running the International Business College in El Paso, Texas. It provided training in secretarial skills and bookkeeping. It was international because it was just a mile from the Mexican border. It was the first institution along the Rio Grande to offer instruction in Spanish, as well as English, for the benefit of recent arrivals from Mexico.

Peter became friends with the local head of U.S. Customs, a tall, rangy fellow also of Irish descent. His name was Pat Garrett. Some twenty years earlier, Pat had achieved a measure of immortality by being the sheriff who shot and killed Billy the Kid.

Charlotte's health improved in the hot dry air of El Paso. In the last month of 1906, she gave birth to another son. He was baptized in the Roman Catholic Church as Francis Joseph Mullin, but from the beginning, everyone called him Joe. I can only speculate about whether sometime in Joe's first year Pat Garrett came by the Mullin house and held the new baby, my father, in his arms. Fourteen months after Joe's birth, Pat Garrett was murdered. He had been riding in a stagecoach on a road some miles north of El Paso in New Mexico. He was shot in the back of the head while relieving himself beside the road.

The strain of childbirth proved disastrous for Charlotte. Her health began to deteriorate, and she died when Joe was two years old.

A few years later, the Mexican revolutionary, Poncho Villa, crossed the Rio Grande. This was when he was still on good terms with the United States. He met with dignitaries of El Paso and specifically asked to meet Peter Mullin. He knew of Peter's work with Mexican immigrants. As a self-styled man of the people, he wanted to express his admiration. Both Joe and Robert accompanied their father to the meeting. For a while, Poncho Villa's main camp was across the Rio Grande from El Paso. Several times, Joe's house was hit by stray bullets from the Mexican side of the river. Joe remembered that, as a youngster, he saw the silhouettes of three men as they rode out a little way from the camp. They came to a tree. Two of the men rode back to camp, leaving the third hanging from a branch of the tree.

CAPONE'S TOWN

My uncle, Robert Mullin, grew up in a West Texas that was still wild and wooly. He knew Pat Garrett, Poncho Villa, and other characters who lived and died by the six-gun. Curiously, his own problems with guns came not in Texas but in Illinois.

Robert became a regional sales manager in Chicago for a major oil company. A reporter from the business section of a Chicago newspaper came to interview him.

The reporter asked about his background and learned that Robert had grown up in El Paso, Texas. There, through his father, he had become acquainted with the Mexican revolutionary, Poncho Villa. Robert also explained how he had run a local oil company. When a major company bought it out, he had joined the larger company. He had been with this company for several years, but this was his first assignment in Chicago.

The reporter asked, "Chicago is Al Capone's town. Does that worry you?"

"No. I'm in the oil business, which Mr. Capone is not. I do not see why we should have any conflict of interest."

The next day, the business section of the paper ran a headline: "Mullin Says He Will Handle Capone Like He Handled Poncho Villa."

About 11:30 A.M. Robert's secretary buzzed him. "Mr. Mullin! Mr. Mullin! There is a man here you have to see."

The man came into Robert's office. It was not Al Capone. It was one of his henchmen who was so well known that the secretary did not have to ask his name. The man stood in front of Robert's desk. He reached under his coat and pulled out a large revolver. He did not point it at Robert. He leaned across Robert's desk and placed the gun directly in front of Robert. The muzzle pointed toward the man, not toward Robert. The visitor sat down. The pistol was inches from Robert and several feet from the man.

"Are you gonna handle Mr. Capone?"

"No! No! No! The reporter got it all wrong. I never said that. You know how the press is."

"Dat's what we thought."

The man stood up, leaned over to retrieve his revolver, and left Robert's office.

Robert evaded both El Paso bullets and Chicago gangster gunfire. Nevertheless, some years later, he was shot.

His wife found out that he had a mistress. She delivered an ultimatum. "Either give her up or leave me and our daughters. You can't have both."

When Robert told his mistress that he was leaving her, she was furious. She had been dreaming that he would leave his family for her. Robert made it clear that their relationship was over. As he reached for the door to leave, she grabbed the small pistol she kept for protection. The bullet hit him directly in the rear end. I suspect that she had been aiming elsewhere, but Robert turned around at just the right moment.

Poor Robert had to spend the next week in bed on his stomach, while his angry wife brought him his meals.

A LITTLE RESEARCH

Both my brother and I always called our father "Joe." We addressed our mother as "Mom" but our father as "Joe." It was not, as some people thought, a sign of disrespect. In fact, it was said with deep affection. Almost everyone called him "Joe" although it was really his middle name.

In an April 1963 article about Shimer College in Mt. Carroll, Illinois, where he was president, *Time* magazine described Joe Mullin as "a burly, bespectacled physiologist with a West Texas drawl." He was "Joe" to me, but he was also someone who made it clear that he expected his sons to pursue excellence. He was not interested in half-hearted efforts.

He often expressed great admiration for anyone who was willing "to stand up and be counted." However, he was also a man who gave much time to his sons, whether it be playing ping-pong or fishing with them, or making sure he was present at any important event in their lives. It always delighted me that for four years Shimer College needed its president to make a business trip east just at the time of the Harvard versus Yale track meet. He knew what it was to be an adolescent without parental support, and he made sure to give it to us.

Joe was orphaned when he was fourteen. For the next two years, he was traded among relatives and friends. He spent the fall of his high school sophomore year in Washington, D.C. During that one semester in Washington, he played football for Sidwell Friends School. In fact, when I called my father to tell him that I had been selected as headmaster of St. Albans, his first words to me were, "Why don't you go to a good school?" Eighty-four years after Joe attended Sidwell, it reentered the Mullin family. Our son, Sean, married Kristen McElhiney, an Upper School English teacher at Sidwell Friends. It was good to have another teacher in the Mullin tribe. In April 2007, Kristen gave birth to Leo Francis Mullin. His middle name was Joe's first name as well as Martha's mother's first name.

For two years Joe never stayed more than six months with any one family. As he put it, "I was moved often because no one could stand me for very long." Luckily, as he entered his junior year of high school, his mother's sister, Josephine Norville, took him in. His aunt never married and since childhood had suffered from considerable deafness. As a long-time high school teacher and librarian in the small Missouri town of Chillicothe, she understood teenage boys. She knew how to handle her nephew, a young man whose yearbook quote would be, "The census embraces one hundred and ten million women. I'd like to be the census." She provided the stability and guidance Joe needed. Moreover, her influence eventually led Joe to leave the Roman Catholic Church of his Mullin relatives and join the Episcopal Church of the Norvilles. If Joe had not been orphaned, he probably would have remained a Roman Catholic. If he had, I would have been raised as one also. By such circumstances, our fates are determined.

Having been business manager of his high school paper, Joe was certain that he should have a career in journalism. He enrolled in the

University of Missouri. He soon decided to study psychology. To better understand the physical causes of psychological behavior he switched to physiology. He began to date a coed named Alma Hill. Her father and uncle were co-owners of a general store in the little town of Piggott, Arkansas. She went on to get a master's from Northwestern and then teach college English. Alma and Joe married while he was pursuing his Ph.D. at the University of Chicago. They were married for sixty-one years. At Chicago Joe worked with one of the pioneers of the study of the physiology of sleep, Nathaniel Kleitman. Joe wrote his doctoral dissertation on the effects of alcohol on sleep. Well into his eighties, he would say to my mother, "I think I'll do a little research this afternoon." Then he would have a nip and a nap.

The 1990 movie *Flatliners* is an early Julia Roberts film about graduate students in Chicago volunteering to have their hearts stopped in early experiments that paved the way for open heart and heart transplant surgery. The emphasis of the movie is on the bizarre near-death experiences they have when their hearts are stopped. Only when I was an adult did I learn that my father had been a real flatliner in the 1930s. He never mentioned it to me. One day I found the Walter Reed Medal he had been awarded for risking his life for science. I asked him why he had done it, and with typical modesty, he joked, "I was afraid that if I didn't volunteer they would not give me my Ph.D." When I asked him if he had had any out-of-body experiences while his heart was stopped, he deliberately changed the subject.

I never knew why he would not talk about it. It might have been modesty. After all, he never told me about what he had done until I found his Walter Reed Medal. It is also possible that he had an experience that was so bad that he did not want to revisit it. My own theory, however, is that not much happened. Joe was enough of an Irishman to avoid telling a story that was not entertaining.

After Joe got his Ph.D., my parents moved to Galveston, Texas, where Joe taught at the University of Texas Medical School. My older brother, Mike, was born there. To continue his research on sleep, Joe rigged up a device much like a seismograph. It was attached to the mattress of my brother's crib. Whenever Mike moved, a pen recorded a mark on a slowly revolving drum. Because the device was homemade, it was a confusion of wires, a clock, the seismograph cylindrical chart, and an arm holding a pen. All were attached to the crib.

Word must have spread in the neighborhood that the professor was torturing a baby. All sorts of people showed up at my parents' door saying they wanted to see the new baby. However, they looked, not at the baby, but at the strange and frightening device attached to the crib. Joe was happy to leave them with their suspicions. My mother, Alma, however, hastened to explain that nothing touched the baby; it was just measuring motions of the crib mattress. Being the unaware subject of scientific research was a prophetic start to my brother's career as a distinguished scientist.

THAT RED HAIR'S NO LIE

Shortly before I was born, my parents returned to Chicago. My father, Joe, continued his career at the University of Chicago as a researcher, teacher, and later, dean. The United States entered World War II seventeen months after I was born. For a while, my father and other physiologists ate only army K rations so that they could carefully measure the effects on their bodies. However, his greatest sacrifice to the war effort was an involuntary one. Joe loved playing handball in the courts under the west stands of Stagg Field, the University of Chicago's football stadium. The handball courts were suddenly closed, and the only explanation was that it was for the "war effort." It was only after the war that Joe learned that the handball courts had been turned over to Enrico Fermi and the other atomic physicists at the university. As they began to unleash the secrets of the atom, they did not know whether or not they could control their experiments. They thought that, as a minimum precaution, they should conduct this work in a windowless handball court under a concrete stadium. When I was less than five years old, I was three short blocks away from the first man-made sustained nuclear reaction in history. Whether or not that left me with a certain glow, I have no idea. I do know that growing up amidst the Gothic buildings of the University of Chicago gave me a taste for the medieval world. I felt at home riding my bicycle into cloistered courtyards, surrounded by leaded windows and graceful stone arches.

From nursery school through the eighth grade I attended the University of Chicago Laboratory School. About half of its students had parents who taught at the University of Chicago. Thus, its students were highly academic. Having an excellent grade school education was immeasurably beneficial to me. The Lab School also served the university's Department of Education as a place for teacher training. Because so many of us had parents who were teachers, we were not intimidated by teachers in training. We provided good (and perhaps combat) experience for those in preparation to be teachers. It always surprised me that we did not drive more of them out of the profession.

The other important institution in my life in Chicago was the local Episcopal Church. My father rarely talked about his own beliefs. I think he was probably closest to a Jeffersonian deist. However, he thought that going to church was a way to inculcate values in the young. He had been raised as a Roman Catholic but, under the influence of his aunt, became an Episcopalian. Both traditions gave him an appreciation of liturgy. From our earliest years, he sent my brother and me to the Episcopal Church near the University of Chicago. The rector, Father Lickfield, also valued ritual. Instead of regular Sunday school, he organized a children's service in a meeting room while the parents were worshipping in the main church. For some of us, wearing little robes, marching in, lighting and putting out candles, and bowing to the cross seemed much more adult than learning Bible stories.

By the time we were eight, we were allowed to join the choir of men and boys. Now I felt really grown up, with vestments, processions, bowing, and genuflecting as a group, and being an important part of the adult service. My brother, Mike, was a better singer than I, and he sang solos. Music kept him going to church all his life even though his beliefs were even closer to agnosticism than my father's. I have no doubt that it was the ritual that first appealed to me. As soon as I was confirmed, I became an acolyte and, thus, even more involved in the liturgy. There was something else I felt. I believed that I was participating in something very important, something beyond normal life, something sacred. It would be years before I heard the word "transcendent" and even more years before I understood it as Paul Tillich used it. Though I could not explain it, I sensed that the transcendent was present in the rites of Holy Communion.

As I entered seventh grade, Father Lickfield started a special class that met each Saturday morning. There were five boys in the class. Four of us had parents who taught at the University of Chicago. We were used to asking questions. And that is what Father Lickfield encouraged us to do. He took us slowly through the Communion Service, including the Creed, the prayers, and the consecration. We talked about the meaning and the theology that underlay each part. Father Lickfield was wonderful in showing us that one could have faith, yet ask questions and try to understand intellectually the things one believes. It was just what I needed as a preadolescent. I credit that class with saving me from the crisis of faith so many young people have as teenagers or in college. It was during this period in my life that I first began to think about being a priest.

We lived on the south side of Chicago about a mile from where I had choir practice two afternoons a week. Between the church and my home was the dreaded Dorchester gang. It was a group of seventh- and eighth-grade toughs who enjoyed harassing choirboys. I found that if I jogged home, members of the Dorchester gang would yell insults at me. However, they were too lazy to chase after me, and I would arrive home untouched.

The gang never hurt me, but thirty years later it almost cost me my credibility with the St. Albans Search Committee. While I was being interviewed to be headmaster, the Committee asked me how I got started running. I laughingly told about the Dorchester gang. I thought it was a fun story, and I did not mean to imply anything about the circumstances of my childhood. Sometime later, the Committee sent two people up to Choate to ask about me. One of them said, "We think it is so impressive that Mark grew up in a part of Chicago that was so tough that he had to run home, but he still managed to get himself into Harvard."

A Choate faculty member, who knew me well, said, "Well, he may have run home, but it was to a home full of books. His father was a professor at the University of Chicago."

While I was in grade school, there was considerable publicity about the attempts to run a mile in less than four minutes. Some people said it was impossible. Others speculated about when and by whom it would be done. As early as the sixth grade I began to fantasize about being the first man to run a four-minute mile. That summer I timed myself running a mile on a gravel road in Wisconsin.

When I finished the seventh grade, I decided that I would try to run a six-minute mile before I turned thirteen and became a teenager.

I had one month to do it. I did not train. Three times I ran a mile on the University of Chicago track. The best I did was 6:03. That was probably very inaccurate since I was timing myself with my own wristwatch. I told no one of these attempts.

In the spring of my eighth-grade year, Roger Bannister of Oxford became the first man to run a mile in less than four minutes. I was both disappointed (amazing arrogance for a thirteen-year-old who had never even seen a track meet) and fascinated. His accomplishment increased my desire to be a miler.

From the late 1930s into the 1950s, NBC broadcast nationally a radio program originating in Chicago. It was called "The Quiz Kids" and featured a likeable quizmaster, "Genial" Joe Kelly. He asked questions of five rather precocious children between the ages of six and thirteen. It was broadcast every Sunday afternoon when families could listen together. Every time a child appeared, he or she received a $100 U.S. Savings Bond. Each week, three of the children would be told that they could come back the next week. The other two would be off the show for a few weeks and then invited back.

A friend of my parents was an associate producer of the Quiz Kids. She knew that both Mike and I were reasonably bright but not geniuses. However, at age six, I had a lisp that she believed would sound cute on the radio. She asked my parents about the possibility of my becoming a Quiz Kid. Since my father was only making $100 a week as a faculty member at the University of Chicago, those savings bonds looked very good. Nonetheless, my parents said that I could only be on the show if Mike was on it also. My parents were not interested in sibling rivalry. They did not make a big deal of the audition. I remember that it was fun to answer the questions that the very nice Mr. Kelly asked. Thus, Mike and I became Quiz Kids.

People have asked me if the show was rigged or if we were given the questions in advance. We did not know the questions until they were asked on the air. However, sometimes there was a general theme. When there was a guest on the show, my parents would have me study up on his area of expertise. Other than that, we did no preparation. Mike soon established himself as an expert on nature. I charmed people by being one of the youngest, having a buzz haircut, and lisping my answers.

John Dunning's 1998 book, *On the Air: The Encyclopedia of Old-Time Radio*, says, "Mark Mullin went into such detail on the mating habits of the grouse that an embarrassed Joe Kelly had to change the subject." I suspect that Mr. Dunning has confused me with Mike. At that stage in our lives, Mike, who was older, knew more than I did about the mating habits of any creature, grouse or human.

My parents insisted that we not take being a Quiz Kid too seriously. They wanted us just to enjoy the experience. There was one aspect of it that I loved. For someone who had never gone far from Chicago except to my grandmother's home in Arkansas, the best part of being a Quiz Kid was the travel. Once a year the show would be broadcast from some distant place. Trips as a young child to Syracuse, Houston, Montgomery, and Denver gave me my first taste of travel.

My biggest disappointment as a Quiz Kid also created a lifelong affection. One Sunday there was a visitor who had something to do with agriculture. He presented each of us with a live, cuddly, baby pig. I was enchanted as I held my pig and tried to answer the questions. At the end of the show, Joe Kelly said, "Well, since you all live in Chicago, you can't actually raise a pig. So we'll take the pigs back and give you a piggy bank instead." I never thought of Joe Kelly as "Genial" again. When we first started dating, Martha jokingly called me "Piglet" and was surprised at my immediate response. Now there are hundreds of pigs, made of all sorts of materials from wood to porcelain to cloth, in our home.

A few years after I joined the Quiz Kids, the show began to be televised. Strangely, I was on NBC national television several times, and my family did not own a television set. About a year later I outgrew my lisp. As I was certainly no longer the youngest contestant, my career as a Quiz Kid was over.

A professor of English at the University of Chicago lived across the street from us. He and my father were friends, and he even had a go at teaching my father fly-fishing. Years later I went to see the movie *A River Runs through It*. My son, Sean, had recommended it to me because of the interaction between the minister and his two sons. Halfway through the movie the name of one of the sons clicked in my head. "Norman. Norman Maclean. My gosh, he lived across the street from us in Chicago."

I did not remember Norman Maclean because of fly-fishing. I remembered him for something else. It was a talent he exhibited on a number of occasions, but one day in particular stands out in my memory. It was a warm spring day. New private automobiles did not become available until a few years after World War II. Norman Maclean knocked on our door. "I just bought a new car. Come and see it." He led my father and me across the street. There sat a shiny new car. It was the first new car we had seen on our block. Then, Mr. Maclean noticed the hood and the windshield. There was clear evidence that a Chicago pigeon had scored significantly. What issued from Norman Maclean's mouth left me standing speechless. Later in life, I worked on farms and served in the U.S. Army, but I never heard anyone equal Norman Maclean for depth, duration, or inventiveness of profanity. He was a master.

My family had always enjoyed the fact that both my mother and father were of predominately Irish descent. When I was in the seventh grade, my good friend, Bob Strozier, and I went to the Tivoli Theater on Fifty-third Street in Chicago to see *The Quiet Man*. I watched in awe as the beautiful scenery of the west coast of Ireland served as a backdrop for John Wayne's courtship of Maureen O'Hara. Barry Fitzgerald's character summed up Maureen's personality. "That red hair's no lie."

When the movie ended, Bob was all excited. "Oh, that Maureen O'Hara reminds me of Ginger. I'm so lucky she's my girlfriend." I, on the other hand, was silent. A resolve had grown in me during the movie: I would marry an Irish redhead. Never mind about seventh-grade girls. It sounds like the plot of a silly romantic comedy that a seventh-grade boy sees a movie and decides he wants to marry an Irish redhead. It was romantic, but it was also prophetic.

When I was finishing grade school in Chicago there were three things I thought I wanted to do in my life. Young people often develop strong ideas about what they hope to accomplish. How often do these dreams come true? New opportunities present themselves, there are disappointments, and goals change. I am not quite sure what it says about my personality that my grade school dreams stayed fixed in my heart and remained an important part of my life. Moreover, my goals were unusually specific.

By the time I was in the eighth grade I had three life dreams: first, to be a mile runner; second, to be an Episcopal priest; and third, to marry an Irish redhead. Interestingly, being a headmaster was not on the list. It never occurred to me that I would spend twenty-five years running schools. Yet, each of those youthful goals contributed to my becoming a headmaster. They shaped both my destiny and the sort of headmaster I became.

Running the mile led me to independent schoolwork. I had gained so much from my track experiences that I wanted to give some of that back to young people. Yet, I never had a desire to be a full-time coach. I was initially drawn to independent schools so that I could coach while also being involved in academic work.

Being an Episcopal priest was a call to service. I came to believe that I could be of most service in schools. It also meant that I was most comfortable working in schools with a religious foundation. The beliefs and practices of the Episcopal Church shaped my ideas on education. When I became a headmaster, I tried to base my decisions on those beliefs.

Martha, the redhead I married, very much encouraged me to look at schools rather than parish work. Then she gave of herself unselfishly to four schools, attending a multitude of school functions and being a wonderful hostess to so many members of the school family in our home. Being a headmaster allows a man to share his professional life with his wife in ways that are true of few occupations.

Although I did not dream of being a headmaster, it is hard for me to imagine my being a headmaster if these three dreams had not been part of my life. They are too interwoven into who I am and what I did with my life.

THE GRAVEL PIT

While I was growing up in Chicago, my mother, Alma, my brother, Mike, and I spent a month each summer with my grandmother in the Arkansas town of Piggott. I have such happy memories of summers there. Just the name "Piggott" conjures up a rush of images.

When there were rainstorms in Piggott, Mike and I would strip to our underwear and run around Grandma's backyard. We had some kind of game filling cans and pails with the water that came shooting out of drainpipes. The biggest thrill was just the running around with almost nothing on, the rain pounding on our heads and bare backs, and our bare feet slipping on the wet grass.

Grandma's house was one story, but it had been added on to so often over the years that you had to go up or down a couple of steps to go from room to room.

Mike and I liked sitting on the floor using our hands to pump the large metal foot pedal of the old sewing machine. We pretended that we were operating a train. The other piece of ancient machinery in her house was the telephone. It was a wooden box attached to the dining room wall. To make a call, one lifted the earpiece, cranked the handle, and when the operator came on, told her to whom you wanted to talk. You could be sure the operator would listen in if she thought it was going to be an interesting call.

Even better was sitting on the railing of the side porch as I pretended to drive a stagecoach. Mike sat beside me and shot his BB gun to defend the stage from bandits and American Indians in the person of a tin can placed in the yard.

The musty smell and lack of light in the barn behind Grandma's house cast a magical spell. Here, Uncle Rudy kept his equipment, and we went with him to collect eggs from the nests of the chickens Grandma kept in a fenced area of the backyard.

We watched in silent awe whenever Grandma cut the head off a chicken to be fried. She would then release the headless body that would run a lap or two around the chicken yard with wings flapping before it collapsed.

We loved riding in Uncle Rudy's old Ford truck. It was fun to sit beside him in the cab and see the dust rise from the cloth seats each time we took a bump. But it was even more fun to ride in the back of the truck, waving at pedestrians as the wind swept over our young faces. Uncle Rudy, who was older than my mother, had been born with birth defects. He lived with my grandmother all his life. He was less than five feet tall, walked with a limp, and had a childlike innocence about him that made him a great companion for us. He seemed like another kid—a kid with a driver's license. Up in the cab of his truck, driving around town or out in the country, he was the king of the road.

Going to Uncle Davis's general store on the town square was always a treat. There we would see boots and overalls waiting for the strong workingmen and farmers who came to purchase them. I loved burying my hands in the open mouths of huge sacks of grain and then raising my hands to let the grain run out through my fingers. Best of all, just before we left the store, we would press our noses against the glass of the candy counter. After a little hesitation to heighten our desire, Uncle Davis would say, "What would you like?" He was always willing to give us one candy each, but only one.

On Sundays, we all went to church. In those days, churches were not air-conditioned. Each person who entered was given a folding paper fan that carried advertising from the local funeral home. All during the Scripture and the sermon, little signs heralding "Johnson's Funeral Home" swished back and forth in front of each face. Of course, when we thought no one was looking, Mike and I closed our fans and used them as swords on each other.

The church was called the Christian Church and was connected with the Disciples of Christ. Unlike other Protestant churches, it had communion every Sunday. However, people did not come up to an altar rail. Instead, ushers passed around silver trays carrying something that looked like saltine crackers. Each adult broke off a piece and ate it. The ushers came around again with trays filled with what appeared to be shot glasses. They did not contain wine. It was Welch's grape juice. Alcohol was not encouraged among the faithful. I had no religious feelings whatsoever about what was going on, but I longed to throw down a shot glass of grape juice in one swig. It was made very clear to me that this was for adults only.

After church, we always took flowers to my grandfather's grave. Grandma and Mom were a little sad there, but Mike and I loved running over the green lawns of the cemetery.

Sometimes we would all drive to a nearby river, perhaps the St. Francis or the aptly named Current River. We would fish with long bamboo poles. Other times, we would swim and then float in inner tubes, being careful not to be swept too far downstream.

We spent many hours at the public swimming pool that was located on the county fairgrounds. The Fourth of July Fair was the highlight of the summer. First, there would be a parade of homemade floats from the courthouse to the fair grounds. The fair itself had so much to delight a youngster: rides, games, noise, people, and food. For me the greatest thrill was a grape snow cone. What could be more wonderful, more cooling, or more exotic than overly sweet shaved ice on a hot Arkansas evening?

My grandmother's house was just two blocks from the railroad tracks. Only a few trains went through each day. Mike and I spent hours walking for miles along the tracks. Sometimes we carefully stepped from tie to tie. More challenging was to see how far we could walk on a rail. A railroad rail is wide, but if there is any train traffic it is also slightly slippery. There were times we managed to walk hundreds of yards before carelessness or fatigue produced a loss of balance and a step onto the roadbed. Of course, it was most exciting when we had a long walk going and then heard a train approaching. We tried to extend the walk to a maximum before the whistle, roar, and rush of the train scared us off the tracks.

For me, the most magical place in Arkansas was the gravel pit. It was a few miles outside of town. When we were small we had to be taken by car. As we got older, Mike and I would ride our bikes up and down the hills to get there. An area of about fifteen acres had been scooped out to collect gravel for road building. For some reason, steep gravel hills and pillars had been left in the middle. These were difficult to climb and high enough to be quite scary to a young boy. The shapes seemed fantastical to me: castle ramparts or towering mountains. The gravel pit bore a slight resemblance to a small Garden of the Gods in Colorado, or so it seemed to my young mind. There was always a hint of danger there. If we had fallen while climbing on those stone fortresses, we could have been seriously hurt. There was also a less specific danger. We knew that tough teenagers came there at night to drink beer and do unimaginable things in the backseats of cars. We felt lucky that we never saw teenagers there.

Piggott was the county seat of Clay County, and that meant that it had a courthouse square. That gives any small town a certain charm and prepared me for the center of Mt. Carroll, Illinois, where I would spend my high school years. Piggott's three thousand people made it slightly larger than Mt. Carroll. Piggott, however, lacked the advantage of having a college in town. Nonetheless, Piggott achieved more fame because of one prominent native son and two unusual native daughters.

Leslie Biffle had been born in Piggott and, after Truman's surprise victory of 1948, became secretary of the U.S. Senate. The town fathers lured him back for a visit and proclaimed "Leslie Biffle Day." A parade and speeches were organized. Red, white, and blue bunting was hung all over town. On the front of every business establishment hung huge signs proclaiming "Welcome Les." Many found it amusing that the funeral home, provider of the church fans, was eager to welcome Les.

I paid no attention to the speeches but rushed around getting the autographs of anyone who looked important from state police officers to politicians. Even at that young age, I knew that the most important autograph was that of Alben Barkley, Vice-President of the United States, who had come to Piggott to honor Lesley Biffle. I never dreamed that years later I would know four other vice-presidents and visit the homes of two of them.

The unusual native daughters from Piggott were sisters. Their father, Gus Pfeiffer, was the richest man in town. Their home was the most elegant and had the only private swimming pool in the county. Gus's oldest daughter, Pauline Pfeiffer, met Ernest and Hadley Hemingway in Europe. She and Ernest began having an affair. After Pauline became Ernest's second wife, they lived in Key West. Ernest Hemingway dedicated *A Farewell to Arms* to Gus Pfeiffer.

During the time Pauline and Ernest were married, she would occasionally bring Ernest to Piggott for a visit. Pauline's younger sister, Virginia, was my mother's closest friend. Years later, Virginia would be my godmother. At the time Ernest was coming to Piggott, my father was courting my mother. Joe and Alma would often go to the Pfeiffer pool. There they got to know Ernest. Years later, my mother said that Ernest expected to be the center of attention. If she was even knitting while he was holding forth, he frowned at her. Nevertheless, they did become friends. She had Ernest autograph some of his books. I have now inherited them. What makes them fun is the growing friendship and intimacy the inscriptions reveal.

In a copy of *Death in the Afternoon*:
Ernest Hemingway

In *A Farewell to Arms*:
To Alma Hill
with very best wishes
    Ernest Hemingway

In *The Sun Also Rises*:
To Alma Hill with
all Best wishes from
her friend
  Ernest Hemingway
  Piggott
  1928

In another copy of *Death in the Afternoon*:
To Alma Hill
with much affection
—and many wishes for
good luck—
  Ernest Hemingway
  Piggott
  1932

Finally, in another copy of *The Sun Also Rises*:
[In my father's handwriting]
I did not,
  Joe
[In Ernest's handwriting]
Neither did I,
  Ernest

My mother would never tell me what it was that both Joe and Ernest "did not."

Although Pauline Pfeiffer achieved lasting fame by marrying Ernest Hemingway, her sister, Virginia, moved in very unusual circles. She went to Los Angeles where she helped bankroll some of the more famous drug experimenters of the 1950s such as Alan Watts and Timothy Leary. Virginia was an interesting choice of a godmother for a future clergyman. When I was in college, she visited Mt. Carroll one summer. She was the first person I ever heard speak of psychedelic drugs from personal experience.

Many years before that, she had been responsible for the closest I ever got to a mind-bending visual experience. When we were children, she was in Piggott at the same time we were. Virginia Pfeiffer, my mother, my brother, and I were driving somewhere. Mike spotted a large bull snake on the highway. True to form, Mike insisted that we stop the car and inspect the snake. We all got out of the car. Mike found a stick that he used to tease the snake and make it strike. Virginia grabbed her movie camera and filmed the snake. When she sent us the film, she explained that she had already exposed the film at a bullfight in Spain. Now, she had managed to double expose the film. When it was developed and shown, it appeared that a giant snake of dinosaurian proportions was about to swallow a huge bull that was determined to gore the reptile. It made great viewing.

Virginia, who never married, lived in California. She shared a house with her friend, Laura Archera. My mother was visiting Virginia Pfeiffer when Laura married Aldous Huxley, who was then in his sixties. The wedding was kept secret from the press until after it was over. Later, Aldous autographed a copy of one of his books, *Heaven and Hell*.

> For Alma Mullin
> Who helped Laura
> to get married,
> gratefully,
>> Aldous Huxley,
>> 1956

Six years later, Aldous and Laura visited my parents in Mt. Carroll, Illinois. This time Aldous inscribed a copy of *The Doors of Perception*. This was the book that described Aldous's experimentation with mescaline. It was from the name of that book that Jim Morrison chose the name of his band. The inscription read,

> For Joe Mullin,
> In memory of
> A wonderful
> Afternoon in
> The country,
>> Aldous H.
>> 1962

Less than a year later, my mother got a letter from California. It speaks of fear of the press, even in those pre-paparazzi days. It also speaks of the awful dilemma of facing an approaching death.

Dear Alma,

I don't know if you have known that Aldous has been in bad health for quite some time, three years as a matter of date, but since we got back from Europe he is much worse. We have taken great care to keep it out of the newspaper material with the unwanted publicity and so far have succeeded. Only just recently did Aldous himself write his family the situation, and since then we have told a very few close friends of discretion which brings me to you and Jo [*sic*] than which there is no one more so. You may have guessed that it is cancer. It is manifest in the neck, but the rapidity with which he has lost strength and weight, it is almost certain to be rather general. He has been in bed for a month and not out of bed for the past week.

The most enigmatical thing is that he has not mentioned or even inferred that there is not a chance of his recovery! He only speaks of what he will do when well. No one can believe that with his knowledge of the disease, his having written of at least two characters who died of the same thing, etc., his writing and talking of the preparation for death that he could really be unaware of it. But neither is he good at pretending. It seems incredible but true that he does not know. No one, not even the doctor wants to drop the word, without his asking or leaving an opening. What would you do? Of course I can not see that he would do anything different, if he did know.

Do not worry about writing how you feel about all this. I know. It is one of the reasons it seems useless to tell anyone. It is only one more person feeling painfully helpless.

I know I can count on you and Joe. When the press finds out, it will be the end of some of the peace and quiet there is left.

Love,
Jinny

Aldous Huxley died on the same day as John F. Kennedy.

The third of Gus Pfeiffer's children was a boy. He stayed home, ran the local cotton gin, and lived in the family mansion. I found his wife, also named Pauline, to be the sort of person who puts on airs that little boys do not like. She probably thought she was the grandest lady in Piggott and had to play the role. I remember that once Mike made a disparaging remark about the yippy little poodle she treated like a human baby. She drew herself up, sniffed down her nose, and said, "Little boy, that dog is worth more than you are."

When we reported the remark to our mother, Alma said, "I suppose she is right."

SNIPE HUNTING

We usually spent July in Arkansas with my mother. My father stayed in Chicago to work. Then in August we would take a family vacation. In my early years my parents rented a small cabin at the south end of Lake Michigan. The cabin was in the woods but right at the top of a bluff where a sandy path led down to the beach. The sun baked the sand at the top of the bluff, and we always yelped as we walked across it in our bare feet.

Down on the beach we rode the waves on inner tubes and then played Japanese Prisoners of War among the tall sand dunes. I remember walking into our cabin one August day. H. V. Keltenborn was screaming over the radio, "The war is over! The war is over! The war is over!" We knew that was a good thing, but we continued our war games in the sand for several more summers.

With gas rationing over, Joe decided to venture a little farther from Chicago. Friends told him of a great place in northern Wisconsin. For many summers, we spent August at North End Lodge on Long Lake. Ed Duvall had been in the business of making oak barrel staves for the aging of alcohol. Prohibition put Ed and his wife, Millie, in deep poverty. But he never lost his faith in the thirst of Americans. He held onto his equipment. When Prohibition ended, he was back in business before many of his competitors were ready. He prospered. In fact, he was the only man we knew personally who drove a Cadillac.

The Duvalls had a son who was born with a crippled leg and arm. The doctors recommended swimming as a therapeutic exercise. So Ed bought a house at one end of Long Lake in northern Wisconsin. The house had a small guest cabin that relatives occasionally used. Once, when the cabin was unoccupied, a family stopped by the house asking where they might find a hotel. This was before motels dotted every highway. Because it was late, Ed and Millie insisted that the family stay in the empty cabin. The following spring the family wrote and asked if they could rent the cabin for a week. Ed Duvall had a nose for a good business opportunity. By the time we first went to Wisconsin there were nine cabins, and more were added later. Each cabin was also provided with a rowboat for use on the lake.

We loved our summers there. We could swim, sunbathe on a giant rubber raft, explore the woods, and fish. On rainy days we lay in bed and studied the shapes of the knots in the pine walls and ceilings. We would say, "Can you see an elephant?" and the others would look all over for a knot that met the description.

In the early days we dug worms and fished for blue gills and crappies with still lines. As we got older we were able to cast for small mouth bass. I found that the challenge of making a good cast was as much fun as actually catching a fish. The test was to have the lure land as close as possible to a log or the bank without having the hooks get snagged on something. Once each summer we would spend a day floating down the Red Cedar River in canoes, fishing as we went. The beauty of the changing riverbanks, the test of getting the canoe over the occasional stretches of rocks and white water, and the competition of accurate casting from a moving canoe all made for a wonderful day.

Of course, boys rarely have deep woods available to them without yielding to the temptation to take others snipe hunting. My best friend, Bob Strozier, had a younger brother. I can still hear the brother's pitiful cries for help when he realized he was alone and lost at night in deep woods. We really did not leave him that way very long, but it must have seemed an eternity to him. Thirty years later, our victim, Charles Strozier, authored the book, *Lincoln's Quest for Union*. The dust jacket reads,

> Lincoln's own metaphor of a "house divided" referred to both himself and to the nation. Thus Strozier shows in rich detail how Lincoln's arduous mastery of his own divided self enabled him to express, through his absolute command of language and his emphatic grasp of others, the profound political and emotional needs of a divided nation.

Charles Strozier was the editor of *The Psychohistory Review*. Using his own psychohistory methodology, I have wondered if the experience of being divided from his older brother and his friends on a nighttime snipe hunt had shaped Strozier's understanding of Lincoln's sense of being divided.

By the time I was eleven, I had gotten interested in running the mile. My school had no track team until the ninth grade. I wanted to run a mile. From the paved highway in Wisconsin there was a gravel road that went past North End Lodge. One day as we were driving away from our cabin, I watched the odometer carefully and noticed where we were on the gravel road when we have gone a mile. The next afternoon I walked out from our cabin and followed the road to the mile spot. I waited until the minute hand on my wristwatch was on a number and the second hand was on twelve. Then I began to run. I do not remember how long it took me to get back to the cabin. That did not matter. For the first time in my life I had run a mile.

SKATING

When I was fourteen, we moved 130 miles west of Chicago to Mt. Carroll, Illinois. It was essentially a farming community in the rolling hills near the Mississippi River. The town also hosted Shimer College. My father was its new president and would remain there for fourteen years. Shimer was affiliated with the University of Chicago. It offered the same prescribed liberal education and emphasis on the great books that Robert Hutchins had brought to the university. *Time* magazine, in a 1963 article about Shimer, wrote,

> Under the spring sun of the rolling farmlands around the north-western Illinois town of Mt. Carroll, Shimer College wears a mask of nodding tranquility. It might be some 19th century prairie academy trying to drive a little erudition into the neighboring pumpkinheads. Instead, Shimer is one of eleven U.S. campuses that have an ideal "intellectual climate" in the opinion of Syracuse University Psychologist George G. Stern, writing in the current *Harvard Educational Review*. . . . In 1954, Joe Mullin came from a professorship at the University of Chicago medical school to become president of Shimer. By virtue of having taught doctors, he had one driving conviction, that professional men by and large are too narrowly educated and need a broad liberal education before going into graduate school.

In 1964, the University of Chicago Alumni Association gave Joe its highest award, the Alumni Medal. The citation reads,

> Since assuming the presidency of Shimer College he has refashioned Shimer into an experimental college of unique character, nationally recognized for its teaching excellence, its intellectual atmosphere and its demonstration that curricular transfer between dissimilar institutions is feasible. There seems little doubt that Shimer's excellence today is the deed of its president, whose leadership of mind and spirit have been as ample as his practical abilities.

I was never an undergraduate at Shimer College or the University of Chicago. However, for the first eighteen years of my life, many of the adults I knew taught at one of these institutions. Most of them believed in a liberal education and the Chicago great books curriculum. It introduced students to some of the greatest writing in Western civilization. Even science was studied by reading the writings of important scientists. As much as 85 percent of an undergraduate's work was in prescribed courses. This was designed to avoid overspecialization on the one hand or dilettantism on the other hand. My father also argued that having all undergraduates read the same books and share a common intellectual experience added tremendously to their education. If people are reading the same books, so much enrichment occurs after class or in dormitory discussions.

The ideal of a shared educational experience may be difficult to achieve at the university level. However, it seems to me that secondary education loses something when too many electives are available. Often, secondary schools feel that the more electives they have the better they are. I doubt it. I thought it was a shame that at Choate it was quite possible for two roommates to have no courses in common. They would not be able to have an in-depth discussion of their academic work. While I was headmaster of St. Albans, students shared educational experiences. Even seniors, who had many elective choices, shared at least one course with all their classmates.

I loved the move from Chicago to Mt. Carroll, a town of two thousand people. I found it satisfying to live in a community where most people knew each other. Even if people did not know each other's names, they would usually greet one another on the sidewalk.

When we arrived in Mt. Carroll, my father took me to the local high school to register me for the ninth grade. The school secretary arranged my courses and then asked if I wanted to do any sports. All I said was "Track, please." When we were walking back to our car my father asked me if I knew what event I wanted to do in track. The dream was so important to me that I did not want to discuss it. Somehow I felt that would trivialize it. I answered, "The mile." I was grateful that he did not question me further.

When the spring came, I found that I enjoyed track as much as I had dreamed I would. If running was fun, competing was even more so. I loved those four springs of high school track. In the spring of my senior year, I ran in the Illinois State High School Championships. I was leading the race as we ran down the backstretch on the last lap. Then, as we came off the curve and headed for the finish line, Frank Ballinger of Mooseheart came beside me. I tried to accelerate, but Frank was stronger. He finished a step ahead of me. My time was 4:23.6.

After the University of Chicago Laboratory School, I found the work at Mt. Carroll High School relatively easy. Here, half of the students lived on the small working farms that dotted the area. In fact, halfway through each class period a bell rang. The teacher was supposed to stop teaching to allow time for doing homework since so many kids had to do farm chores when they got home. However, one course in which I struggled was Latin. Miss Fetteroff had a great wall chart made like the Circus Maximus. We were each assigned a different colored chariot. Every class day began with each of us being asked a question. A correct answer moved one's chariot forward a space. My chariot spent most of its time mired in Roman mud.

I will always be grateful to Mary McQuaid. She had just graduated from a small Midwestern college. This was her first teaching job. She made us write. She made us rewrite. The amount of writing she made us do—certainly more that all the other Mt. Carroll teachers combined—stood me in good stead when I got to college.

The nearest Episcopal Church was in the next small town, ten miles away from Mt. Carroll. It was a struggling mission church with few members. Father Whitney was a kindly old priest who was delighted to have a college president, my father, in his flock. He was also glad to have two well-trained acolytes to fill out his meager roster. He used Mike and me often, and that kept me involved with the church during high school.

In the middle of my freshman year, I pulled the book *The Robe*, by Lloyd C. Douglas, off the shelf of my high school library. It had the greatest influence on me of any book I have ever read. The dust jacket said, "This is the story of the Roman soldier who gambled for Christ's robe and won." It also quoted the author as saying, "I tried to take the saints out of the stain[ed] glass windows and make them flesh and blood people." For me, the book took Christ out of the ritual and transcendent mystery of the Eucharist and made him a flesh and blood person to whom I could relate. Moreover, by following a Roman soldier who moved, questioning and doubting every step of the way, from atheist to Christian, *The Robe* reinforced the idea that questioning and faith are not incompatible.

My faith was also strengthened by discussions about religion with my good high school friend, Dennis Stiles. Denny lived on a farm, and we spent many hours riding around in his pickup truck. We said that we were looking for girls who might be willing to ride with us. Actually, we spent most of the time talking about religion and the meaning of life. Denny was not a believer. Having to defend my beliefs to a mind as sharp as his forced me to think more deeply and clearly. As for the girls we hoped to attract, only later, when I had actually studied theology, did I learn the phrase, "The triumph of hope over reason."

Mt. Carroll also allowed me to have friends from families that were not academic. Soon after I started high school, a classmate asked me what my father did for a living. When I told him, he replied, "Oh! Then you'll get to go to college." I am embarrassed now that I was surprised by his answer, but all my classmates at the Laboratory School in Chicago took college as a certainty in their future. The jobs I had also brought me into contact with different people. I worked as a thistle cutter and hay stacker on local farms, a dishwasher, and a stock boy at the A&P grocery. I spent two summers working on the maintenance crew of Shimer College. Thirty-seven years later I would be in binding arbitration with the Washington National Cathedral to protect the maintenance crew of St. Albans School.

The people of Mt. Carroll were amused when Blanche Fawcett married Don Trickle. Together, they ran the Trickle Inn, the town's only drive-in restaurant. Most of us who were teenagers in Mt. Carroll spent many summer evenings hanging out in front of its white plywood façade. Part of the appeal was that the Trickles hired the high school cheerleaders to work at the Trickle Inn. Three of them were redheads. I had at least one date with each of them, but nothing much developed. In my junior year, I asked the one I liked best to the Prom. She accepted. But then, a few weeks before the Prom, I had to break the date. It appeared likely that I would qualify for the state championship track meet that was on the same day as the Prom. That ended my courtship of high school redheads.

Of course, spending one's high school years in a college president's house provided unusual intellectual stimulation. I knew many of the college teachers. They loved the academic life. I occasionally attended lectures or concerts at the college. Many fascinating visitors stayed in our guest room. One guest, whom I had never heard of, even had my parents in awe. To me he was just an old man with bushy white hair and a German accent. The night before his lecture, some of my friends and I went skating on the little Wakarusa River that ran on the edge of Mt. Carroll. There was snow on the ground. We built a bonfire on one side of the river. It threw our gliding shadows on the rock cliff across the river. My parents brought the lecturer down to watch the skating. He stood silently for a long time then turned to my parents with tears in his eyes. Paul Tillich, one of the most profound theologians of the twentieth century, said in his thick accent, "It makes me a child in Germany again, before the two wars."

TWO RUNNERS

Dennis Stiles not only challenged my religious beliefs while we were together in Mt. Carroll High School. He also challenged me on the track. When I arrived in Mt. Carroll, he was the best miler in the school. By my sophomore year, I was able to beat him, but not by much. Knowing that if I relaxed in practice or a meet he would be past me was one of the best things that could have happened to me. Because of Denny, I always had to push myself to a maximum effort. We raced against each other, argued religion, and were very close friends. Today, we do not run against each other, and we rarely talk about religion. We do remain very good friends.

Denny's father was in the Civilian Conservation Corps during the Depression. Eventually, he was able to lease a small dairy farm a few miles northeast of Mt. Carroll. Although he had little formal education, he knew how to raise dairy cows and how to raise sons. The Stiles are an American success story. Denny's younger brother became a university professor of aeronautical engineering. Denny graduated from the Air Force Academy. He flew helicopters into North Vietnam to rescue downed American pilots. Later, he was a U.S. air attaché to Egypt and then Austria. When he left the Air Force, he pursued his passion for poetry and became president of the South Carolina Poetry Association. *Saigon Tea* and *Spit* are among the collections of his poetry that have been published. In 1997, the *Rockford Review* published one of his poems.

Two Runners Reach the Age of Heart Attacks

For my friend, Mark Mullin

Late and hot
No wind
No stars
As midnight wanders

past with our youth in tow
we remember the mile run

the cinders, the lime
the way we shook
our hands to loosen the nerves
the crouch in starting blocks
the, "On your marks, get set,"
the shot that let us go.

I was the one
who always finished behind you
who ran beside mirrors in the air
who strummed on the earth
who ran for the whispers

hiding in girls
You were one
who ran to win
who ran like a black spin from Ireland
who ran with lungs rasping
like an engine about to explode
who ran half-blind with effort
mind burning like a fire in the fog.

Now, we see the same shadow
approach across the lawn.

Your heart, you say, feels heavy
like a bag too full of blood.

My heart, I say, feels tremors,
like a cup too full of secrets.

Our lives have been rich
and both of us are drunk
enough to touch for bandages
under the skin.

• *3* •

The Scholar

LEADING TO GLORY

$\mathcal{A}$t the start of my senior year in high school, my father told me that because I could attend Shimer College, where he was president, for no cost, he was not interested in paying for me to go to a college that was not as good as Shimer. He was prepared to admit that Harvard and Yale were better than Shimer and suggested I apply to both. I agreed, being confident that neither would take me, but thinking that by applying I would mollify him. I knew I did not want to go to Shimer. It did not have a track team. Moreover, I had watched my brother spend three years where his father was president. I wanted none of that. Little did I know that each of my own sons would, for nine years, attend a school run by their father.

I had no idea how serious my father was about not paying for other colleges. I knew that Shimer College was so small that it could not pay its president very well. A scholarship would be a tremendous help to my family. I also knew I wanted to run track in college. I set my sights on getting a track scholarship and contacted coaches at several Big Ten universities. Just as the track season was getting started, but before I had registered any fast times, I was admitted to both Harvard and Yale. It was a time when Eastern universities were eager to expand their national base. Fortunately, I had the sense to know I should not turn down both of them. Harvard offered me a Harvard National Scholarship, and I accepted.

By late spring, when I had run some fast high school miles, offers of full track scholarships began to come in. I was glad that I had already settled on Harvard and could just politely decline. One exchange did amuse me. A letter came misspelling my name and saying, "Dear Mr. Mulling: We see that you have run a 4:23 mile. We would like to have you run for the U.S. Naval Academy. If you have not been working as hard as you should in high school and your grades are not up to par, go to any college for one year. If you complete one year's work at any accredited college we can get you admission to the Naval Academy." I wrote back that I would be attending Harvard. Back came an answer, "Dear Mr. Mulling: We see that you have decided to attend Harvard so we assume your grades are pretty good. If, after a year, you find you are not happy at Harvard, we are sure we can arrange a transfer to the Naval Academy." I wondered what sort of letters I would have gotten if I had been in a prestige sport like football or basketball.

I knew Harvard had a track team but knew nothing about the quality of the program. I had no contact with the coach or anyone in the Athletic Department until I arrived in Cambridge. Fate or luck or some other power brought me to one of the great track coaches and one who was just right for me. Bill McCurdy had been National Collegiate Athletic Association (NCAA) Champion at Stanford in the 880-yard run. He was tall, with a chiseled face and close-cropped hair. During World War II he achieved the highest score of all U.S. servicemen on the physical fitness test. When I got to college he was in his early forties and still in excellent shape. Personal example was part of his success. On my third day of practice at Harvard, we all went for a run. Even though I had been a good high school miler, Bill McCurdy, more than twice my age, finished ahead of me.

It was his ability to bring out the best in each runner that thirty years of Harvard runners remember with abiding gratitude. The workouts he gave us were tailored to challenge each of us individually, to demand that we each produce a maximum effort. When he set qualifying times to make the spring vacation trip to Puerto Rico, he set different times for each runner. Thus, each of us, champion and beginner, had to demonstrate improvement if we wanted to go on that trip.

Bill McCurdy made it clear that he valued courage—the courage to challenge a runner who was clearly better than you or the courage to run at a pace faster than was prudent for your ability. He knew that such tactics might produce spectacular failure. That was all right. On the other hand, they might result in surprising success. He had little time for those who played it safe, who were afraid to test themselves to the fullest.

One would expect star runners to admire their coach, but Bill McCurdy also touched those who had little success. Erich Segal never ran fast enough to get a varsity letter in track at Harvard. However, Erich did write the best-selling book, *Love Story*. He also taught at Harvard, Yale, and Princeton. How many people have taught at all three? When Erich was asked to name the best teacher he had at Harvard, he immediately said, "Bill McCurdy."

I would agree completely with Erich. Bill McCurdy was one of the three most influential men in my life. The other two were my father and my parish priest at our Chicago Episcopal church, Bill Lickfield. Being most influenced by a teacher/administrator, a priest, and a coach certainly points toward a career path.

When Bill McCurdy died some twenty years after he retired, former runners came from around the country and abroad to attend his memorial service. Nine of us, three from each of the decades in which Bill coached at Harvard, spoke. We each told a favorite McCurdy story. There was one constant theme. Even in an individual sport like track, Bill McCurdy emphasized the team over individual success. He taught us that one is more likely to accomplish something great when one forgets oneself and works for the good of the group. I did not say it on that day, but I remember the highest compliment he ever paid me: "Mark, did you ever notice that your best races were when the team needed it?"

Bill McCurdy's emphasis on *team* shaped the way I looked at schools when I became a headmaster. I tried to discourage turf wars between teachers or distinctions between teachers and administrators. Actually, the term "headmaster" comes from English boarding schools where teachers were called "masters." Thus, a headmaster is really a head teacher, not a CEO or administrator. I was distressed by those people who would only consider the school from the viewpoint of one constituency. Just as on a track team, athletes compete in very different events, but all work for a team victory; in a strong school, people have different responsibilities, but all should be seeking the good of the whole.

Recently, my hostess at a dinner party told me that one of the guests had been a board member of a local independent school. Unfortunately,

I did not get an opportunity to speak to that guest until people were ready to leave after dinner. I said, "I am sorry we did not get a chance to talk. I understand you have been involved with independent schools."

I was saddened when the guest replied, "Oh, I was on the other side. I was a board member." How tragic for that school if a board member thinks of a school as having different sides rather than being one team.

Two years after Bill McCurdy's death, the suburban Boston town in which he had lived built a track and named it for him. The name of the town is Harvard, but it is twenty miles from the university. I got a call asking if my words from Bill McCurdy's memorial service could be used on the stone and metal plaque at the track. Of course, I agreed. Martha and I went to the dedication service. It is a source of great satisfaction to me that my words permanently honor a man who did so much for me:

> He led us to glory
> To the glory that really matters
> Not the glory of the world
> But the glory that comes
> From reaching deep and doing your best

READING EDMUND BURKE

After a high school where only half the graduates attended any sort of college, the academic work at Harvard was a shock. I did well in any course requiring writing. Calculus and French were another story. Both courses caused me to think carefully for the first time about teaching methods. They also taught me to persevere. I had had trouble with Latin so I was not surprised that French was hard for me. The instructor spoke only French to us. Such a method might work well in an intensive immersion course. It is, after all, how children learn their first language. But in a course that met only three times a week for an hour each time, it was very ineffective. After a week and a half, I turned to the student sitting next to me.

"Are you getting this? I can't even understand what the homework is."

He replied, "Oh yes. I understand it."

"How? This is beginning French."

"I studied at the Sorbonne last summer."

I had not expected to have trouble in calculus, having scored well on the math SAT. But the instructor just did problems on the board and never interacted with the students. Until the first test, six weeks into the course, he had no way of knowing whether his students understood anything he said. I did not. I was also, as a freshman from a Midwestern high school, too embarrassed to tell him I did not understand. I thought the fault must be mine.

At the midterm I had a "D" in both French and calculus. Robert Watson, dean of students, called me into his imposing office in University Hall. I sat there, so nervous that I could not stop picking at my socks. Dean Watson was wonderful. He made it very clear that my situation was serious. But he also said, "I have confidence in you. I know you will improve. Therefore, I will not take away your running eligibility at this time." He realized how important running was to me. By the end of the first semester, I had made the necessary improvement. French was saved for me because Bill McCurdy talked a graduate student, Erich Segal, into tutoring me. By my senior year my grades were good enough that I was a serious candidate for prestigious scholarships to study abroad.

Ten years later, I read that student radicals had physically carried Dean Robert Watson out of University Hall. I was disgusted that this caring man should be so treated by privileged young people. However, at my twenty-fifth reunion, I was lining up with the other class officers. I looked across the Old Yard and saw Robert Watson standing with his fiftieth reunion class. I left my place in line, ran across the Old Yard, and said to him, "I would not be here today if it were not for you. And your example has influenced how I have tried to treat the students in my charge."

While not all of my teachers at Harvard were good in the classroom, many were excellent. There were also many colorful characters. B. F. Skinner taught a psychology course on behavioral conditioning. Each semester he used his conditioning techniques to train a live pigeon in front of the class. W. K. Jordan could make the last will and testaments of Elizabethan Englishmen into fascinating documents. Reinhold Niebuhr helped undergraduates understand how complex and difficult moral decisions can be for individuals and for societies. Arthur Darby Nock fell asleep once in his own class. Karl Friedrich taught the history of political theory. It was in political theory that I majored. Friedrich expounded on all the ways society could be organized from a Platonic ideal, to a Hobbesian autocracy, to Rousseauian general will, to a Lockeian social contract.

The political theorist most appealing to me was Edmund Burke, the Englishman who supported the American Revolution and opposed the French Revolution. Burke said that society must be a contract between those who have come before, those who are living, and those yet unborn. I like to think of a good school as a Burkeian society that extends forward and backward in time. I can understand alumni who want a school to remain as it was in their day. It is not surprising that students resent the influence of alumni or criticize a headmaster for spending time with them. It is hard for students to realize that in a few years they will be alumni themselves. It is also natural for parents to be uninterested in improvements that will come to the school after their child has graduated. However, headmasters, trustees, and others responsible for schools should consider the past, the present, and the future of the school in true Burkeian fashion.

Professor Friedrich knew something of forming societies. He was the American representative overseeing the writing of the West German Constitution after the defeat of the Third Reich. I remember once literally running back to my dormitory from his lecture to read the book he had been discussing.

In the spring of my freshman year, Fidel Castro visited Harvard. He was greeted as a hero because he had just overthrown the repressive Batista regime in Cuba. I joined a crowd of students who surrounded him as he stood in camouflage fatigues outside the Freshman Union. I pushed my way to within a few feet of him but was not able to shake his hand. He spoke that evening to a large and enthusiastic crowd at Harvard Stadium. None of us dreamed that within two years he would be considered such an enemy that the United States would support an armed invasion of Cuba. Certainly, I never thought that he would be the only world leader in office while I was a college freshman who would still be in power when I retired forty-three years later.

As a sophomore, I was appointed to a three-year term as the undergraduate representative on the Board of Directors of the Harvard Cooperative Society. It ran the large campus store. I was diligent about attending meetings but contributed little to the discussions since the other members were either senior faculty or leading businessmen. For the first time, I watched how a volunteer board worked, never dreaming that I would spend twenty-five years being very interested in the workings of boards.

In my junior year, John Kennedy was elected president of the United States. Even those at Harvard who had not supported him were excited at the way this young, appealing Harvard man captured the imagination of the nation. Just twenty-one years before, he had sat in the same classrooms, eaten in the same dining rooms, and studied in the same libraries as we were now. President Kennedy took several Harvard faculty members to Washington with him. One person he did not take was the professor of international relations. I took the international relations course that spring. When the Bay of Pigs disaster happened, the professor stopped his prepared lecture frequently and took questions from the floor. Some of us, with the wisdom of twenty-year-old cynics, sat in the back row and said to each other, "Henry Kissinger is just pretending he is in Washington holding a press conference, but he'll never make it."

At Harvard, seniors pursuing an honors degree were required to write a lengthy thesis. Several people advised me, "Choose a narrow topic that is not well known. Concentrate on just that."

I decided that if I were going to do all the work of a thesis, I should choose a question to which I was genuinely seeking an answer. I decided to write on "Christian Attitudes toward War" because I did not know where I stood on the issue of war. The section in which I looked in the Bible was the weakest part of the thesis because neither my advisor (a political theorist) nor I knew anything about Biblical criticism. I studied medieval just war theory that set down strict conditions about when a country could go to war. Traditional Christian thought has said that there are several conditions necessary to make war justifiable. First, a legitimate authority must conduct the war. Second, it must be only in response to an attack or great harm done to one by the enemy. Third, it must be aimed at combatants, not civilians.

Fourth, peace must be the ultimate aim. I also read pacifist arguments from the Society of Friends and Leo Tolstoy.

I found myself drawn to the position that flows from St. Augustine to Reinhold Niebuhr. It is a view of man that says that because we are members of society and responsible for each other, it is sometimes necessary to do things that, if done solely by individuals, would be morally reprehensible. But one may only do these things under certain carefully defined conditions. As St. Augustine quotes the Psalmist, "From our necessities, Good Lord, deliver us." My thesis was too broad to be really good scholarship. However, I had the satisfaction of investigating a subject that truly mattered to me.

At Harvard there were no regular class officers. Four Class Marshals were elected in the senior year. They planned graduation activities, encouraged classmates to make a first gift to Harvard, conducted Prize Day, led the seniors into the graduation ceremonies, and were the only members of the class to shake the hand of the president of Harvard at graduation. I was genuinely surprised when I was elected First Marshal of the Class of 1962. One of my responsibilities was to ask my classmates to support the class gift. The handwritten notes I put on hundreds of letters were my first experience with fund-raising. However, that experience was of little benefit to Harvard in later years. The Fourth Marshal became headmaster of Deerfield. The Third Marshal was headmaster of Nichols School, Belmont Hill, and Robert College. The Second Marshal was dean of the Law School at Queens College. The First Marshal was headmaster of St. Albans and Casady. We were all too busy raising money for our own institutions to raise much for Harvard.

Because I was competing throughout the academic year in cross-country, indoor track, and outdoor track, I had time for little else than studying and running at Harvard. Nevertheless, I very much value the experience I had there. However, those years also taught me that an academic institution is never right for everyone. I had a good friend who dreamed of Harvard all the way through high school. He was admitted, but when he got to Harvard he found the academic work over his head. He worked very hard but just barely managed to graduate. His low grades made it impossible for him to be admitted to the sort of graduate school he wanted. Getting his "first choice" was the worst thing that could have happened to him. It was a lesson I was not often successful in sharing with my students and their parents. On the other hand, my own Harvard experience was wonderful. It left me feeling an obligation to the university. Although I did little fund-raising for Harvard, I did try to be helpful whenever I could. I particularly enjoyed the term I served on the Board of the Harvard Alumni Association.

While I was at Harvard, I attended the student Episcopal services. The sermons were at a high intellectual level, but it was still the liturgy of the sacrament that drew me. I was also aware that the president of Harvard, Nathan Pusey, was a committed Episcopal layman. He was a man of clear intellectual ability. Moreover, he was a man of exceptional moral courage as he had already demonstrated by being one of the first to stand up against Senator Joe McCarthy's witch hunts. The power of leadership by example was impressed on me.

My faith in Christ remained strong. Under the influence of the Harvard faculty, however, I found my thoughts turning more and more toward university teaching. In my senior year I sought an opportunity to study in England, and I planned to pursue a Ph.D. when I returned to America.

SO RUN THAT YOU MAY ATTAIN IT

Every two years, a combined track team from Harvard and Yale competes against a combined team from Oxford and Cambridge. This is the oldest international track meet in the world, predating the Olympics by one year. The meet was scheduled to be held in London at the end of my freshman year. Two Americans were to run in each event. For most events, Bill McCurdy and the Yale coach could agree about who should compete against the English. I was running about as fast as the varsity milers at Harvard and Yale, but as a freshman I had never actually run in a meet against them. Bill McCurdy and the Yale coach decided on a run off. On a cold rainy Tuesday afternoon, four Harvard and three Yale runners were lined up; only two of us were freshmen. "There will be plane tickets waiting for the first two runners to cross the finish line." I wanted a ticket. Neither my parents nor my brother had ever been to Europe. I took the lead right at the start, determined that no one would pass me. I was still leading at the finish line. I would go to England!

Of all the races I ran, I think this was the most thrilling for me. Even though the track was muddy, I had run within one second of my personal best. As a freshman, I had beaten all the varsity milers at Harvard and Yale. I had had the courage to dominate the race by leading all the way. And it meant that I would be the first member of my family to go to Europe.

We stayed at Oxford before the meet. I was assigned a room on the top floor of University College. To get to it, I had to pass a statue of the poet Shelley who had studied at University College. The statue was life-sized and portrayed his dead body as he lay on the beach after drowning in Italy. At night, a faint light gave the marble the bluish tint of a drowned person. It was a chilling sight on the way to my room. Nonetheless, I loved being at this ancient university with its beautiful Gothic buildings, deep-rooted traditions, and gowned students. The experience of living in an Oxford college for a few days inspired me to try to return after I had completed Harvard.

We trained at the Oxford track where Roger Bannister had run the first four-minute mile. I could not believe I was there. After the Oxford-Cambridge versus Harvard-Yale meet in London, we also competed in Dublin and Belfast. The Dublin track was the one on which, just a year before, Herb Elliott had set a new world record for the mile run. I did not have any success in those meets yet was thrilled to run on the track where the first four-minute mile was run and the track where the current world record had been set. They were hallowed places for any aspiring miler.

While we were in Dublin preparing to run there, I met a real Irish redhead and took her dancing several times. Then I had to go on to Belfast for another track meet. That dream remained elusive.

After the competition in England and Ireland was over, I spent eight weeks traveling in Europe. Being far from home, the awareness of the centuries of Christianity in England, visiting actual locations in Rome that were mentioned in *The Robe*, all strengthened my faith at a crucial time in my life. Most important was the surreal experience of running alone under the midnight sun north of the Arctic Circle in Norway. In that unusual light, in those beautiful woods, I knew Christ's presence in a new way. It was a breakthrough of a new reality.

While I was in Norway I had another sort of experience, one much less spiritual. After the track meets, I had gone to Helsinki to join two friends from Harvard. They had purchased a VW bug, and we drove it all the way north through Finland and then to the top of Norway. As we were driving south through the fjord country, one of my friends tried to pass a bus on a narrow dirt road. The bus hit us, and the VW was knocked upside down. Amazingly, none of us were hurt. The people got off the bus, and there were enough of them to roll the car right side up. We drove on, although we had to sit hunched down because the roof had been slightly flattened. After we had been driving for half an hour, the friend in the back seat became to scream. "Stop the car! Stop the car!" The battery in a VW bug was under the back seat. While the car was upside down battery acid had leaked out, been absorbed by the seat cushion, and was now working its way through his trousers.

In my sophomore year I became the fastest miler in Harvard history and won the Ivy League Championship. I got four rungs up a six-rung ladder to make the 1960 U.S. Olympic team, but as a sophomore I found the West Coast runners too much for me.

In track there are events for most body types. Hurdlers and high jumpers are tall. Distance runners are thin. Sprinters are solid. And weight men, who throw things, are big. That was helpful on that California trip. We were staying in Palo Alto preparing for the national championships that led to the Olympic trials. One evening, Ed Stowell, the Harvard assistant coach, was driving us to a local restaurant for dinner. We were headed for a restaurant that promised an "all you can eat" dinner. That is attractive to young trackmen who burn thousands of calories in each practice. Ed, who was from the East, had trouble finding the restaurant. At one intersection he realized that he was in the wrong lane and abruptly switched lanes cutting off the car behind us. The other driver hit his horn, lifted his middle finger, and pulled around us blocking our way. Three big tough-looking goons got out of the car and headed for ours.

Ed Stowell was not tall and had the trim build of a distance runner. As the toughs approached our car, Ed said, "Howard, Fitzgerald, Mullin, out of the car." All of us were thin distance runners. At 145 pounds, I was the heaviest. We got out of the car trying to look fierce. The three toughs began to laugh. This was going to be fun.

"Alright," Ed Stowell said. "Nichols, Bailey, and Doten, out of the car." At an even six feet, Nichols was the shortest of the three. He weighed 235 pounds. Bailey was taller but weighed only 198. However, he was so strong that he was the first man to weigh less than 200 pounds and throw the hammer more than 200 feet. Then there was Doten. When we were in Puerto Rico for spring training, people called him "The Mountain." On the flight to California he got in trouble with the stewardess for breaking his seat belt. He had forgotten to un-buckle it when he stood up.

When Nichols, Bailey, and Doten joined Howard, Fitzgerald, and Mullin, the toughs leapt back into their car and left rubber on the pavement as they sped away. I felt as though I had been in an old Charles Atlas advertisement.

Although in other years I had run well on muddy tracks, in my jun-ior year I had trouble with rainy days. Tracks in those days were still made of cinders. A heavy rain could turn them into mush. The Penn Relays were held on a miserable wet day, but we were still confident that Harvard could win the four-times-one-mile relay. There were four good milers at Harvard that year. We all wanted the neat wristwatches that winners were given. The watches said Penn Relays Champion on their faces. My teammates gave me a ten-yard lead as I ran the anchor leg. On the muddy track it was difficult to know pace. I led for three and three-quarters laps. With fifty yards to go, Ergas Lepps, the Big Ten Champion from Michigan, blew past me. As I headed for the showers, cold and disappointed about not getting watches for the other milers, one of the sprinters shouted to me, "Hey, Mark. What time is it?"

Things went better two weeks later on that same Franklin Field track in the Ivy League Championships. On the last lap, Yale's Bobby Mack, who had beaten me indoors, challenged me twice but was un-able to get past me. My time of 4:07.1 set a new Ivy League record. Only the next day, when I read it in the newspaper, did I learn that I had run the fastest mile ever run in the University of Pennsylvania's Franklin Field Stadium. The old record had been set by Roger Ban-nister when he was an undergraduate at Oxford.

Three weeks after that, on another cold rainy day on Randall's Is-land, New York, Spike Paranya, of Wesleyan, beat me in the Intercol-legiate Championships. The race was so close that we recorded the same time. Although we were rivals on the track, Spike became, and remains, a good friend. The Paranyas and the Mullins still visit each other every couple of years.

In June of my junior year, the Oxford-Cambridge versus Harvard-Yale meet was held at Harvard. Herb Elliott was at Cambridge University. He held the world record in the mile run, was the 1960 Olympic Champion, and had never lost a mile race in his life. But his serious running days were behind him, and he was not in top shape. He chose to run the 880 instead of the mile in the Oxford-Cambridge versus Harvard-Yale meet. People kidded me that the greatest miler in the world was afraid to run against me, but that was completely unfair to Elliott. In fact, a young Oxford runner, John Boulter, did unexpectedly beat me in the mile. It is a part of the cycle of life that the next guy is always right there, panting at your heels, ready to overtake you.

During the indoor season of my senior year, we knew that the Harvard-Yale-Princeton meet would be extremely close. Every point would matter. I had beaten Bobby Mack of Yale outdoors but had lost to him twice indoors. On the Sunday before the meet, the bulletin in the Episcopal Church I attended had on its cover a simple drawing of a runner and a quote from St. Paul's First Letter to the Corinthians. "So run that you may attain it." Six days later I beat Bobby for the first time indoors, and we won the meet. It was the fastest mile I had ever run, and the fastest mile anyone had run in Yale's Coxe cage. The cover of that bulletin, framed, has been kept where I can see it ever since. It captures what I think track teaches about life: set a goal, then have the discipline and make the sacrifices necessary to move toward the goal. This applies whether the goal is athletic success, career accomplishment, a good family life, or one's relationship with God.

During the outdoor season of my senior year, I was undefeated in the mile run. In my last race for Harvard, I won the Intercollegiate Amateur Athletic Association of America Championship, breaking the record set four years earlier by the 1956 Olympic Champion, Ron Delaney. My time was 4:06.4. I felt very blessed that the last time I wore an "H" on my chest I set the intercollegiate record.

Track runners know that their sport does not get the interest or attention that some other sports receive. Therefore, I was honored to receive the "Bingham Award for Integrity, Courage, Leadership, and Ability on the Athletic Field." It is considered Harvard's highest athletic award. In retrospect, I realize how important the first three qualities are for a headmaster: integrity, courage, and leadership.

Although I had no thoughts of being a headmaster, Harvard track did get me thinking about teaching in boarding schools. Jack Richards had been captain of Harvard track eight years before me. When he graduated from college, he began teaching at Andover. A few years later, he took a one-year leave of absence from Andover to get his master's degree in education at Harvard. While he was working on his master's, he also coached the Harvard freshman track team, of which I was a member. Jack and I became friends. He returned to Andover and continued to coach there.

Just before I graduated from college, he invited me to visit him and his young family at Andover. They had a nice apartment attached to a dormitory. Jack showed me around the impressive Andover campus. He spoke of how much he enjoyed teaching bright students, coaching track, and getting to know students as only a dormitory master can. It looked like a very rewarding life. I could imagine myself leading such a life. However, I was headed for advanced study at Oxford. My thoughts were still on university teaching, which had, at that time, replaced my eighth-grade desire to be a priest.

THE GRECIAN URN

The speakers at Bill McCurdy's memorial service were right about his emphasis on team. He made it very clear that he would rather have the team beat Yale than have one individual win a national championship. I am glad that we did not lose to Yale in an outdoor track meet during my three years on the varsity.

One Yale meet gave my mother, Alma, a little publicity. When my brother and I were small children in Chicago, there was an empty lot half a block from our apartment. We often played there after school. When it was time for dinner, my mother would step out on the back porch, put two fingers in her mouth, and whistle. But to call what she did a whistle is like comparing a canon to a cap gun. It was shrill; it was loud; it was long; and it was audible at great distances. Any sailor on shore leave would have envied it. When we heard that whistle, we ran home as fast as we could because we knew that dinner was ready.

When my mother started watching me run in track meets, she would wait until sometime during the last lap. Then she put two fingers in her mouth and blasted out. We joked about it making me run faster as a Pavlovian response. Whether or not it had any effect on my running, it certainly had spectacular results on those sitting near my mother. As the wife of a college president, my mother usually looked quite respectable as she sat quietly in the stands during a track meet. People hardly noticed her. Then there would be an ear-splitting, brain-piercing sound, leaving those around her partially deaf and wondering what had happened. My mother would smile demurely and say, "That's my son, there, running."

At the Harvard-Yale meet my junior year, the sports reporter from the *New Haven Register* picked up the story and talked to my mother about her whistle. The next day a headline read, "Mother's Whistle," and the article began by saying that it was not "Whistler's Mother" but "mother's whistle" that had brought victory to the Harvard team.

At that same meet someone from the Harvard Athletic Department took a picture of the finish of the mile. It appeared in *The Second H Book of Harvard Athletics*. If you are partial to the color crimson, it is a great picture. I am breaking the tape at the end of the mile run. Chris Ohiri, the Nigerian Olympic soccer player and Harvard long jumper, is throwing his arms around me, as he always did when I finished a mile. Looking very tired and strained, Bobby Mack, a strong distance runner, is two yards behind me. The letters "Y A L" are clearly visible on his chest. The "E" does not show.

In the 1980s, J. August, a venerable old Cambridge clothing supplier, remodeled its store on Massachusetts Avenue. It began selling only clothing with Harvard insignia on it. To add to the Harvard atmosphere, it placed large photographs of Harvard athletics high on the walls. There is an aerial shot of the Harvard crew on the Charles River. And over one of the counters is a ten-by-three-foot copy of the picture in which I am beating Bobby Mack.

When we are in Cambridge, which happens every two or three years, I sometimes stop by J. August to see if the picture is still there. One time Martha told a clerk that I was the runner in the picture. He was unimpressed. I am sure he was born after the picture was taken.

The picture was still there last time I checked, which was in 2006. One of these days J. August will remodel again, and I'll be hauled away with the rubbish.

While I was at Casady School in Oklahoma, the National Association of Independent Schools met in Boston. We were delighted that Will Billow, the St. Albans chaplain, was at the meeting. It is always fun to see him. He said, "Some of the boys tell me that there is a picture of you at Harvard. I'd like to see it."

When we got to the J. August store, there were two men standing directly under my picture. From their conversation, we could tell that one was the manager or owner, the other a salesman. Will could not resist telling them that the picture was of me.

The manager got agitated. "Well, you know, once the university releases a picture we are allowed to use it." I realized that he thought I might cause him some sort of trouble about the picture or demand a royalty.

"Oh, I hope you'll keep the picture up there for a long time. Just make sure that Yale runner never catches up to me."

The manager relaxed. "Don't worry. It's just like the runners on the Grecian urn. He'll never catch you."

DREAMING SPIRES

Having been to Oxford with the Harvard track team after my freshman year, I was eager to return as a student after college. The Rhodes Scholarship had a reputation for wanting scholar-athletes so I thought I might have a chance at that. One day, I was standing looking at bulletin board announcements for both the Rhodes and the Marshall Scholarships. Marshall Scholarships are patterned after the Rhodes Scholarships but are paid for by the British government. It was a thank you to America for the Marshall Aid Program. A holder of a Marshall may attend any British university, while a Rhodes must go to Oxford. In those days, the Rhodes was limited to men, while the Marshall was open to anyone. As I was looking at the bulletin board, a Harvard professor came along. He was someone I had never liked very much because of his abrupt and arrogant manner. Yet I will always be grateful to him, because on this day he gave me excellent advice. As we stood there I asked, "I am applying for Rhodes. Do you think I ought to also apply for the Marshall? I hear it is more academic than the Rhodes."

His answer was quick. "Of course you should. Your grades are good. You have a chance. Go for it."

For Thanksgiving during my senior year in college, my roommate, Dave Ruschhaupt, invited me to a dinner given by a local alumnus. Don Hurley liked to entertain students who could not go home for Thanksgiving. I was reluctant to go.

"I don't want to spend Thanksgiving with a bunch of strangers."

Dave urged me to go. "I think Mr. Hurley is very well connected. He probably knows people on the Rhodes Selection Committee."

This caught my attention. I went to the Thanksgiving dinner for the wrong reasons, but then the law of unintended consequences took hold. Mr. Hurley's niece, Martha Jane Leamy, a redhead of Irish decent, sat across from me at dinner. She was very attractive. However, she was dating a classmate of mine, and we merely exchanged pleasantries.

As I was leaving the party I saw a picture of Mr. Hurley standing with the editor of the *Christian Science Monitor* who was also the chairman of the New England Rhodes Committee. I seized my opportunity and told Mr. Hurley that I was applying for a Rhodes. He graciously said he would drop a note to the chairman about me.

Both the Marshall and the Rhodes Committees had their interviews the same week in December. I believe there was a decisive moment in each interview. At the Marshall interview one member of the committee asked, "You have applied for both the Marshall and the Rhodes. If you get both which will you accept?"

I assumed that they wanted me to say I would take the Marshall. But I felt that I had to be honest. Without hesitating I said, "I'd take the Rhodes."

At the Rhodes interview, I was asked about the provisions of the Monroe Doctrine that set U.S. policy toward Latin America. This was less than a year after the Bay of Pigs incident. One could reasonably expect a government major at Harvard to know the provisions. Unfortunately, most of my course work had been in political theory, not political practice. I had looked at the Monroe Doctrine in Henry Kissinger's course, but I had not thought about it in seven months.

"I am afraid I do not know," I answered. I did know that I would not be a Rhodes Scholar.

To my surprise, the British government granted me a Marshall Scholarship for two years of study at Oriel College, Oxford. Apparently, the Marshall Committee liked honesty. Years later, I thought often about those two interviews during the six years I served on the Marshall Scholarship Selection Committee.

For me, Oxford is one of the most magical places on earth. The Gothic buildings, the gardens and lawns, the meadows and parks, and the two rivers make it a city of spectacular beauty. More than any place I know, it combines the past, the present, and the future. The past is everywhere at Oxford. So many of the buildings are ancient. Where else could one of the colleges have been founded in 1379 and still have as its official name today "New College"? So many of the people who have shaped Britain throughout its history have been associated with Oxford as students or teachers. Yet Oxford is very much in the present. It is a place of young people. Everywhere one looks during term time, there are students. And it is a place of the future, preparing young people in every field to be tomorrow's leaders.

Oxford has so many traditions that it is hard to imagine being part of the start of a new tradition. Because of my friend, Stuart Cohn, I did get to do that. Stu was the Big Ten fencing champion from the University of Illinois. He fenced at Oxford in the winter season, but I never saw him in a match. In the spring he told me that he was going to start a new event. "We are going to have fencing out-of-doors. But each time someone touches an opponent, he has to drink half a pint of beer. Why don't you come and cheer me on?"

"Sounds fun. I'd be glad to come."

"But I expect you to drink a half pint every time I do."

I do not like beer but agreed anyway. The match was held on the lawn of Merton Lane near Christ Church Meadow. The day turned out to be unusually warm with the strong afternoon sun beating down on us.

Because Stu was an expert fencer he scored a number of touches early in the afternoon. A couple of quick pints on a hot afternoon can leave one the worse for wear. I quit drinking, pretty sure that Stu would not notice. I was right. He had two more victories but then no more. By now his opponents had a distinct advantage.

Stu went on to become a professor of law at the University of Florida. He has told me that the spring beer fencing continues at Oxford to this day. In the 1990s, the Vietnam government paid Stu to lecture there on business contract law. I think of those 50,000 Americans who died, vainly trying to keep Vietnam from going Communist. Today, its government is paying to learn about capitalism.

There were a fair number of Americans at Oxford while I was there. Several of them were classmates from Harvard. One of our most unusual classmates was Saul Kripke. Most of us first noticed him in the Harvard library. He always seemed to be there. But what caught our attention was his rocking. Most of us bent way over our books, or slouched in our chairs, or put our feet on the desk. Not Saul. He rocked! Saul would lay his book flat on the desk. His hands would be at his sides. And he would rock rapidly back and forth from the waist, his head covering an arc of almost two feet. Saul had a disheveled, slightly exotic look anyway, but when he was in motion at a desk, he was a sight not to be forgotten. And so, early in our freshman year, he became one of the best-known members of our class. At least he was well known in the sense of notoriety. I suspect that few of us knew him well. The times I tried to talk with him I found myself merely exchanging polite banalities. We never seemed to get beyond the weather as a topic of conversation. The reason, of course, was that Saul's depth of thought was so far beyond mine that there was little we could talk about.

All through college, Saul rocked away. We rarely saw him taking any notes. The motion of his upper body seemed to move information directly from the printed page to his brain. How he managed to stay focused on the page as his shoulders and head moved quickly back and forth I did not understand. I was sure he had the strongest and most elastic eye muscles in the world. A friend from New York explained to me that Orthodox Jews often pray standing up with the same rocking motion. Saul, the son of a rabbi, had obviously transferred the motion from prayer to study. Given the esoteric nature of his academic work, there may have been no line between study and prayer for Saul.

Although we were impressed, few of us were surprised to learn that while he was still an undergraduate at Harvard, Saul was also teaching mathematical logic to graduate students at MIT.

When we were at Oxford together, I only saw Saul a couple of times. I used the Oriel College library most of the time. I did not know where Saul studied. Wherever it was, I was sure that he was in perpetual motion. The last time I saw Saul was in the spring. There is, perhaps, nothing as lovely as a spring evening in England. Because of the northern latitude, the light lasts long after dinner. The air is soft, the temperature just right for a light jacket. At Oxford, the ancient college buildings add a stately and timeless grace. If one has access to an English garden, of which there are dozens in Oxford, it is hard to imagine a more wonderful or romantic place.

On just such an evening, I went for an after-dinner walk with some of my friends. A couple of them had been classmates at Harvard. We walked around Christ Church Meadow. In this meadow, many years before, a mathematics professor had told two little girls a story he made up as he went along. The story involved a white rabbit. One of the girls was named Alice.

As we walked in the meadow, we somehow got talking about Saul Kripke. We, who were his classmates at Harvard, told the others how unusual he was but also how brilliant he was. No one said anything particularly mean, but we did talk about how different and out of it he seemed.

Then to our surprise, there was Saul, walking toward us and also enjoying the evening air. We greeted him with that mixture of friendliness and embarrassment that people have when they meet someone they have just been talking about.

We walked past him. When we were far enough past him that there was no chance that he could hear, I said, "Think about what just happened. We were talking about how out of it Saul is. We are walking in an incredibly romantic situation with a group of guys. Saul was walking with a girl. He is more with it than we are."

I never saw Saul again. However, I was not surprised by an article in the *New York Times* on January 28, 2006. "Saul Kripke turned 65 in November. In many circles, Mr. Kripke, who in 2001 was awarded the Schock Prize, philosophy's equivalent of the Nobel, is thought to be the world's greatest living philosopher."

One day in November of my second year at Oxford, one of the London papers carried an article about the next American presidential election that was a year away. The headline read, "The Man Who Is

Gunning for Kennedy." There was a large picture of Barry Goldwater dressed in Western gear and holding a high-powered rifle. The article told how Goldwater hoped to win the Republican nomination and then run against Kennedy. Because Goldwater was from Arizona, the article played up his Western heritage, hence the rifle.

Later that same day, I was walking back to my room to get ready to go out to a dinner party at a friend's home. An English student passed me in the first quad. "Your president has been shot." I ran to my room, turned on the radio, and heard that President Kennedy was being operated on in Dallas. I knelt down and prayed, "Lord, let him live. Let him live."

By the time I got to the dinner party, the news was reporting John Kennedy's death. I was impressed by the reaction of the English. Several times in the next few days, total strangers, recognizing me as an American by my clothes, stopped me on the street to say, "I am sorry about your president."

Kind as the British were, I think most of us who were abroad at the time felt very cut off from America. I found myself drifting to the rooms of other Americans. We did not have much to say to each other, but we needed to be with others who had shared the experience of growing up in the United States. In a time of crisis or sorrow, any sense of familiarity, of home, is welcome.

An Oxford education consisted of two parts. Least important were the lectures. There are three terms in each academic year. Every term, dons gave a variety of lectures. One did not sign up. No attendance was taken. One just went if a lecture looked as though it would be helpful.

The heart of the Oxford education was the tutorial. Each term a student was assigned two tutors. The tutors might well be senior faculty members. A student met each tutor once a week. The tutors assigned a paper topic and suggested books that might be helpful (never something as simplifying as page numbers). The next week the paper (usually about twenty pages) was presented to the tutor. Thus, two lengthy papers were prepared each week. The student did not have to spend time typing the paper. He or she just read it to the tutor. Such an education teaches research skills. That much writing usually brings improvement. The student gets instant feedback from the comments the tutor makes. Worse than any red pencil marks I got on papers at

Harvard was the time I was reading a politics paper to Mr. Hugh Seton-Watson. I looked up and said, "Sir, are you awake?"

He shook himself and sputtered, "Yes, yes. Of course."

I resolved to improve my writing. How proud I was a month later when Mr. Seton-Watson interrupted me as I read my paper about the role of the executive in government. He said, "I did not know that."

All of this was in preparation for examinations, which were held at the end of the student's time at Oxford. The student took eight three-hour exams over a five-day period covering two years of study. The results were published in the *Times* of London for all the world to see. No wonder, on the last day of exams in a particular subject, one's friends waited outside the Examination Building with champagne. During the last frantic fifteen minutes of writing one could hear corks popping.

I chose to study (the British would say "to read") what is called P.P.E. It combines philosophy, politics, and economics. In the old days it must have been a good course of study for those preparing to run the British Empire. But now, of course, there is no empire. Today one needs to specialize in just one of those disciplines. It was, as it turned out, good training for me. At the time, I had no idea I would become a headmaster. When I did become one, I found that a headmaster needs a little philosophy, some economics, and a lot of politics.

I enjoyed running at Oxford and earning a "Blue," which is Oxford's equivalent of a varsity letter. However, I only ran competitively during my first year there. I missed Bill McCurdy's leadership and the sense of team he instilled in all of us. I never ran quite as fast as I had in America, nor was I undefeated. England has always produced good milers. Over the years, three Oxford runners have set the world record in the mile.

Two races, however, gave me particular pleasure. I was thrilled to win the mile in the Oxford University versus the Amateur Athletic Association meet on the Oxford track. It was in this same meet, on the same track, nine years earlier that Roger Bannister had run the world's first four-minute mile. My last competitive race was for the Oxford-Cambridge team against the Harvard-Yale team. Winning the mile against my former teammates and friends, Ed Hamlin and Ed Meehan, and helping the Oxford-Cambridge team to win, was a good way to end my running career.

I was pleased that my parents came to London for the Oxford-Cambridge versus Harvard-Yale meet. It was the first time either of my parents had been to Europe. I did tease my father a bit about the fact that this time he had to admit that he had come just to see me run. He had not been able to dream up any Shimer College business in England.

In those years, Guinness stout was not widely available in the United States. It may have been served in some Irish pubs in Boston, but not in Illinois. My father had never tasted it until that trip to England. He loved it and expressed regret that he would not be able to get any when he returned home.

Early the next November, I wrote to the Guinness brewery in Dublin. I said that my father's birthday was on December 16 and that I would love to get him some Guinness. "Please tell me how I can order some in the United States for him and what I should pay." I heard nothing back from the Guinness brewery and assumed that my project was a failure. I sent him a book for his birthday.

On December 16, my father was at home in the little town of Mt. Carroll, 130 miles west of Chicago. The doorbell rang. When my father answered it, a well-dressed stranger stood there. "Mr. Mullin?"

"Yes."

"I have a present for you from your son. Here is a case of Guinness stout."

I was definitely son of the year on that birthday.

While I was running in England, an old man used to show up for the important meets. He would shake our hands and say, "Well run, my boy." Everyone treated him with respect, and I knew that he had once been considered the world's fastest man. Only twenty years later, when the movie *Chariots of Fire* came out, did I learn the full story of Harold Abrahams and his rivalry with Eric Little.

I did run in one more track meet. The year 1995 was the centennial of the Oxford-Cambridge versus Harvard-Yale meet, one year before the centennial of the Olympics. The meet was held at Oxford. Along with the regular student competition, former winners were invited to run in special veterans' races. Although most of us were no longer running competitively, this gave us a chance to relive our youth. I trained for a while with Skip Grant, the St. Albans coach. Then I pulled my hamstring and could only train lightly.

When I got to the meet I was impressed to find that Chris Chataway and Chris Brasher were running. They were the two men who paced Bannister to the first four-minute mile. Bannister himself was at the meet, but he had given up running after an automobile accident some years earlier. Because the meet was at Oxford, it was held on the same track where Bannister had run the first four-minute mile forty-three years before.

In the mile, I was afraid my injured leg might give out. Above all, I wanted to finish. Therefore, I ran carefully and did not really try to run fast. I finished in 6:29. When the Harvard track newsletter reported the meet, someone made a mistake and my time was listed as 4:29. That is about as fast as extremely fit fifty-year-olds could run. I had letters from several Harvard friends congratulating me. I am not the sort of person who likes to complain. I never asked Harvard to correct the printing error.

DECISION IN DEVON

While I was at Oxford, I went to my college chapel regularly. One day in late November 1962, John Evans asked me to go to church with him the next Sunday evening. John had been a year ahead of me at Harvard and had been on the track team. I would not describe him as a close friend, but he had looked me up when I got to Oxford. Why he asked me to go with him to his church that particular Sunday evening I never knew.

The preacher was very clear in his message. It is not enough to try to be a moral person; none of us is good enough to meet the standards God sets. We all are selfish at times. It is not enough to go to church. It is not enough to say "I believe in the Christian faith." Christ asks more. He asks us for a personal, loving relationship with Him. He asks us to make him Lord and Master of our lives. He is not trying to turn us into slaves or robots. He asks us to allow him to direct our lives as a good coach directs a runner. The runner must still run the race. But he follows the instructions of his coach. That was a message I could understand. That was a message I could accept. This was not a conversion experience, but it was a moment of commitment.

Of course, the coaching analogy has its limits. A good coach's instructions are clear. That is not the case with God's will. It is sometimes difficult to know what God wants for us. God's will is revealed subtly, through a variety of sources: the Bible, tradition, the church, other people, circumstances, and our inward longings. One of the things I value about the Episcopal Church is that it teaches that we are imperfect human beings and can never arrive at absolute truth. We must always be searching for understanding of theology, morality, and God's will. It warns us to be suspicious of those who claim certainty about God's will. However, the difficulty of knowing God's will is not a reason not to seek it. I find no contradiction in saying that I must pray earnestly, "Thy will be done," but have trouble discerning that will.

I did not immediately sense any calling to the priesthood. I still thought I would be a university teacher. What I did have was a great feeling of relaxation and confidence that God would lead me to what I should do. However, during the next nine months my feeling that I must be a priest grew gradually.

The summer between my two years at Oxford I spent a month working with the Children's Special Service Mission in Cornwall. In the spectacular scenery of the cliffs above the ocean, I found satisfaction in working with young people and sharing my faith with them.

At the end of the summer, I returned to Oxford before classes began. I set aside two days. I spent both days in the University Church of St. Mary the Virgin, an ancient and beautiful church. Its tower is one of the "dreaming spires" of Oxford. In St. Mary's there is a sign that reminds visitors, "For 900 years men and women have been worshiping on this spot." St. Mary's is also where Thomas Cranmer, author of the English *Book of Common Prayer*, was put on trial under Bloody Mary. He went directly from this church to be burned at the stake on Broad Street. I spent two days in that ancient church, praying and reading a book on prayer. I ate no lunch, but each afternoon went for a long walk in the Oxford parks and gardens. During the walk on the second day, I became certain that I should seek ordination. Not to do so would be to be disobedient to God. Years later, if people asked me why I wanted to be a priest, I usually replied, "I didn't want to. I *had* to."

I wrote to Bishop James Montgomery of Chicago to begin the process that would lead to ordination while I proceeded with my last year at Oxford. In March of that academic year, something happened that I am reluctant to write about. I do not want to imply that I expect this sort of thing to happen often. However, to make this story complete, I must tell it. For eleven years, I had dreamed of marrying an Irish redhead. In February of that year, I began to realize that, while I had committed my professional life to God, I was still holding on to one major point: whom I would marry. I realized that to be truly obedient to God I had to turn over all of my life.

During spring vacation, I went to Devon with a group of Oxford students on a volunteer work project. After work on St. Patrick's Day, I walked into the Valley of the Rocks near Lynton. There, I made a conscious decision that I wanted God to direct all of my life. I had turned my career over to Him. Now, I would turn my marriage (or nonmarriage) over to Him. Ten days after making that commitment, I had my first date with Martha.

EASTER MORN

During my second year at Oxford, I learned that Martha Leamy was living in Germany. I had met her two years earlier at her uncle's Thanksgiving dinner but had not seen her since then. She had broken up with my classmate. She was teaching U.S. soldiers in Germany who did not have high school diplomas. It is fair to say that as a single, young, red-headed girl, she had her classes' attention. I invited her to visit Oxford. She arrived on Good Friday. I booked a room for her at the Tackley Hotel. It was a funny old hotel, located on High Street, just a block from my room at Oriel College. The Tackley was housed in a building that had been the original site of Oriel College. Narrow staircases led to odd-shaped rooms, whose charm came from age, not décor.

The first evening, I took Martha walking among the ancient buildings of Oxford. Because most of the students were away for spring vacation, the university that night was quiet, deserted, and seemingly asleep. The old buildings, with their towers, arches, and crenellation stood in their places, waiting for the return of young people. We walked under Hertford College's full-size replica of the Bridge of Sighs. Then I led Martha down an unlit narrow passage between two college buildings. It was dark and deserted. There was no sign to indicate where we were heading. I could tell she was just a little nervous. She did not know me that well. After twenty yards, the passageway made a sharp right turn, and we emerged into a little courtyard. We crossed it and entered the warmth of one of Oxford's oldest pubs, the Turf. There, under the low-beamed ceiling, Martha had her first pub grub.

Saturday, I suggested a tour of Oxford. We began by climbing the high circular staircase of the tower of St. Mary's Church. St. Mary's is in the center of Oxford. The view from the tower is marvelous. We could see how the colleges are laid out in quad after quad in every direction. A few blocks to the south we saw beautiful Christ Church Meadow and beyond it the River Thames. For the rest of the day, Martha and I pretended to see the sights of Oxford, yet it was clear that our attention was on each other.

Saturday evening we took a bus into the countryside. The lovely Trout Inn is built beside the Thames. Here, the river is small, hardly bigger than a stream. We sat on stools at the bar. The steaks were good. The wine was tasty. But it was not the wine that made me giddy. We knew we were falling in love. I had gone with other girls and had been close to a couple of them. I had never had the experience of completeness, of rightness, of joyous certainty, that I had immediately with Martha. On Easter morn, as church bells rang from several towers, I kissed Martha for the first time.

She spent five more days in Oxford and then we went to London for the weekend. Each day I thought I was in love only to find the next day that I was even more in love. We did not talk of marriage. However, I hoped and believed that a lifetime together was where we were headed.

After ten days in England, Martha had to fly back to Germany. Several days after she left, her first letter came to me. It told how her plane had caught fire over the English Channel and had made an emergency landing near Canterbury. No one was hurt, and eventually another plane took her to Germany. I wrote back and asked a question that was very important to me. "Who were you sitting next to?"

Her reply was what I had hoped for. "I was sitting next to a nun. Why do you ask?"

I answered that when I was a junior in college, a girl from my hometown had flown to Boston to go to the Harvard-Yale football game with me. On Sunday evening, I put her on a plane to return home.

The next morning, when I returned to my room after breakfast, John Valentine, one of my roommates, greeted me with the heart-stopping words, "Sharon's plane crashed." Then he added, "But she is okay." Her plane had caught fire on Sunday night but had landed safely. For the next year and a half we had a long-distance romance, only seeing each other during vacations. Then, just after I graduated from college, I got a "Dear John" letter from her. It told me that when her plane from Boston caught fire, she grabbed the hand of the man sitting next to her and went down the escape slide with him. Now she was planning to marry him.

Martha understood my relief that she had been sitting next to a nun. She said nothing about the apparent danger of flying after visiting me.

Martha is of Irish descent, as am I. However, she really became Irish for me when we went to Ireland two years after we were married. We rented a horse-drawn gypsy wagon and drove through the back roads of County Galway. One day we even drove through the village of Cong where *The Quiet Man* was filmed. Our horse had the dashing name of "Sultan." He also had two speeds: slow and stop. That meant that in the time it took us to pass a farmer in a field we could have quite a conversation with him.

We passed one farmer who asked, "How long have you been married?"

"Two years."

Being Irish, he did not ask if we had children. "How many children do you have?"

"None."

"Ah, the fresh air will do you good."

That night we parked our wagon fifteen feet from the waters of Galway Bay in the little hamlet of Caramore. Sure enough, nine months to the day, our first daughter was born. We named her "Cara," which means friend in Irish.

• *4* •

The Seminarian

THE HOSPITAL

$\mathcal{A}$s I was finishing up at Oxford, Bishop James Montgomery wrote saying that he felt I had had too much of the academic life. I had literally lived all my life in buildings owned by colleges. He said, "I want you to join the army before you go to seminary." I negotiated with him, and he agreed to six months active duty with the army reserve for me.

The bishop was right that it was a good experience. Until the draft was ended a number of years later, serving in the military was an experience most American men had. It was good for me to share it. It also put me in contact with men from very different backgrounds than mine. It turned out that I often needed their help. When I was sent to ordnance supply school I had to deal with automotive parts. I knew little about them. When the sergeant would say, "Mullin, get a differential axel," I was dependent on help from high school dropouts who had worked on cars all their lives.

However, after we did bayonet training, I could not resist writing to the bishop and saying that I found sticking my bayonet into a dummy and yelling "Kill! Kill!" a strange way to prepare for the Christian priesthood.

There were two other reasons why my military experience was not so bad: location and timing. After basic training at Fort Leonard Wood, Missouri, I was the only one in my unit to be sent to Aberdeen, Maryland. There, I was just an hour and a half from where Martha was teaching. We were able to spend every weekend together. Then, the same month I was released from active duty, the United States went from 15,000 troops in Vietnam to 50,000. The buildup was on, and I missed it.

That fall I entered the General Theological Seminary on the west side of Manhattan. I have to describe the experience as a disappointment. I wanted to be trained as a priest, to know the things a priest needs to know. Instead, General Seminary tried to give us an academic education but did not do it as well as the divinity school of a major university would have done. For example, during the three years I was there I probably wrote twenty academic papers with footnotes. That is not a skill a parish priest (or even a school chaplain) has to have. On the other hand, I was required to write only two sermons, something most priests will need to do fifty times a year for their entire ministry.

The good thing about General was its location on the west side of Manhattan and the opportunities to do interesting fieldwork. One year I taught released time religion classes to high school students in Brooklyn. I found, not to my surprise, that I really liked working with young people. The next year I was working at a parish in Spanish East Harlem when Martin Luther King was killed. Everyone in New York City was nervous. I went out to Brooklyn to accompany Martha home from the school where she was teaching. However, New York remained much calmer than some other places.

The rector of the parish had me do an interesting experiment. He asked me to buy three everyday necessities in East Harlem: a loaf of bread, a quart of milk, and a bar of soap. Then he told me to take the cross-town bus to Morningside Heights, where Columbia University is located. He told me to buy the same three items and then take the bus back to East Harlem. In those days East Harlem had only small mom-and-pop stores. These stores could not buy in the discount volume that the larger stores near Columbia could. Moreover, because of their rough neighborhood, the East Harlem stores paid high insurance rates. Thus, these stores had to charge higher prices. It turned out that if a resident of East Harlem had the time, he or she could save money by paying for bus trips to and from Morningside Heights just to buy a loaf of bread, a quart of milk, and a bar of soap. It was an important lesson to me about one of the reasons the poor remain in poverty.

The summer after my first year in seminary, I worked as a chaplain intern at St. Luke's Hospital. Every patient got at least one visit from a chaplain or chaplain intern. If anyone indicated a desire for other visits, we made it a point to come back. I had to learn that the first thing I needed to do was to assure patients that a chaplain visited everyone. Some people thought the arrival of a chaplain meant he knew something bad that the doctors had not told the patient. Most people in hospitals, however, are glad for a visit, even from a stranger. Some have a sort of foxhole mentality. It makes them particularly appreciate contact with someone who just might have "a little pull upstairs." However, most people stayed in the hospital for such a short time that it was hard to develop meaningful relationships.

Emergency situations made me face the question of the role of a clergyman. If someone had a cardiac arrest, there would be a special code signal. A team of specialized doctors and nurses rushed to the patient. The chaplain was also called. We Americans are used to being involved, useful, and active. I found it quite difficult just to stand there while five or six other people worked frantically to save the patient. Of course, I prayed at such times, but I could have done that in the chaplain's office. Why was I there? This was a particularly challenging question when there were no family members to be comforted. I suppose I had been such an active person that I needed to learn something about the ministry of presence. When I became a priest, I found that presence, just going to the home of a family in grief, was tremendously helpful. What I said was not as important as being there.

At St. Luke's Hospital, I learned more about the importance of presence one day when I sat with an elderly man. I had never seen any visitors at his bedside. He was drifting in and out of consciousness. One day, when I had seen all the new patients, I sat holding the man's hand for twenty minutes. He said nothing, but I could tell that during his conscious moments he wanted to hold on to someone. Suddenly, I was aware that there was a senior doctor standing in the doorway. When he saw what I was doing, he put his hand on my shoulder and said, "God, I wish I had time to do that. It would do my patients such good."

As a priest-headmaster, I learned that immediacy is as important as presence. I tried to follow the example of my predecessor, Canon Charles Martin, who was a tireless visitor. My administrative assistants got used to there being an urgent phone call for me. I would then fly out the door, saying, "Reschedule any appointments in the next two hours." I would head for the home of a student who had just been killed in an automobile accident, a teacher who had just learned that his two-year-old son's cancerous eye had to be removed, or the trauma unit at the hospital where a faculty member who had been struck by a car was slowly gaining consciousness.

On two occasions, I have been the first non–family member in the door of a home after a suicide of a young graduate. Suicide of a son or daughter is the worst nightmare a parent can face. There is nothing a priest can say, but just being there right away is never forgotten. I never had a current student commit suicide, but six of my former students took their own lives before they were twenty-five. Five were from St. Albans, and one from Casady. A Washington reporter once called me and said he wanted to do a story on the suicides, which, he was sure, were caused by all the pressure at St. Albans. He decided not to write the story after I told him that I had attended a small-town high school where there was almost no pressure. Nonetheless, two of the twenty-three boys in my high school class committed suicide within a few years of graduating. In the suicides of the young men I have known, I believe that substance abuse was a factor in some. A failed romance, compounded by racial discrimination, was a factor in another. Fear of disgrace in the military was another. I have no knowledge of why the others took their own lives. All I could offer the distraught parents was the assurance that their son was remembered fondly and the comfort that the presence of a priest brings to some people.

I think presence matters even after death. Twice, when a faculty or staff member died unattended, I stayed with the body for over an hour until the coroner arrived.

Presence matters also in joyful times. On July 23, 1966, Martha and I were married at the Cathedral of St. John the Divine. It is just two blocks from St. Luke's Hospital where I was working. It was a relatively small wedding, but it was good to have our families and special friends present. Of course, we made sure that my former roommate, who had introduced us, was there. We had a two-day trip to New England, but we saved our real honeymoon, a trip to Quebec City, until the end of the summer.

In August of that summer, the staff at St. Luke's was amused when for one week the number of maternity cases doubled. It was nine months after the great Northeast Blackout had left New York without lights for most of the night. Candlelight and no television encourage romance.

Months later, as I made plans for fieldwork for my last seminary summer, I heard of a program for chaplain interns working with the U.S. Sixth Fleet in Nice, France. That sounded like a good summer for Martha and me. When I went to sign up, the advisor asked, "Would you put Alaska as a second choice?"

"Of course."

It was one of those cases where getting one's second choice is so much better than the first choice. We've been to France many times since then, but living in a log cabin in an Indian village in Alaska is something we will probably never do again.

HUSKIES

Martha and I flew to Seattle and then on to Anchorage. The next day, an all-day train trip brought us through Denali Park and finally to Fairbanks. Bill Gordon, Bishop of Alaska, took us immediately to his single-engine plane that he piloted himself. We flew off, over the Alaskan wilderness. Hour after hour we flew, seeing no signs of human presence. It was light throughout the late afternoon and evening. Bishop Gordon did swoop down to give us a closer look when he spotted some moose feeding at a river's edge. Finally, we circled over the village of Huslia, thirty or so log cabins scattered haphazardly about one hundred yards from the banks of the Koyukuk River.

We landed on the sandy strip at the edge of the village. People rushed from the village to the plane. It was obvious that they were glad to see Bishop Gordon and curious to meet us. We learned later that whenever a plane landed, all of the children and most of the adults hurried to the runway to see who had arrived. In such a small and isolated village, people were eager to see any new face. It was fifty miles to the next village of the same size, but there were no roads connecting the villages. Until the snow came, all travel was by river or air.

We walked to the far side of the village where the church stood next to the two-story log cabin that was the vicar's home. The vicarage had interior walls of plywood. There was an indoor outhouse; it was, of course, my job to carry the honey pot to the outdoor outhouse that stood thirty feet behind the vicarage. In another little shed was a diesel generator. Bishop Gordon explained, "You won't need to run the generator for lights until mid-August because it will always be light outside. But if you run it for an hour or so a day, the electric pump will pull water up from the well to the storage tank. Then you can have cold running water."

To me, the most interesting feature of the house was the basement. One entered through a trap door in the living room. The basement was about seven feet down, its walls unfinished dirt. The permafrost started at about four feet during the summer, and the basement remained the temperature of an electric refrigerator. We were able to keep milk, butter, and meat there for days, and eggs lasted over a month.

Bishop Gordon stayed less than an hour and then took off for Fairbanks, leaving me in charge of the church and both of us very dependent on the Athabascan Indians for managing life in the wilderness. We found the people very eager to help and to include us in whatever they were doing.

The oldest people of Huslia spoke primarily Athabascan. Most of the adults spoke a mixture of Athabascan and English. However, they made a real effort always to speak English in front of their children. This was very helpful to the young people. When they grew up and left the village, they were fluent in English. The sad thing was that few of them knew their native language. Huslia was unusual because it had voted not to allow alcohol to be sold there. Occasionally, someone would bring a few bottles in, but it was quickly consumed. In general, Huslia avoided many of the problems with alcohol that afflict some American Indian communities.

Alaska is one area where Christians cooperated rather than competed. One village would be all Episcopalians, another Methodists, and another Baptists. Thus, Huslia felt like a medieval village where everyone went to the same church. It was also medieval because no one came to church until I rang the bell. When I was ready on Sunday morning, and again on Wednesday evening, I would ring the bell. The people would stop what they were doing and come to church. They did not put on fancy clothes. If women had their hair in curlers, they left the curlers in. They came as they were. The church was built of logs. There were rough benches and a log altar covered with beaded moose skin.

I think it was very good for me that the first congregation to which I preached regularly was composed of people who lived off the land. They needed concrete examples and stories, not theological abstractions or ecclesiastical conundrums. Like the people Jesus preached to, they lived in a small village and were dependent on the fish they caught. Even a superficial reading of the New Testament shows that most of the time Jesus told stories. I would spend my ministry preaching to adolescents who were significantly better educated and more sophisticated than the Alaskan Athabascans; however, they were adolescents who were required to attend chapel. A good story was more likely to hold their attention than anything else. I had a professor in seminary that told us, "Marry a girl who is not interested in theology. If she likes your sermons, the people in the pews will also." No one ever followed his advice more faithfully than I. Martha helped keep my sermons centered on what people needed to hear rather than what I wanted to say. One time at St. Albans, when I thought I had been particularly eloquent, she commented, "Mark, that was a pretty good sermon, but you mentioned God too much."

There were one hundred and fifty Athabascan people in Huslia. And there were at least three hundred husky dogs. Each family kept a team of huskies for pulling sleds in the winter. The dogs were chained near each family's log cabin. In the summer, the dogs would dig down into sandy soil to get cool and escape insects. In August, when we began to have a few hours of darkness, one dog would start to howl at night. Dozens of others would soon join in. It was a haunting and beautiful sound.

Beginning in July, the people set nets in the river. As the salmon came up the Koyukuk River on their way to spawn, the people netted them, gutted them, and hung them over smoldering fires to cure. All over the village, beside every log cabin, hundreds of salmon hung drying over smoky fires. In fact, it takes about three hundred dried salmon to feed one dog for a winter. At the height of the salmon season, not everyone could spread nets near the village. Some of the people went to fish camps a few miles up or down the river. The fish camps not only increased the take of salmon but also gave the families a change of scenery and a tenting trip for a couple of weeks.

One Sunday afternoon, Martha and I went in our outboard motor boat to visit some of the families in fish camps. The families had not been able to get to church. Because of the possibility of being attacked by a bear or a moose, we were told never to leave the village without a rifle. I did admit to myself that perhaps Bishop Montgomery had been right about military service. I was glad I had been sufficiently well trained by the army to earn a marksman medal. Fortunately, I never had to use that skill.

The first camp we visited was that of old Chief Henry and his wife, Bessie. He invited us into his tent for moose meat stew. If I had not known it was moose I would have thought it was slightly tough beef. When we finished, Chief Henry, whom I had already known for six weeks, put his hand on my shoulder. "Now we have eaten together. Now we are friends." The old man, who could barely read and had certainly never studied theology, taught me more about the sacramental power of sharing a meal than any professor I had in seminary.

Along with conducting services in the log church, I saw our chief task as working with the teenagers. Huslia had a small grade school. When they were ready for high school, Huslia adolescents were sent to Indian boarding schools in Alaska and in the Lower Forty-eight. When they came back to Huslia for three months in the summer, they were bored. We played many volleyball games that went on late into the night because it was always light. I particularly enjoyed the volleyball because, at five feet eleven and a half inches, I was taller than most of the residents of Huslia. We also organized massive games of capture the flag, ranging over several miles of scrubby woodlands. Later in the summer, when it began to get dark late at night, we had great bonfires to roast bear and moose meat. The best celebration of the summer was the Fourth of July. The people were very proud of being Americans and spent the whole day at games and contests. The biggest competition was a tug-of-war between all the men and all the women in the village. When the signal was given, the women immediately pulled us off our feet. We claimed that we had not been ready and demanded a rematch. The women just smiled and repeated the process with the same result.

When there was a big forest fire somewhere in Alaska, the Fire Service would send a plane to Huslia and take the able-bodied men of the village off for a week or two to fight the fire. The men loved the adventure. It was also one of their few chances to make considerable amounts of cash. One time, when most of the men had gone to fight a fire, a fifteen-year-old boy let a cherry bomb go off in his hand. Amazingly, he did not lose any fingers, but the cherry bomb's packing was embedded in his palm. His mother brought him to me to get the packing out. I poured after-shave on his hand to sterilize it and had a razor blade as the sharpest possible knife, but nothing to ease his pain. I asked two of the teenage girls to come into the room where I was going to try to remove the packing. When the young man saw the girls, he stuck out his hand and said, "Cut." He never flinched as I used the razor blade to open up his palm.

Huslia gave me my first experience of disciplining teenagers. I noticed that some candy was missing from the storage shed behind the church. It was candy for the Bible School. A couple of days later, I caught two of my acolytes sneaking into the shed. They were very embarrassed and confessed their theft. I told them that I would not tell their parents if they would do enough work around the church to pay for the candy. They proved to be good workers. How I wish that all the disciplinary problems I faced as a dean or headmaster could have been solved so easily.

One day, the woman in the cabin nearest ours asked if we would like one of the husky puppies that her dog had just delivered. We accepted readily and named the puppy "Minga," which means beautiful lake. When we got back to New York for my last year of seminary, Minga made our lives much more interesting. Housebreaking a husky puppy provides considerable exercise when you live in a fifth-floor walkup apartment. All huskies contain some wolf blood, and our dog had markings that made her look very wolflike. It was deceptive. Her wolf blood made her loyal to her pack. Minga decided that all human beings belonged to her pack. She greeted everyone with much tail wagging and as much licking as permitted. The dean of the seminary once said in a sermon, "If half the Christians in this place were as friendly as a certain dog, this would be a much better community." Everyone knew he meant Minga. We enjoyed walking Minga to Washington

Square. People would stop to pet her and then talk with us. We met a lot of interesting New York characters that way.

Years later, when the new Bishop of Washington spoke to the faculties of the Cathedral Schools, he mentioned that he remembered our friendly husky dog from his time at the seminary. How many Alaskan huskies have been preached about by both a seminary dean and a bishop?

Although she was always friendly, Minga was not always well behaved. In fact, she once almost burned down our apartment building. One long weekend, we left New York but let the girlfriend of a seminarian stay in our apartment. The seminarian promised to walk Minga regularly. In the middle of the night, the girl called him saying that she smelled smoke. He rushed over to our apartment. Apparently, he had not walked Minga enough. When Minga lost patience waiting for a walk, her urine shorted out an electrical wire.

During my last year in seminary I began to think and pray more and more about being a school chaplain. Martha encouraged this because she thought my academic and athletic experiences would be valuable in a school. However, a number of faculty members at the seminary told me that I really ought to do a few years of parish work before doing anything else. I have always thought there is a strange contradiction in the Episcopal Church. Seminaries try to train people for parish work, yet the number of people who attend Episcopal parishes continues to decline year after year. Seminaries offer almost no instruction in being a school chaplain, yet most Episcopal schools are thriving.

Bishop Montgomery of Chicago said that he would allow me to go directly into schoolwork if I could find a position. "I think a man does his best work when he is where he wants to be." However, he did ask me to talk with the rector of Lake Forest, Illinois, about being his curate. "He, like you, was an athlete at Harvard. I think you two would get along well." Martha and I stopped in Lake Forest on our way to Mt. Carroll for Christmas vacation. When the rector learned that we had spent the past summer in Alaska, he told us a strange story.

"I once had two parishioners, Ted and Sue, who fell in love and wanted to marry. Ted announced that he was interested in becoming an Episcopal priest. Although they were active parishioners, Sue's parents were against the match. They knew that marriage to Ted would probably mean a very different lifestyle for Sue than the one they had provided her. To test his vocation, Ted went as a volunteer to work for the Episcopal Church in a remote Alaskan village. After Ted had been there several months, Sue came to see me. 'Please, you've got to try to contact Ted. I woke up last night with a terrible feeling that something awful was happening to Ted. Something is really wrong.' I called the Fairbanks office of the Diocese of Alaska, which said it would try to contact Ted by radio. The next day, before I had heard from Alaska, Sue came back to see me. 'Don't worry about contacting Ted. He's fine. Last night I had the feeling that he is happier than he has ever been. I don't know why I was so worried before. I guess I just miss him.' An hour later I got the call from Alaska. Ted had contracted meningitis. He suffered greatly for thirty-six hours and then died."

The rector was a sophisticated man, proud of his rationality. I was certain the story was true. It confirmed my belief that there can be ways of communicating that we do not yet understand. This is particularly true between people who love each other. For all our modern knowledge of various means of producing power, we know very little about the power of love.

• 5 •

The Dean

THE PROPELLER

In the winter of 1968, Martha and I visited the Choate School so that I could be interviewed for the position of chaplain. Choate was a boarding school for boys in Wallingford, Connecticut, halfway between New Haven and Hartford. The assistant headmaster, Gordon Stillman, met us at the train. He was tall and thin. His silver hair added to his aristocratic appearance. He was gentlemanly and yet reserved. He was just what I expected in a New England schoolman. He took us to the headmaster's residence where we were to stay. As we left our bags, Gordon explained that the headmaster, Seymour St. John, was down at the gym watching the varsity basketball game. He aimed us toward the gym and said that the headmaster would find us after the game. When we got to the game, we sat on the side opposite the team benches. I soon noticed a man sitting on the end of the Choate bench. He was not taking part in the coaching, but he followed the action of the game with total concentration. He was not a tall man but looked physically fit. He was partially bald. Even from across the basketball court I would have described him as intense, rather than aristocratic. I was not surprised when, after the game, he walked up to us and said, "Are you Martha and Mark? I'm Seymour St. John"—nor was I surprised when he led us to a Mustang convertible. That kind of car seemed to fit him. "Oh, I know my house is within walking distance.

But I drive everywhere on campus. If I walk, people will stop me and want to talk. I would either have to be rude to them or be late for my next appointment."

In those days, Choate had a required chapel service after dinner on Saturday evening. I was the guest preacher and told some stories about our time in Alaska. Later that night, Seymour invited us into his kitchen for a late night snack. He almost made it seem as though we were children, sneaking into our parents' kitchen to take forbidden cookies. We sat talking about Alaska and flying in small planes. Seymour said, "I used to fly my own seaplane. One time I was landing it on an inlet where we have a house. I was alone. I stepped out of the cockpit and onto the pontoon to keep the plane from hitting the pier. I slipped and fell forward. My head was hit three times by the spinning propeller. I passed out, but when I fell into the cold water I woke up and was able to crawl up to the house to get help. See the scars on my head?" I wondered what it would be like to work for a man who had been hit three times on the head by a spinning airplane propeller and lived to tell the tale.

Seymour did offer me the position of chaplain at Choate. I was also offered a similar position at another New England boarding school. On the last day before we had to make a decision, Martha and I went to bed thinking we would go to the other school. When we woke up, we turned to each other in bed and both said, "Choate."

Two of our children were born while we were at Choate. When Cara was two years old, there was a street fair a few blocks from where we lived on the campus. At the fair, we bought her a helium balloon. Unfortunately, on the walk home, it escaped. She was still crying when we got back to campus. We happened to run into Seymour St. John. He asked why Cara was crying. We told him and went on into our house. Fifteen minutes later, there was a knock at our door. There stood the headmaster, holding a new balloon. The busy man had gone down to the street fair, bought a balloon, and returned to present it to Cara. It was typical of his care not only for faculty but also for their families.

Seymour St. John set two other examples that were important to me. In my third year, a retired faculty member died. He was a man that I had gotten to know well. Although his funeral was held at a church in town, I thought it would be nice to have a little memorial service in the Choate Chapel. After I announced the service, Seymour called me to his office.

"Mark, you need to know that I feel that if I do not attend the memorial service for Ed Berry, people will think that I am slighting him. I've had to cancel a meeting in New York with an important donor. Next time please check with me before you schedule anything that I should attend. I know, however, that your intentions were good. Please, please, just because I pointed out to you how you caused a problem for me, do not stop taking initiative. Just check with my schedule."

Seymour could have said nothing to me, and I would have learned nothing. He could have reprimanded me in a way that made me afraid to take initiative. Instead, he took the time to help me to learn, and he did it in a way that did not make me feel insecure.

The third example Seymour set was about housing. At a boarding school, housing is very important. Salaries are universally low, but the quality of faculty housing varies tremendously. In fact, at the first faculty party we attended, more people asked me, "Where are you living?" than asked, "What are you teaching?" In the eight years we were at Choate we lived first in a second-floor apartment where the student hallway went between our bedroom and our living room, then in a duplex, and finally, for five years, in a beautiful colonial home built in 1774 with a walk-in fireplace in the living room and another small fireplace in the master bedroom. It was the house in which Judge Choate was living when he founded the school. We shared all these residences with students. Seymour St. John used housing to retain teachers he thought were valuable to the school. It gave the headmaster considerable power to reward faculty he wanted to keep at Choate. But, of course, it opened him to the charge of favoritism.

When Seymour retired, the system changed. In the name of fairness, housing was assigned strictly on the basis of seniority and number of children. Such a system avoided any decision making by the administration and thus any criticism. When we left Choate, the teacher who moved into our colonial house was an average teacher who contributed little to the extracurricular life of the school. It was a good example of an institution accepting mediocrity in the name of fairness. Systems based primarily on seniority or systems in which leaders can avoid decision making usually encourage mediocrity.

At Choate I taught religion and ethics, and I also taught two sections of the required tenth-grade course in European history. I had sixteen students in each section. It was easy to engage the students in lively discussions of the events that had shaped modern Europe.

One fall, another teacher who also taught a section of European history was out for six weeks. His section happened to meet at the same time as one of my classes. The headmaster asked me to teach the two classes together until my colleague returned. Of course, I agreed. I was the same quality of teacher that I had been before. The students were the same quality. But now, there were thirty-two of them in the classroom. The quality of what we got done declined dramatically. One does not have to be an expert on education to know why. During a forty-five-minute class with sixteen students, a conscientious teacher can call on each student every day, making sure that they stay alert and finding out what they are learning. Doing that with thirty-two students leaves little time for anything else.

Recently, I listened to the audiobook *Teacher Man* by Frank McCourt. The book is a wonderfully funny and thoughtful tale of being a classroom teacher. His rich Irish brogue makes it all the more delightful to hear on audio. McCourt tells of teaching English in the New York public schools to 176 students each semester. The most conscientious teacher imaginable would have difficulty finding the time to read carefully and make helpful comments on 176 papers if he gave his students frequent writing assignments. And if students do not write frequently and receive comments on their writing, few of them will develop the ability to write well. Of course, reducing class size means spending more money. It means hiring more teachers, and it may mean building more classrooms. Reducing class size is, however, the first place I would put money in any school or school system that runs classes larger than twenty students.

BUFFALO BOB

When I became chaplain of the Choate School, I also taught history and served as a housemaster. I particularly enjoyed coaching cross-country in the fall and track in the spring during the eight years we were at Choate. I often ran with the boys, but it seemed to get harder each year to keep up with the varsity.

We arrived at Choate in the fall of 1968 just as the Cultural Revolution of the sixties was beginning to be felt in secondary schools. It has been my observation that student trends move from colleges to secondary schools rather than the reverse. The sixties were late in coming to Choate.

Required chapel was a natural and easy target for students who wanted to reject authority and tradition in the name of independence and individuality. It was a tough time to be a school chaplain, conducting services for students who made it very clear they did not want to be there. The first article I ever published was about my experiences as a chaplain in those years. It was titled, "Should Buffalo Bob Come to Chapel?" The students of those years had been the first generation to spend all their lives with television. They were used to being entertained. Buffalo Bob had been a character on the *Howdy Doody Show* and was having a comeback making guest appearances at colleges. I, too, tried to entertain the students in chapel. I had guitars, folk singers, modern dancers, movies, outside speakers, and anything that I thought might catch their attention. They remained resistant, sometimes hostile, to chapel services.

One time my attempt really backfired. I wanted to show them that the issues addressed by religion were such universal human issues that advertisers appealed to them. I had what appeared to be faith statements (but were actually advertisements) written on large cardboard sheets. A student would hold up the sheet, then turn it over to show what was being advertised. The best example was "Something to believe in," which turned out to be an ad for Buick automobiles. The disastrous sign said, "Try something different tonight." When it was turned over it showed the ad "Try rice tonight." I was unprepared for the roar of laughter. Then I saw that the boys were all looking up in the balcony where the sixteen-year-old daughter of English teacher David Rice sat very red-faced.

In the spring of my first year, Bishop James Montgomery of Chicago came to Choate to ordain me to the priesthood. He told me that at the end of the service he would invite the students to come forward to kneel at the altar rail and receive an individual blessing from the new priest. That made me nervous. Given their attitude toward chapel, I was afraid that very few would come forward.

During the ordination, and even during his sermon, Bishop Montgomery made it clear that he was not there to entertain or impress the students. He was there as a bishop in the Apostolic Succession to ordain a man to the priesthood. The students responded to his sincerity of purpose. When he invited them up to receive my blessing, more than three-quarters of them, including nonbelievers, came forward. A friend from seminary, who came to Choate for the first time for my ordination, expressed it best. "When I walked into that brick New England chapel I thought, 'This is not where Mark Mullin should be ordained,' but Bishop Montgomery turned it into a Gothic cathedral."

I came to see that the best way to reach students is to be authentic to oneself. They may or may not agree with what you say, but they will have something to which they can react. I saw this also when, in my third year, I was asked to join other teachers in a special sex-ed program for tenth graders. The program would have six evening meetings. The plan was that one of the teachers would give a lecture, and then we would break up into small discussion groups led by the teachers. All the other teachers stressed that it was very important that we be "value-neutral" so that we did not impose our views on the students. It was the only time in my life that I have had trouble getting adolescents to talk. The lecturer presented facts about sexuality, but there was really nothing to discuss. Of course, few fifteen-year-old boys are willing to admit in front of their peers that they have questions about sex. The last half of the last lecture was given to the chaplain. By then I had had it with "value-neutral" education. I told the tenth graders that I was going to speak from a Christian perspective. I spoke specifically about different sexual acts and what Scripture and Christian tradition had to say about them. When we broke into discussion groups, I could hardly control my group. All the students wanted to talk, to argue, to react. Leaders of the other discussion groups reported the same experience.

LIGHTS OUT

Teaching religion to ninth graders is fun. They are developing the intellectual tools to question seriously the certainties of childhood, but they have not formed the layers of pseudosophistication sometimes attached to older students. They are much more likely to be skeptics than cynics.

Part of the charm of some ninth graders is that they think a clergyman will be shocked by their challenges to religion. Of course, getting them to ask tough questions about religion is just what a good teacher wants. Once in a while, however, it was fun to shock them.

One dark, rainy New England day at Choate, my ninth-grade religion class seemed particularly affected by the weather. Most of the students were dispirited, but several were amusing themselves by expressing total disbelief in anything religious. Halfway through the class I heard a member of the maintenance staff using the electric buffer on the floor of the hallway outside my classroom. Suddenly, the lights went out, and the classroom was plunged into semidarkness. I heard the maintenance man walk down the hall and out the door. He must have been new because he did not know where the circuit breaker, which had been tripped by the buffer, was located. He had gone to get the head of the maintenance department.

"All right you guys," I proclaimed. "You don't think prayer works. I am going to pray and make the lights go back on. But it is better to pray alone so I'll go in the hall and pray by myself."

I went out of the room and to the alcove where, I knew, the circuit breaker was. I flipped the switch, and the lights returned to the classrooms. When I got back to my classroom, the ninth graders were laughing but unconvinced.

"Yeah, yeah, Mr. Mullin. You did something in the hall to fix the lights."

"Okay. This time I will stand in front of the room where you can all see me. I'll pray and make the lights go out again."

I caught the eye of the student sitting in the back row nearest the door. I gave a tiny nod toward the light switch and saw in his eyes that he got my meaning. I turned my back to the students, raised my arms toward heaven, and began to chant. "O Lord. O Lord. Let the lights go *out*."

Instantly, the room was dark again. For a few seconds I had a room full of devout believers. Then they spun around and saw the grin on the face of the student sitting next to the light switch.

Some years later, John Geoghegan was a freshman in that same religion class. John had been raised as a Roman Catholic, but his natural inquisitiveness made him a young man ready to challenge any statement of faith. Every day in class he went after anything I said. However, his easy charm and delightful manner soon made him one of our favorite students, and he spent a lot of time with Martha and me.

In the summer after his sophomore year, we took John and three other Choate students to Ireland and England. Even on the trip, John teased me about religion in a friendly sort of way. One of our stops was in Oxford. When we arrived we found the St. Giles Fair in full swing. Since the Middle Ages, the St. Giles Fair has taken up four blocks of the main north-south street in the center of Oxford for a few days. Whatever entertainment was provided centuries ago by jugglers, fortune-tellers, and gypsy musicians has been replaced by those portable mechanical rides that move from fair to fair. They ranged from a merry-go-round to a small roller coaster. One of the most popular rides was a giant upright barrel. Six people could stand in it at one time. As it spun with ever increasing speed, the centrifugal force pressed them tightly against the wall. There was a catwalk above the barrel from which their friends could watch.

We persuaded John Geoghegan to have a ride in the barrel. We did not tell him what would happen when it reached top speed. Martha and I stationed ourselves on the catwalk and waved to John as the barrel began to spin. As it gathered speed, John was pressed against the wall. He smiled bravely at us to show that he was enjoying it. The barrel moved faster and faster.

Suddenly the whole floor of the barrel dropped away. We knew that it was supposed to do that. Centrifugal force would keep the riders safely pressed against the wall. John, however, was not anticipating this development. As the floor dropped away, a look of total fright came to his face. My classroom skeptic began to cross himself vigorously and repeatedly.

PEAT

The trip with John Geoghegan was not the only time we took students to Ireland and England. Five other times we shared our favorite places with students from Choate, Blue Ridge, and St. Albans. For most of them, the highlight of the trip was staying with James Fair at the Murrisk Abbey Hotel on the west coast of County Mayo, Ireland.

I first got to know James Fair when he was the trainer of the Harvard track team. In fact, he makes a brief appearance in Erich Segal's bestseller *Love Story*. Erich, who had been on the track team at Harvard, used a different name for the character. But he gave the character the initials J. F. From the way the character speaks, it is clear that he is a portrait of James Fair.

James had been born in County Mayo and trained as a physical therapist in Dublin. When he came to America, he soon began working with Harvard athletics. He saved his money and eventually bought back the land in Ireland that the British had taken from his ancestors more than a hundred years before.

In the summer after my first year in Oxford, I went to Ireland to help James build a hotel on that land. He named it the Murrisk Abbey Hotel, after the five-hundred-year-old ruins of the nearby Murrisk Abbey.

It is in one of the most beautiful places I have ever seen. Directly in front of the hotel, the waters of Clew Bay stretch northward. Separating Clew Bay from the Atlantic Ocean is a mile-long strand of sand dunes and beaches. Behind the hotel is a small wooded area. Then there are some lovely green fields, framed by stone walls. At the edge of the fields, a path climbs twenty-five hundred feet up the rocks of Croagh Patrick, Ireland's holy mountain. It was here that St. Patrick spent Lent in prayer and fasting before beginning his great missionary effort in Ireland. Every year, tens of thousands of pilgrims climb Croagh Patrick on the third Sunday of July. Over the years, I have climbed it many times. However, when I was there on the Sunday of the pilgrimage, James and I were down below parking cars in his fields at two shillings a car.

After my second year at Oxford, Martha flew over from Germany to join me in Murrisk for three weeks. It was wonderful to have that time together in Ireland, so early in our romance.

Two years after we were married, we returned to Murrisk. It says something about the Ireland of those years that we had to be chaperones for James. He was in his forties. He wanted to date a woman in her thirties. We were in our twenties. However, only when her father learned that we were married would he allow her to go with James and us. I suspect that those days are now gone forever in Ireland.

When we took students to Ireland we usually included a visit to the Medieval Banquet at Bunratty Castle. As soon as we entered the hall, I would tip the steward to make sure that during the banquet one of our students was put in the dungeon. The others loved it when the victim was forced to sing a solo in front of all the guests to gain his release.

A couple of times our trips provided students with athletic training. Running up and down the sand dunes of the strand was a great strength exercise for aspiring football players or distance runners. In the summer of 1970, James used a horse and plow to construct a rough track around one of his fields. He announced a track meet, and a large crowd of locals turned out. The American students and I had a great time competing against and getting to know Irish young people. It was that sort of contact that made the time in Murrisk so special. We knew enough local people that our students were made to feel at home. This was still in the days when most of the cottages in Ireland were heated by open peat fires. The rich, sweet smell of smoldering peat was one of the great charms of Ireland in those years.

Whenever we entered an Irish cottage, we were always greeted with hot tea and homemade Irish soda bread. At the end of a visit, the host would usually say, "Now you can't leave without a little sing-song." Everyone was expected to join in.

The best singing, however, was on the beach. We were friends with a young woman who lived near the Murrisk Abbey. She would join us for a bonfire on the strand. She sang in Gaelic. The haunting, mystical sound of her voice took us back through the centuries to a wild and magical Ireland.

HOW DID YOU KNOW?

When I had been teaching at Choate for a few years, my good friend from the Harvard track team, Pat Liles, brought his family down for a visit. Pat was now a professor at the Harvard Business School. He explained to me that the Business School had been a pioneer in teaching by using case studies. He suggested that I might do the same thing in the religion and ethics class I taught to ninth graders. Case studies for ninth graders were not common in the early 1970s.

I wrote a number of cases that presented the sort of issues that teenagers and young adults might face. They dealt with honesty, academic cheating, turning others in, drugs, and love and sex. Some cases I made up. Some I based on real events that I had known in my years as a teacher. The cases generated considerable discussion in my classes. I hoped they also taught students to think more deeply and clearly about ethical issues.

One of the cases my students most enjoyed discussing was based on real events at Choate. Chuck, a junior, was caught smoking. It was a suspension offense. However, Fred, the head of the student Judicial Committee, had been smoking with him and had just left the room when a teacher walked in and discovered Chuck. The situation was more complicated because Fred had been awarded a Morehead Scholarship, which pays all expenses to the University of North Carolina. That would have been very helpful to Fred's family who were middle-class people with several children to educate. However, the Morehead Scholarship required that winners stay in "good academic and social standing" for the remainder of their time in high school. I was chaplain at the time. Fred came to see me to discuss whether or not to turn himself in. We talked late into the night. I did not tell him what to do but encouraged him to explore the consequences of different options. Fred finally decided to turn himself in. Fortunately, the Morehead people realized that he had done a very noble act, and he kept his scholarship.

Two years later, Fred showed up at our home at Choate.

"I am about to lose my Morehead Scholarship."

"Again?"

"Yes. I got arrested marching for civil rights in North Carolina. Getting arrested for anything is against the Morehead rules."

I knew of a Choate graduate who had been a Morehead Scholar and had marched for civil rights at Selma, Alabama. Now he was at Harvard Law School. I called him and he immediately drove to Wallingford. He listened carefully to everything about Fred's situation. At his suggestion, Fred contacted the American Civil Liberties Union (ACLU). The ACLU convinced the Morehead people that, because the charges against Fred had been dropped, he could not be considered guilty. Fred kept his scholarship. Today, he is teaching ethics at a law school.

Several years later, there was a senior at Choate who was interested in teaching. He got permission to earn academic credit in the spring semester by being a teaching intern in my ninth-grade class. We reserved a period of time immediately after the class so that we could meet to critique and analyze what had gone on in the class.

I let him teach about a quarter of the time. He was a tall, mature young man who captained a varsity sport. The ninth graders certainly looked up to him. I found that analyzing what had gone on in each class was very helpful to my own teaching. A third party who can watch both the teacher and the students can often make useful comments.

The teaching intern particularly liked the case studies and was intrigued by the fact that some of them were true. He used to laugh and say, "Someday, you'll write a case study about me. Then I'll be famous."

One day I was sitting in my office. The teaching intern walked in.

"What are you working on?" he asked.

"I'm writing a new case study."

"Tell me about it."

"Once there was a student in a boarding school who fell in love with his French teacher. They began seeing each other."

He gasped, and then flushed crimson.

"How did you know? Does everybody know? How did you know?"

"Martha knew."

"How?"

"It was at that game last week. She saw you look at each other. You weren't even talking together. When we got home she said to me, 'Those two are in love.'"

"Have you told anyone?"

"No. You are only a month from graduation. And the French teacher has already said she will not be back at Choate next year. We will not tell anyone."

A teacher having an affair with a student is totally unprofessional. In this case, however, it was not sordid. He was a mature nineteen-year-old. She was twenty-five. It was clear that they were in love, not just having a fling. I was glad that I was not in a position of authority at Choate so that I could treat it with the confidentiality of a clergyman.

A few days later, the senior came over to our house and talked to Martha about it. Afterward he told me, "You know, when you are in love you want to shout it from the rooftops and we can't. I have not been able to tell anyone. I'm so glad I can share it with you two."

THE SPIRITUAL CRISIS

The closed community of a boarding school means that teachers spend many hours discussing not only academic matters but also all the problems associated with the residential lives of adolescents. Because so many teachers also coached in the afternoon, Choate held its faculty meetings at night, usually once a week. The meetings began right after dinner at 7:30 and sometimes lasted until 10:00 or 11:00.

One year, I mentioned to Martha that I had noticed that frequently the school doctor, who lived on campus, was called out of the faculty meeting sometime after 9:00 P.M. I wondered, "Could there be that many nighttime medical emergencies?"

At the next meeting, precisely at 9:00 P.M., the phone in the faculty room rang. A teacher answered it, listened a minute, and then said, "Mark, that was Martha. There's a boy having a spiritual crisis. He's at your house and needs the chaplain. Go home right away."

I rushed across campus. When I got to our house I found no student waiting for me. Martha just smiled and said, "You owe me one!"

Because a boarding school is a closed community, one often socializes with the same people, time after time. I think it was at this stage in my life that I developed my dislike of cocktail parties. Much as I liked and admired most of the Choate teachers, I found little enjoyment in standing around with a drink in my hand talking superficially to someone I had worked with earlier in the day.

Martha developed the style of entertaining we liked best. She always had a sit-down dinner so that people could talk leisurely and uninterruptedly. Whenever possible, she included guests from off campus to broaden the conversation. At some parties we had dancing and arranged a schedule so that people had to switch partners. Most important, she gave each party a theme. She encouraged guests to dress for the theme, which put them in a party mood right away.

We started, of course, with St. Patrick's Day parties. From there we moved to a Medieval Banquet. We borrowed life-size stocks from the drama department. Then we provided chunks of bread to be thrown at any miscreants the other guests decided should have some time in the stocks. One January, we decided we needed a beach party. We brought several hundred pounds of sand into our living room, and Martha built a cardboard beach buggy for couples to sit in. After we spent a month in Peru, we had a Peruvian party. It was when the students were away. We got old refrigerator boxes and built an Inca tunnel in the boys' part of the house. After roasting meat over the open fireplace and drinking a fair amount of sangria, guests had to crawl through the Inca tunnel.

We continued the tradition of theme parties in Washington. Once, for St. Patrick's Day, we hired the sort of double-decker bus used in Dublin. It drove our guests past the illuminated monuments of Washington at night. Another time, we got hold of round tables and umbrellas for a French sidewalk café in our living room to thank Peggy Steuart for chairing St. Albans's Seventy-fifth Anniversary Celebration.

One party proved to be prophetic for Martha and me. We asked all the guests to come dressed as their dreams if they were not living their present life. One woman came as a geisha. Our Washington neighbor, Thor Halvorson, came as a Viking. With the help of some large safety pins, one guest squeezed into the naval officer's uniform that he had worn in his twenties. "My dream is that it would still fit." Martha came as an artist in the south of France. I came as a writer on the west coast of Ireland. After we left schoolwork, we did rent a farmhouse in Provence for two weeks. While we have not been back to Ireland recently, I have certainly enjoyed having time to write.

PICTURES

In the year Seymour St. John retired, he asked me if I would serve as a dean the next year. I agreed but found it a painful job because this was the early 1970s. Drug use was heavy among students. In a boarding school they were frequently caught and had to be severely punished. Moreover, I was pretty sure that most of the time we caught and punished the experimenters. The hard-core drug users knew how to hide their activities.

I believed that a school must maintain a strong stand against drugs, alcohol, and violations of honor. Yet it was so sad to see students cause themselves and their parents such distress when they were caught doing things that many of their contemporaries were doing. One time a student with whom I was close asked me, "Mr. Mullin. Why do you serve as a dean? It clearly causes you so much pain to suspend or expel a student. Why not just be a teacher?"

"The day I can expel a student and not feel pain is the day I'll stop being a dean."

Of course, there is a code among adolescents that condemns anyone who turns in a fellow student. But if the offense is egregious enough, some students will not tolerate it. Once, I received information from an eleventh grader that a classmate of his, named Oliver, was selling speed on campus. I went to Oliver's room. He was not there. It was always my policy not to search a student's room unless he was present. I waited until Oliver returned.

"I'd like the speed you have."

"What speed?"

"The 350 hits of speed that you have left of the original 500 you brought on campus that you have been selling for a dollar a hit and that you are keeping in the trunk under your bed."

"I guess you've got me, don't you?"

"Unfortunately, Oliver, I do."

When Oliver had been sent home, I called the school doctor. "I've got 350 hits of speed. Can they be of any medical use? What should I do with them?"

"There's no way to know their purity or strength. You might as well flush them down the toilet."

In 1974, my salary was about $275 a month, plus housing and meals for all my family. I still remember that moment of flushing drugs worth more than a month's salary down the toilet. My real pain came a few days later. I was preparing some students for confirmation because the Bishop of Connecticut would soon visit Choate. I happened to look at the list from the year before, and there was Oliver's name on it. I was some school clergyman! One year I was preparing Oliver for confirmation and the next year expelling him for selling a significant quantity of drugs.

A few weeks later our family went to Disney World for spring vacation. As we were getting on the monorail, there was Oliver.

"My father felt so sorry for me for being thrown out of Choate that he sent me to Disney World to cheer me up."

An even more painful situation involved a student named Tom who had gotten connected with some hard-core New Haven drug dealers. They had given Tom a fairly large supply of marijuana on consignment. He was to sell it at Choate and then give them half the money. He kept both the marijuana and the money in a box under his bed. However, someone stole his box. When he tried to explain it to the drug dealers, they said, "It must have been one of your customers who saw you take the stuff out of the box and put the money in it. Show us a school yearbook with pictures of all the students you sold to."

The drug dealers, who were white, decided that the thief must have been the only one of Tom's customers who was black. His name was Billy. The drug dealers went to Billy's dormitory room. They held Billy and his roommate at gunpoint for half an hour while they searched the room for Tom's box. Billy insisted that he had not taken it from Tom. Eventually, the drug dealers left but only after they had relieved Billy and his roommate of their watches and what little cash they had.

Billy and his roommate then executed a very traditional punishment on Tom. They took him to the basement of a dormitory and shaved his head. This was at a time when almost every teenager had shoulder-length hair. It was immediately apparent that Tom had been punished, and the story was soon all over campus. Tom, of course, was expelled for selling drugs. Billy was a more difficult case. Two weeks before he had been put on school probation for getting caught with a beer. In the drug situation he had only been caught because Tom had been dealing with New Haven toughs. Moreover, he had already suffered the frightening experience of being held at gunpoint for half an hour. Yet he admitted that while on probation he had purchased marijuana from another student.

Billy was a senior and already accepted by an excellent college. Choate offered seniors the opportunity to live off campus and do an individual project in their last semester. Billy had been approved for a project that was to begin in two weeks. Rather than expel him, I told him that he should leave campus immediately and not return. He could do his project, get the credit, and we would mail him his diploma.

When he came to pick up his son, Billy's father came to see me. He was a soft-spoken, humble man. Without any trace of bitterness, he said to me, "You know, we live in Harlem. Billy's brother was shot there. So I sent Billy to Choate where I thought he would be safe. Instead, drug dealers held him at gunpoint in his room."

"It is awful and I am terribly sorry. This is one reason why we take a strong stand against drugs. It may bring our students into contact with very dangerous people. Billy knew our rules and he chose to violate them. But I am going to let him get credit so he can go on to college."

"No one in our family has ever graduated from high school."

"Well, Billy will be a Choate graduate. He just won't attend the ceremony."

Slowly and sadly, Billy's father said, "There won't be any pictures."

My heart broke as I realized I had actually punished the father instead of the son.

NATIONAL SECURITY

While I found being a boarding school dean in those years to be frequently painful, I like to think that one time my work as a dean served the national security of the United States.

When I first started teaching, Choate was an all boys' school. Soon it was announced that Rosemary Hall, a girls' school, would be moving to Wallingford to establish a coordinate relationship. A new campus was built about half a mile from the nearest Choate dormitory. Between the two campuses there was a stretch of woods crossed by a couple of paths.

What the campus planners did not anticipate was that this was an ideal arrangement for panty raids. The dormitories were just the right distance apart. It was fun for teenagers to run through the woods at night to the other dorms, run through the halls looking for underwear, and then race back through the woods.

One day a Choate secretary found an interesting document that had been unintentionally left in a copy machine. It was an elaborate set of plans for a massive panty raid. Group A would go past the infirmary at five minutes after midnight. Two minutes later, group B would move around the Arts Center. Meanwhile, group C would be coming down from the upper woods. These are just the sort of plans that teenage boys relish devising and then implementing.

Ten minutes before the raid was to begin, two other deans and I stationed ourselves in strategic places in the woods to intercept the raiders. As a group of six Choate students ran toward the Rosemary Hall dormitories, I popped out from behind a tree and yelled, "Back to your dorms, gentlemen." Five of them fled in confused surprise, but one kept going. I was young, foolish, and a little upset that he had not obeyed me. I tackled him. When I had him on the ground I realized that it was the junior varsity quarterback. I learned later that he, an aspiring football star, was highly embarrassed about being tackled by a faculty member.

A year later, I gave up tackling students forever. This time the dean's office had no advance notice when the girls raided the boys. The girls ran through the boys' dormitories and then started back to their own. I went out in the night to keep the boys from chasing the girls back through the woods. I yelled at a group of boys to get back to their own dorm. Once again, several turned around; one kept running toward the girls' dormitory. I tackled him. When I got him to the ground, I realized to my horror that she was a girl. Her shoulder-length hair, army fatigue jacket, and blue jeans had given her the same appearance in the night as almost all the boys. Visions of lawsuits danced in my head. I drew myself up and said in my most deanly voice, "Young lady, get back to your dorm." Of course, that is where she had been heading anyway. She hurried off through the dark. I heard nothing more about the incident. I suspect she was as relieved to avoid trouble for being on a panty raid as I was relieved that there was no complaint about my tackling her.

Many years later, I was at lunch at St. Albans when a naval officer appeared at the door of the Refectory. His uniform indicated that he was of significant rank. I saw him ask a question of a student, who then pointed in my direction. As the officer came toward me, I realized that it was the junior varsity quarterback from the panty raid, now all grown up. After we greeted each other, he told me that he was stationed at the

Naval Intelligence School. It was just a few blocks up Massachusetts Avenue from St. Albans.

"I am training young Naval officers in intelligence and counter-intelligence. Do you know what the first thing I teach them is? I tell them, 'Do *not* leave the original document in the copy machine.'"

REVOLUTION

I always enjoyed teaching at the Choate Summer Session, and for a number of years I was its assistant director. Some students were there to make up academic deficiencies. The majority were high school students who came to have a brief boarding experience and for the academic enrichment of a school such as Choate. We were allowed to offer courses that were more creative than the regular school year fare. It was also Choate's practice to have college students as teaching interns in the summer. I always liked working with an intern, sharing my ideas on education and benefiting from his or her feedback about my teaching.

One summer I offered a course entitled "Revolutions." We looked at the French Revolution, the Russian Revolution, and the Nazi Revolution. Using these examples, we also tried to draw conclusions or general principles about the revolutionary process. The course met for six weeks every weekday for an hour before lunch and an hour after lunch. I was assigned a teaching intern, an earnest young man who was a rising senior at Amherst.

On the first day of class, I asked the students to suggest things that are necessary for a successful revolution. Soon we had a list on the board:

Real grievances
Repressive regime
Revolutionary leader
You may need to be willing to lie and deceive people.
While the regime has to be repressive it also has to vacillate in its
    response. If it is too repressive it will just crush the revolution.
You have to be sure the revolutionaries keep up a united front.
If you really want to stir up the people, you need martyrs. Even
    better, get the regime to kill children.

All of the students in the class were new to Choate. I knew none of them. But I watched them carefully during that first discussion. I asked Sam to stay behind after class.

"In three weeks I am giving a major test on the first half of the course. If you can create a revolution in the class and get the students to refuse to take the test, I will give you an A for the whole summer. The only condition is that you must tell no one that I put you up to this."

The look in Sam's eye told me that I had chosen well. He readily agreed to try. We arranged to meet secretly once a week so that he could report to me on his progress. I assured him that the teaching intern would know nothing of this.

This was a summer in the early 1970s. The revolutionary excitement of the sixties was still in the air. At first, Sam tried stirring up resentment toward me. Happily, that did not get far. As we got closer to the announced test, he tried bribery. If he offered a small amount of money no one was interested. If Sam offered a large amount no one believed he would actually pay.

Two days before the test, Sam reported, "I'm finally having some success. But I have had to lie. I told John that Bill would refuse to take the test if he would join us. Then I told Bill that John would join if he would. I think I'm making some progress, but they are still not sure what they will do."

"Let me give you some help and give them a real grievance. I have promised a two-hour review tomorrow. I'll deliberately waste all the time so they will feel unprepared for the test and feel that it is my fault."

During class the next day I could sense the growing frustration as the time went by and I did nothing to prepare them for the test, which would be the following day.

The test was scheduled for the hour before lunch. I told the intern that I had to stop by the Summer Session office and that he should get the students started on the test. I deliberately arrived ten minutes late and found the intern talking with the class.

"What's going on?" I demanded.

"Well, Sam has collected everyone's test and the class is refusing to take it. I'm discussing it with them to find out why they won't take it."

"Discuss it? What's to discuss?" I grabbed the last copy of the test from the intern's hand and glared at the class. "I'm going to make new copies of this. You've got until I get back to make up your minds to take the test." I slammed the door on my way out.

A few minutes later I charged back into the classroom. "Now, who is going to take this test?"

One girl's eyes welled up. "I've got to have the credit. I'll take it." With that, all of the class except Sam asked for the test.

I said to the intern, "You continue to proctor the test." Then turning on Sam I growled, "Come with me, young man." We barely got out into the hall before we both burst into laughter. "At lunch, I want you to tell the others that I said you would be expelled."

At lunch, the intern approached my table. "Sam is saying that he is going to be expelled. All the other students are really mad. Now they are about to revolt. What are we going to do in class after lunch?"

"I don't know what you are going to do, but I am going to tell them how Sam and I plotted the whole thing together."

The poor intern almost dropped his tray of food. However, he was very gracious in accepting my regret that I could not let him in on the plan. "I just did not know you well enough to know what kind of actor you could be."

After lunch we had a wonderful class on revolutionary strategy. We saw how lying helped the cause. We noted the importance of a real grievance (my wasting the two-hour review period). We found that too much conciliation does not help (the intern talking with the class rather than making them take the test). We looked at the show of force that broke the revolution's united front. Finally, the impact of a martyr was clear (the class was ready to revolt when it thought Sam would be expelled).

Sam got his A for the summer.

WAR

My early years at Choate were during the Vietnam War. Like many Americans, I started out supporting the war. We had been alive during World War II and the Korean War. Those were wars in which our country's purpose seemed clear, and most Americans believed our government's assertion that the wars were necessary. We started with that assumption about Vietnam. As we learned more about the corruption and unpopularity of the South Vietnam government, we began to have doubts. If Buddhist monks were willing to set themselves on fire in opposition to the South Vietnam regime, why were we fighting to support it? Then, when the Tet Offensive showed how vulnerable our position was in Vietnam, many of us had another realization. If the U.S. government has been misleading us in saying that we are making progress in Vietnam, why should we continue to trust that government? It also became clearer and clearer that this was America's first major war that made class distinctions. Even before Richard Nixon ended the draft, it had become apparent that those born to privilege were doing significantly less of the dying than those with fewer advantages.

I used to read to my students an article by James Fallows. He talked of the guilt he felt that he and his fellow Harvard students found ways to avoid the draft or get safe assignments within the military during the Vietnam War. But the working-class boys from South Boston did what they were told and went to fight and die. This was clear to anyone who looked in the Choate Chapel. There was a plaque listing many names of Choate graduates killed in World War II. A smaller plaque listed those lost in Korea. Choate lost no one in Vietnam.

My attitude toward the war turned from support to opposition. Yet I never joined in any of the protest demonstrations. I was busy with my early career and my growing family. To this day I carry some feeling of guilt that I neither fought in Vietnam nor protested the war. I believe that it would have been patriotic to do either or both. Timing and circumstances allowed me to avoid taking a public stand on the most important public issue of my young adulthood.

THE MATHEMATICAL DOG

When Martha and I decided that the time had come to leave Choate, we looked at a number of schools around the country and the world. One was a school in paradise. The Bishop's School in La Jolla, California (where the weather is always perfect), was looking for an assistant headmaster. However, the head was in her first year. While I also looked at nonadministrative positions, I thought that if I were going to be an assistant headmaster, I ought to work for a head who was experienced. I said no to La Jolla.

A week later, I was in bed with pneumonia. It was April. It was snowing in Connecticut. I said to myself, "Mark, you really are dumb. You just turned down a job in La Jolla."

I found the experienced head I wanted in Hatcher Williams. He had been headmaster of the Blue Ridge School for twenty years. The school was at the base of the Shenandoah National Park, thirty minutes from Charlottesville, Virginia. Hatcher spoke with a slow North Carolina accent but had a quick wit and a sharp mind. He could get his hand in and out of a donor's pocket before the donor felt a thing. He reminded me of Senator Sam Ervin who had, just a few years before, drawled on about being "just a country lawyer" while he exposed the evils of Watergate. I learned much from Hatcher, but Blue Ridge had another appeal. Its stated mission was to help students who had run into academic difficulties at other schools.

Before we made our decision, we explained our options to Martha's then ninety-nine-year-old grandmother (she lived another eight years). "Go where you can do the most good."

We tried to follow her advice. We found that Blue Ridge was really helping boys. We only stayed a year because St. Albans called. However, we remain close to Blue Ridge. In 2004, I gave the graduation address there. I had also given the graduation address in 1977. I must add that it was a different speech. It is meaningful to me that I spoke at a Blue Ridge graduation a month before I became a headmaster, spoke at my last St. Albans commencement, spoke at my last Casady School graduation, and spoke again at Blue Ridge after I had stopped being a headmaster.

I have also returned to Blue Ridge several times to perform weddings of faculty children. We knew these young people, Margaret Davis, Coby Frye, and Dan Frye, as small children during the year we were at Blue Ridge. What a joy it was to participate in their weddings now that they were grown up.

It is not surprising that we remain close to some Blue Ridge faculty members. The school was so isolated that the faculty had nowhere to turn for entertainment except their own parties. At a boarding school, most people live on campus and so can walk home from a party. The head football coach made wicked daiquiris, and in good weather the hills surrounding the school were great places to play. During the one year we were at Blue Ridge, there were three faculty parties at which blood was shed, never in anger, but always in joie de vivre. It wasn't fighting but falling down stairs or off rock walls that produced the blood.

The headmaster, Hatcher Williams, wisely turned a blind eye to our socializing, as long at it did not come to the attention of the students or affect our teaching. However, I suspect that he inflicted a subtle punishment on us. If he knew that some of us had stayed up too late the night before the administrators' meeting, he would deliberately drone on and on at the meeting. I think he enjoyed watching us jerk our heads as we fought the temptation of a quick nap during the meeting.

While we were only there a year, I have always felt that one of my greatest, or at least most fun, moments as an educator occurred at Blue Ridge.

Blue Ridge is a boarding school for boys. In early September, parents nervously said goodbye to their sons in the shadows of the mountains. Phone calls and letters gave some measure of how the boys were doing. However, parents eagerly awaited the October Parents' Weekend so they could see for themselves how their sons were getting on. Almost all the parents came, no matter where they lived.

On the first evening of the weekend, the parents gathered in the theater. After Hatcher Williams welcomed the parents, he introduced me, the new assistant headmaster. I told the parents that I had come to Blue Ridge because I believed in the mission of the school. In the month and a half that I had been there, I had seen how well the school carried out that mission. "We believe that we can teach every student any subject. As a matter of fact, a dog wandered on the campus today, and we decided to see if we could teach it mathematics. Bill, will you bring that dog on stage?"

With that, the football coach came out followed by a golden retriever.

"What is two plus two?" I asked.

The dog barked four times, and the coach gave the dog a biscuit.

"What is five minus three?"

The dog barked two times and got another biscuit.

"Let's get tough. What is the square root of twenty-five?"

Five barks, another biscuit. The parents were amazed.

"Okay," I said. "You may think this is all rigged. I'll take questions from the floor. Try anything, as long as it has a numerical answer."

Several hands shot up. The dog got each answer right. The parents were really excited and ready to believe that we could teach their sons anything. Of course, most of the time they were watching the dog and counting the barks. What they did not notice was that the football coach would hold a biscuit in his fist, extended toward the dog. The dog (who had been the coach's pet for several years) would begin to bark. When the dog reached the correct number of barks, the football coach would turn his fist over and open his hand to reveal the biscuit. The dog would immediately stop barking and come get his reward. I had no worries about the dog making a mistake. But the football coach . . .

· 6 ·

The Headmaster

THE FIRE POLE

$\mathcal{T}$here are usually many reasons why one is selected for a desirable position. I suppose that was the case when I became the fifth headmaster of St. Albans School. Certainly, the fact that I am an Episcopal priest made me attractive to the Search Committee. The school had a long tradition of priest-headmasters. I believe that another factor was that I was only thirty-six years old and really did not think that I had a chance of being chosen. I relaxed and enjoyed myself during the interview process. This helped the way I presented myself.

I have joked about three incidents during the selection process that impressed important constituencies. One may have gotten me the vote of the Search Committee. Another won over some of the faculty. The last brought me student support.

The first interview was in December 1976. It consisted of a tour of the school followed by lunch with the Governing Board Search Committee in the Burling Lounge. Several members of the committee made a point of saying that we were having the same food as the students were being served that day. I did not realize at the time that they were subtly apologizing for serving it to a guest. It was noodles, ground beef, tomato sauce, and some other unidentified objects all stirred together. I later learned that for visual reasons the students called it "train wreck." Nevertheless, I enjoyed it and without thinking about it, I asked if I might have seconds. There was a little stir and a sense of surprise in the room. Then I noticed that no one else had taken seconds. At first, I thought I had done an "Oliver Twist." Perhaps there was a rule against seconds at St. Albans. Finally, one of the Governing Board members said, "You must be a real schoolman if you want seconds of that stuff."

My second visit to St. Albans was a three-day event in January. At one time, I was asked to meet with a group of teachers in the headmaster's Sitting Room. After we had been talking for about half an hour, I stood up and said, "Does anyone mind if I shut the window? I'm freezing." I pushed the heavy window down. I could feel a ripple of response in the room. This time it was not surprise but gratitude. Only later did I learn that the retiring headmaster, Charles Martin, thought heaven was exactly like Vermont. He was famous for throwing windows open in the middle of the winter. I also learned that one faculty member said after that meeting, "I know all I need to know about Mark. At least he won't freeze us."

Martha had not come to the December luncheon, but during the three-day January visit, she won over the students. I had already had a tour of the school. While I was meeting with some administrators, she was shown around the school. On the tour, she was taken to Tom Sole's old art studio in the basement of the Lower School building. It was a two-story space in which he had built a loft office. There was a stairway up to the office and a fire pole for a quick return to the main floor. When Martha arrived on her tour, Tom Soles was in his art studio, but there were no students present. Martha looked around and asked Tom about the work the students did. She expressed her admiration for their accomplishments. Then she looked up at the fire pole and said, "May I try that?"

"Of course, go on up," Tom replied.

Martha, strikingly attractive in her early thirties, started down the fire pole, her skirt and long red hair flying upward. At that moment, a class of boys came into the studio.

"Who is that?" the students shouted.

"She," answered Tom Soles with a grin, "is the wife of one of the candidates for headmaster."

MAINE GRANITE

I was serving as assistant headmaster of the Blue Ridge School near Charlottesville, Virginia, when I was selected as headmaster of St. Albans. People at both schools began to tell me about the late Sam Hoffman because he had taught at St. Albans during the regular school year and at Blue Ridge in the summer session. Everyone said he was a great teacher. However, he did have a drinking problem. Although it was a serious problem, it did not interfere with the quality of his teaching. No parent ever complained about him. In fact, there is a plaque in the Little Sanctuary at St. Albans that reads, "Sam Hoffman. He believed in his students so much that they came to believe in themselves."

At St. Albans, Sam also served as starter for track meets. Tom Soles loves to tell about the time Sam, who had undoubtedly begun his afternoon cocktails before the track meet, managed to discharge the starter's pistol while it was still in his pocket. Although starter's pistols only fire blanks, the noise, smoke, and Sam's response were spectacular.

Hatcher Williams, the headmaster of the Blue Ridge School, told me of an incident that happened one summer. Before the first faculty meeting of the summer session, a new teacher had struck up a conversation with Sam. The two men clearly enjoyed talking together. After the faculty meeting, the new man spoke to Sam.

"I really enjoyed talking with you. Would you like to get together for a drink some time?"

"Sure," answered Sam. "Are you free second period?"

I succeeded Canon Charles Martin as headmaster of St. Albans in 1977. He had been headmaster for twenty-eight years. Moreover, he was born in the same year as both of my parents.

Four years after we moved to Washington, I wrote the afterword to *An Illustrated History of St. Albans School*. I wrote,

> Becoming headmaster of St. Albans, with its surprises and many happy moments, has been a little like becoming the new son-in-law in a large, lively, and slightly eccentric family. The headmaster of any school necessarily faces many challenges. Can he keep the institution financially solvent in the face of inflation? Can he maintain a faculty

whose members will provide a vigorous academic program and serve as role models for impressionable young men? Can he run the school in such a way that the needs of each boy will be met without sacrificing what is good for the group as a whole? The headmaster of St. Albans, whether he is new or experienced, faces an even more exacting challenge: can he, in a secular age, keep the school true to its calling as a cathedral school, a place of Christian education?

I was thirty-six years old, and a majority of the faculty was older than I was. I found them easy to work with. Most of them were happy with what they were doing. I had enough respect for their experience that I listened carefully to their views on the school. Years later, I found it harder to be as patient with parents or board members who had less experience in education than I did.

Although I was young, two things carried me through those early years. I was able to express my ideas clearly and concisely whether in letters, articles, or speeches. All the writing I had been made to do at Harvard and Oxford, all the many sermons I had given to unwilling adolescents, proved beneficial. It was even more important that I had an image and view of what St. Albans should be. I was not always sure how to get there, but I knew what sort of school I wanted it to be.

Being an Episcopal school was part of that vision, and I carried on the tradition of priest-headmasters. However, it was not my custom to wear my clerical collar on most days. I found that sometimes it creates a barrier that may make people ill at ease. Coming to the headmaster's office makes some people nervous anyway. I did wear a clerical collar when I was doing something sacramental such as celebrating Holy Communion. I also wore it if I went to visit someone in the hospital. A clerical collar gets one past nurses and limited visiting hours.

The night before my first St. Albans commencement, a senior was in a serious car accident. He broke several bones. When his mother called me to tell me of the accident, she asked if her younger son (a St. Albans sophomore) could come forward to receive his brother's diploma. I readily agreed.

As soon as commencement was over, and I had made a polite appearance at the reception, I headed for the hospital where the injured boy was in traction. As always, when going to the hospital, I wore my priest's collar. The hospital was in a northern Virginian suburb that I had not visited. I soon found myself lost. When I stopped at a red light, I began to study a map. I could not even find where I was on the map, much less how to get to the hospital.

Suddenly, a loud and furious honking began behind me. I looked up and saw that the light had gone green. I looked in the rear view mirror and saw an angry woman pounding on her horn. I also saw a plastic Madonna on her dashboard.

With the light still green, I got out of my car and hurried back to the woman. I had a worried look on my face. In my most earnest voice I asked, "Do you need a priest?"

The woman began to cross herself vigorously and repeatedly. "Oh no, Father. I'm so sorry, Father. Forgive me, Father."

Being an Episcopal school gave St. Albans a special identity. Of course, the school chapel, the Little Sanctuary, was very important in maintaining that identity. Here, students were asked to consider the most essential questions facing us as human beings. They were pointed away from their natural self-absorption and toward the transcendent and the eternal. Moreover, they were regularly exposed to Scripture and to some of the finest music ever written. In how many American schools do students regularly listen to readings from the Bible and get repeated doses of Bach, Hayden, and Mendelssohn? I believe strongly in the separation of church and state. It is good for both the country and the church. I presently serve as a judge for the Council for American's First Freedom National High School Essay Contest. However, just as all high school students should be exposed to Shakespeare, I wish there were a way for them all to have some exposure to the Bible, one of the most influential books in human history.

The Little Sanctuary was used not only for regular student services but also for weddings, baptisms, and funerals by alumni, students, faculty, and parents. One day I was talking about the building in Lower School chapel. I explained how people frequently used it for special ceremonies. To illustrate my point, I mentioned that on the next Saturday I would be performing the wedding of a young couple. Neither of them had attended St. Albans, but the bride was the daughter of an alumnus who still valued his time as a student in the Little Sanctuary.

That night, after supper, a St. Albans mother called me at home. I could hear the laughter in her voice even as she identified herself. "Congratulations. I hear you are getting married on Saturday. Does Martha know about this?"

"What do you mean?" I could not think what she was talking about.

"At supper tonight, Fred told us that the headmaster said that he was going to marry the daughter of an alumnus."

That was not the only time a sermon got me in trouble in the Little Sanctuary. Another time it involved a baptism. Most baptismal fonts are ornate and beautiful creations, about as removed from a riverbank as you can get. However, the baptismal font in the Little Sanctuary was a large rock. It had a small indentation scooped out of the top to hold water. I have no idea if there are rocks in the Jordan River where Jesus was baptized, but if there are, this could have come from there. Its sides were worn smooth by thousands of years of moving water, so it certainly came from a river or the edge of the sea.

In fact, it came from Maine. Mimi Crocker gave it to the school in memory of her late husband because they had spent summers in Maine. It was the best baptismal font I have ever seen.

One year, a St. Albans family asked me to baptize their fourth-grade son in the Little Sanctuary. We chose a Saturday. The family and several of their friends gathered around the font. I knew that the boy and his family summered each year in Maine. I began to preach what I thought was a magnificent sermon about the boy's life at St. Albans, his life in Maine, and his new life in Christ all coming together in this piece of Maine granite. The nine-year-old looked up at me and said, "Don't you know it's illegal to take granite out of Maine?"

CHAMPAGNE

While many weddings were held in the Little Sanctuary, on one occasion it was used in a slightly different way. There was a young alumnus who was two years out of college and now in graduate school. There he met a young lady. They fell in love. One weekend he brought her to Washington to meet his parents. His girlfriend had never been in Washington so they spent the weekend seeing the major sights.

On Sunday evening he brought her by St. Albans to see where he had gone to school. As they left the school it was just getting dark. The view of Washington from Mount St. Alban is always impressive. It is magical when the lights of downtown Washington begin to twinkle at dusk.

"This building is where we went to chapel twice a week," he told her. "Chapel was compulsory."

"It's a funny old building."

"Yes. I'd like you to see inside it. I think they hide a key under a rock here."

She was a well-brought-up young lady. "If it's locked we shouldn't go in."

"Here's the key. I found it. Come on in. Don't worry. It's Sunday evening. Nobody is around. Who can object if we go into a church? Besides, I'm an alumnus."

They went in and he switched on the lights. It was too dark outside for the great stained glass window to show.

"Gosh, these benches are hard. Did you really have to sit on them?"

"Yes. That's what kept us awake. Come on up these stairs. I want to show you the view from the second-floor tower. It's wonderful when the lights are on in Washington."

"Oh no. We shouldn't go up there."

"Come on," he urged.

When they got to the room at the top of the stairs there was a trail of rose petals on the floor leading from the stairs to the windows. The windows looked out at Washington. One could look down on the Capitol and the Washington Monument, both illuminated by spotlights. Facing the window was a small sofa. Between the sofa and the window was a bottle of champagne in a bucket of ice and two glasses.

She still didn't get it.

"Somebody is going to have a party up here. We've got to get out of here."

The young man walked over to the bookcase. He pulled out a book. It was one of those fake books, which have been hollowed out. Inside was a ring.

Early the next morning I went to the Little Sanctuary to collect our ice bucket, glasses, and key. The rose petals that Martha had laid down were still there. I found a one-word message waiting for me.

"Yes!"

THE CURSE OF TOURS

I preached to the students once a week all the years I was a headmaster. There is no way of knowing how much of what I said remained with them. There was, however, one story that students liked enough that they asked me to repeat it.

We were in France in the summer of 1983. Mutual friends arranged for us to stay in a house a few miles south of Tours. This was, of course, in the Loire Valley, where the magnificent chateaus are not only beautiful but also filled with history and legends of evil deeds. Our youngest child, Kevin, stayed with his grandparents in America, but Cara and Sean came with us.

The house south of Tours was in the country, set in ancient woods. We arranged to arrive the day before the owners left on their vacation. They wanted to show us the things we needed to know about the house. The family had two daughters. One was about Sean's age, almost twelve, and the other was younger. Soon after we arrived, the mother suggested that the older daughter take Sean on bicycles and show him the path through the woods to the lake. I could see that the younger daughter was upset. She looked sad, and her lower lip curled downward. I did not blame her. This stranger (who did not even speak French) had ridden off on her bicycle. Because there were only two bicycles she could not go along. A little while later, I noticed that she was drawing with chalk on the concrete walk in front of the house. After she went into the house, I wandered over to see what she had drawn.

In chalk, on the concrete, was a face of a girl, smiling. Next to it was a skull and crossbones. Next to that was a face of a boy, frowning. There was a line across his forehead, an *X* over his left eye, and a line across his right cheek.

It was some time before the two bicyclists returned. Sean's face was covered in blood. As they had ridden through the woods toward the lake, Sean had raced ahead, even though he did not know where they were supposed to go. He did not turn right when he should have done so. The density of the woods made it difficult to see the barbed wire strands that had been stretched across the left-hand path. He hit them first with his face. As always, facial wounds bled profusely.

As we cleaned up his face, it became clear where his wounds were: on the forehead, just below the left eye, and on the right cheek. I did not mention the chalk drawings to anyone that night. After the French family left for their vacation the next day, I took a couple of photographs of the chalk drawings. I half expected that when we got them developed they would be blank. In fact, the drawings showed quite clearly in the pictures. After I took the pictures, I washed off the chalk drawings, wanting to get rid of them before Sean got up and saw them.

I did not know what had happened. I did not know whether the little girl drew the pictures before Sean hit the barbed wire or afterward. Did she predict the accident, see it in her mind's eye as it happened, or did she cause it? I did not know. What I was certain of, however, was that she made the chalk drawings before Sean returned to the house and she saw him. She had the locations of the injuries exactly right.

Two years later when this French family came to Washington to stay with us for a few days, I was very careful to do nothing to upset the younger daughter.

The only point I could make to the students when I told this story is that I believe we know as little about the power of the human mind or spirit to transcend time or distance as Benjamin Franklin knew about electricity. He knew there was some power out there, but he had no idea how to harness it or put it to use. Yet, two hundred years after Franklin flew his kite, we think nothing of using electricity to light the darkness, cool our buildings, and communicate immediately with people thousands of miles away. I believe this is particularly true of the power of love. That was demonstrated to me five years later, when Sean was sixteen.

During the twenty-one years we lived on Woodley Road in Washington, fire trucks or ambulances went by our house several times a week. We were very accustomed to sirens, whether it was day or night.

One night, about midnight, we were asleep when a siren went past our house. Martha sat up and said emphatically, "That one is for us." She had never said it before, and she never said it again.

I did not argue but threw some clothes on and started walking in the direction the siren had gone. I went a block and a half to Thirty-fourth Street. Up the hill, at the corner of Thirty-fourth and Lowell, I could see flashing lights and a car against a tree. Before I had gone twenty yards up the hill, Sean came running down the street into my arms. A classmate who had just gotten his license had been driving him home. Oncoming headlights had confused the young driver. He had hit the car coming toward him and then run into a tree. Mercifully, no one was hurt.

THE YARMULKE

Whether or not students remember the content of sermons, sometimes regular services in the Little Sanctuary had moments of grace. There were several hymns that were particularly popular and that students sang with unusual gusto. Sometimes we were able to use a chapel service to honor an individual. At those times the students always showed generosity of spirit. On several occasions, it was in the Little Sanctuary that I shared with the students the news of a death of a faculty member and some of my feelings about the person. I believe that doing it in that setting made a significant difference. During the course of the 1991–1992 academic year three faculty members died. Two of them were department chairs.

Tiger Ferris ran the indoor tennis club and helped with intramural sports. One gets none of the excitement or glory of a varsity coach, and the students in intramurals are rarely volunteers. Yet, Tiger Ferris served faithfully for many years despite being afflicted with Crohn's disease. He set an example to our students of dedication to duty despite personal pain. When I spoke to the students after his death, I said that they had been privileged to be witnesses to such faithfulness.

Henri Billey became Dean of Students when I came to St. Albans. He was very much a Frenchmen. He had a wonderful ability to insist on proper behavior yet do it with a sense of humor that meant that only the most recalcitrant students failed to enjoy his company. He also had an intrinsic sense of when to cut a student some slack and when to stick to the letter of the law. All of the students addressed him simply by his last name: "Billey." It was pronounced "BA" and was a sign of respect and affection.

Billey was also successful as a French teacher and chairman of the Foreign Language Department. As a Frenchman, he taught in a style that was more Continental than American, more 1950s than 1980s. He hectored and bullied his students and kept them constantly on their toes with quick questions and demands that they get it right. Many were intimidated at first. After awhile, most realized that this was a different method of teaching. They found that behind this style was a man who cared passionately that they learn his beloved French. Many also came to know him as a friend who was deeply concerned about them as people.

Billey carried that Continental style into every area of life. He drove with reckless abandon. I refused to ride with him after my first trip with him at the wheel. He thought peanut butter was an abomination and that Coca-Cola would "rot ze stomach." He always attended the Prom but usually came looking like Humphrey Bogart in "Casablanca."

After Billey had been teaching for many years, he decided to learn Japanese. He got a tutor and worked diligently. One summer he spent a month in Japan speaking only Japanese. When he got back to Washington, he told me of his frustrations.

"There were some things in Japanese I just could not get, try as I might. That will make me a better teacher. Now when an English-speaking student tells me he cannot get something in French I'll understand that it is not just lack of effort."

In the summer of 1989 *Vanity Fair* magazine published an article about some of the problems that had occurred that year with student publications at St. Albans. The author of the article chose to quote two seniors who made Billey sound like someone who took pleasure in torturing students. (I did not fare well in the article either.) Billey was visibly upset when he came to see me about the article.

"I've tried so hard to be a good teacher. Now I'm made to seem like a sadist."

"You just have to ignore the press. Everyone—students, parents, your colleagues—knows that you are a good and caring teacher. And they know that those two students were mad at St. Albans in general and just sounding off. Don't worry about it."

However, he did continue to worry about it. During the fall I could see that having such things said about him in print in a national magazine was eating at him. Four months later he was diagnosed with cancer. He continued to teach but over time grew weaker and weaker. During Christmas vacation of the 1991–1992 academic year he died.

When I had been at St. Albans some years, we had an educational guru speak to the faculty. He purported to be able to tell much about a person just from seeing the SAT scores. He claimed to be able to tell what position someone played on the football team by looking at the ratio of the player's verbal and math scores. We gave him a number of scores of present students. He was right enough of the time to be entertaining, but I am not sure what, if anything, our teachers learned from him.

The guru claimed to have another skill that interested me. He said he was an expert at discovering the real person just from reading someone's resume. Headmasters have to decide which candidates to interview from hundreds of resumes. I also wanted to know if there were ways I should shape an interview based on the individual resume. I met with the guru in my office.

"Here are the resumes of three people currently working at St. Albans, so I know them well. I've blanked out the names but copied the resumes exactly as they were sent to us. What should I have been looking for in the interview?"

The guru studied the first resume.

"This is a bright man. He will relate well to students and will keep a good balance between his professional and personal life."

"You've described him well." I handed him a second resume. He studied it a bit longer.

"This is an interesting fellow but one who will get bored teaching four or five classes a day. He is all over the map. I would not hire him as a teacher."

"That was my resume. And yes, headmasters have to jump from talking to a student in trouble to interviewing a teacher candidate to working on a budget question to writing a speech to thanking a donor all in the space of just one morning. Now here is the third resume."

Although there was nothing about the man's appearance on the resume, the guru spoke with great certainty.

"There is something strange about this man's physiology. He is extremely thin, unhealthily. And it is not hereditary. It is something else."

The guru was right about something physical being unusual, but he had one detail wrong. The teacher in question was extremely heavy. In fact, when Donald Brown had interviewed to teach at St. Albans I had worried about his weight. Would it slow him down? How would the boys react to him? However, he was so bright and such a strong mathematician that I decided to hire him.

Donald Brown soon became the star and then the chairman of the Mathematics Department. He wrote a calculus textbook. He was a very demanding teacher but utterly devoted to his students. Every night of the week he was in his classroom from after supper until midnight. Any St. Albans student could come and get personal help. If I had reason to be at school in the evening, I would usually stop by his classroom because it was such fun to visit with him.

As far as I know there was only one punishment he ever inflicted on a student. A late assignment or any other infraction meant that the offender had to wash all the blackboards in Donald's classroom and clean the chalky erasers. And they had to be left immaculate.

I knew that a mind as sharp as his would challenge our brightest students. For a while, I worried about whether he was too tough for the less gifted. Then, one Thanksgiving vacation, I was talking with a young alumnus who had, I knew, struggled with math at St. Albans. I asked him about his college experience.

"I haven't had any teachers in college as good as Mr. Brown. He's the greatest."

Donald never did get his weight under control. After he was diagnosed with diabetes he cut back from two six-packs of Coca-Cola a day to one six-pack.

Then one day during the 1991–1992 academic year, the chief custodian, Leroy Weaver, sent word that he had gone to Donald Brown's apartment in the True-Lucas Building and something was wrong.

I hurried to Donald's apartment. There he was, a very large man sitting lifeless in an easy chair. He looked very peaceful. I hoped he had been asleep when an insulin reaction killed him.

In the Little Sanctuary, I spoke to the students about Donald Brown's death, the third faculty death of that year. Shortly afterward, a student stopped me in the hall.

"Mr. Mullin, we have watched you try to hold this community together through the shock of three deaths during this year. You have tried to give strength and comfort to us. But I know that those men were also your friends, not just teachers. You must be feeling great personal pain. I want you to know how sorry I feel for you."

Sometimes the moments of grace in chapel came from what the students did. During my early years at St. Albans, the Student Council would organize a Crazy Hat Day once a year. Students were allowed to wear a hat all day at school if they paid a dollar. The money then went to a charitable cause decided on by the Student Council. Any hat was allowed, but unusual and outlandish hats were encouraged. Of course, only the truly daring or suicidal would wear a Dallas Cowboys hat in Washington.

In those days, we still had chapel first thing in the morning. As we sang the opening hymn on Crazy Hat Day I glanced over the student body to see what was being worn. There was the usual collection of baseball caps and a fair number of more creative objects perched on heads. Then my eye fell on a student in the third row. He was from a major Muslim country in the Middle East and was attending St. Albans while his family was on assignment in Washington. Securely on his head was a yarmulke that he had borrowed from a Jewish friend. We were singing Martin Luther's great hymn, "A Mighty Fortress Is Our God." I said to myself, "There really is hope for the future," and offered up my thanks to God.

SANTA CLAUS

St. Albans is very fortunate to have its own chapel. The intimacy of the Little Sanctuary is wonderful for regular school services and sacramental events such as baptisms and weddings. However, for state occasions such as commencement and the Christmas service, being able to use the magnificent Washington Cathedral is a great blessing. Every year St. Albans and the National Cathedral School for Girls had a combined service of lessons and carols that filled the Cathedral with students, parents, and alumni. Both headmasters and the bishop always took part and sat up in the Great Choir.

When our son Kevin was two years old, Martha decided to take him to the service. She knew the limits of patience of a two-year-old and planned to sit in the back, prepared for a quick exit. However, as she entered the Cathedral, she ran into the head verger, John Kraus. He, of course, believed that things should be done in the proper way and insisted on escorting Martha to the seats he had saved for her in the front row. Martha was fond of John and did not want to argue with him. Against her better judgment, she and Kevin sat in the front row.

Things went well for a while. Then Kevin, seeing older children performing, decided that he should join them. While the music director conducted, Kevin stood on the kneeler to do his own conducting. While "Silent Night" was being sung, Kevin presented his own version of "Jingle Bells." Bishop John Walker and I, in the Great Choir, were far enough removed that we could exchange amused glances with each other. Martha, on the other hand, was not having a good time. Trying to shush a two-year-old without creating a bigger scene is not an easy task. Finally, Kevin decided he had had enough fun and it was time to go. He stepped into the aisle and started the long way toward the back of the Cathedral. Martha, of course, had to go after him. As the congregation realized to whom the little blond boy belonged, a wave of laughter swept down the length of Washington Cathedral.

Sometime after we had gone to sleep that night, Martha sat straight up in bed. "Tell me it didn't happen. Tell me I dreamed it." I awoke, laughed again, and tried to assure her that she had the sympathy of every St. Albans mother who had ever tried to control a rambunctious little boy.

At another Christmas, I was the one who was embarrassed in the Cathedral. The Lower School music teacher thought it would be good to have an afternoon service a few days before the major Christmas service. This would allow the younger musicians a chance to perform more than they could in the more formal evening service. She wanted to keep the whole thing light and fun. She thought it would add to the occasion to have Santa Claus make an appearance and throw candy canes to the grade school students.

Someone told her that I owned a Santa Claus suit. She soon came to my office to ask if I would make an appearance in that suit. I readily agreed.

"Let's keep it a surprise. You'll need to get there about forty-five minutes early because the student orchestra will arrive half an hour before the service. You hide somewhere. Then, during the last song, which is, 'Santa Claus Is Coming to Town,' you pop out and throw candy canes to the kids. Okay?"

I figured that in a great Gothic cathedral that seats three thousand people there would be plenty of places to hide. When I actually arrived in my Santa suit, dutifully forty-five minutes before the service, I realized that any place on the main floor might be discovered while the musicians and later the other students arrived. Grade school children are more prone to investigate nooks and crannies than to go quietly to their seats. Then I found what I thought was the perfect hiding place. I went up to the Great Pulpit. By sitting down on the floor of the Pulpit with my back toward the congregation, I was completely hidden from anyone on the main floor of the Cathedral. All of the students and teachers would be on the main floor.

Fortunately, I had remembered to bring a book with me. So there, before any students arrived, sat Santa Claus on the floor of the Great Pulpit reading a book. What I had forgotten was that there were still tourists in the Cathedral, and many came into the Great Choir for a better view of the High Altar and the reredos. From there they could see me quite clearly. Several tourists took my picture. I heard one woman exclaim, "My, these Episcopalians have strange rituals."

GIFTS

Christmas was not the only time I got in trouble in the Cathedral. Commencement is the last chance for seniors to have a little fun with the headmaster. My fourth commencement at St. Albans was a special one for me. These boys had come into the ninth grade just as I became headmaster. We had gotten to know each other well during the past four years, and I felt particularly close to them. Moreover, Bishop John Walker had a son in the class, and the Walkers and the Mullins had become good friends. I was pleased that Bishop Walker would be the commencement speaker and that he and I would stand together handing out diplomas.

St. Albans always gave diplomas in alphabetical order. When the second senior came up for his diploma, he seemed a little nervous. After he got his diploma, he looked back at his classmates and then put three jellybeans in my hand. From then on, most of the students handed the bishop or me a few jellybeans. Bishop Walker and I were in clerical vestments, which meant that we had no pockets. One can hold half a dozen or so jellybeans in a hand, but after that it gets difficult. We began to drop jellybeans that bounced vigorously on the stone floor of the Cathedral. Most of the congregation could not see what was happening but wondered why the people in the first few rows were giggling. As we worked through the seventy members of the class, the situation got worse. It was a hot June day, and the jellybeans began to melt in our hands forming a sticky mess.

We neared the end of the alphabet. Tommy Walker, the bishop's son, came up for his diploma. The mischievous grin on his face showed that he had been in on planning the prank. After giving his son his diploma, Bishop Walker grabbed him by the neck with one hand and stuffed a glob of melted jellybeans into his jacket pocket. After the service several people said to me, "It was so touching the way the bishop hugged his son after he gave him his diploma." I did not correct them.

The custom of giving me a slightly embarrassing gift at commencement persisted for a number of years. Three years after the jellybeans, about half of the class handed me an egg. This time I carefully set the gift down before receiving another. I had no desire to use the stone floor of the Cathedral to find out if the eggs were hard-boiled or raw.

After that commencement service, I heard a reporter ask one of the graduates why the seniors had handed me eggs. Any other graduate would have simply said, "Oh, we wanted to give the headmaster a hard time on our last day as his students." But this particular graduate, when asked about the eggs, showed both his paternal legacy and his future as a U.S. Congressman. Eighteen-year-old Jessie Jackson Jr. answered expansively, "The egg is a symbol of new life. As the chick bursts from the egg, we burst from St. Albans into our new life as college students."

THE DANCER

The Cathedral could be a place of worship or a setting for great music. It could also be where one was moved at the deepest levels. John Mastny was a very talented young man and actor. He had made a marvelous Mercutio in a school theater production.

When John graduated from St. Albans, he headed for the University of California at Berkeley. In California, his interest moved from acting to dance. He fell in love with a California girl who was also a dancer. I have always thought it would be wonderful to be a trained dancer and then dance with someone you love. John and his girl must have had something very special.

One night they were walking home from a dance rehearsal through the streets of Berkeley. A young man approached them.

"Give me your money."

"Why?" asked John.

The bullet went straight into John's heart. He fell to the ground. His girl threw herself on him, screaming. The young gunman fled.

John's memorial service was held three thousand miles away in the Washington National Cathedral. Chairs were set on three sides of the large flat area of the Great Crossing. Prayers were said. I read a Scripture lesson. A couple of people talked about John. Then, in total silence, John's girlfriend stepped to the center of the Great Crossing. High above her the Gothic arches supported the Gloria in Excelsis Tower. She stood motionless, with that graceful, erect posture that dancers often have. There was no sound. Then the haunting music of the hymn "Lord of the Dance" filled the Cathedral. The girl danced, pouring her love for John and the pain of her loss into every motion of her body. It was as true a sacrament as was ever offered by a priest in that spot, the spiritual and the physical perfectly combined.

A girl dancing for her lost love moved many of us to tears. A graduation speech once had the same effect. It was the custom at St. Albans to have a parent speak at commencement. When a class was in its junior year, I would begin to think about which parent might be the appropriate speaker. The Class of 1984 had two famous parents, both named Jackson. Henry (Scoop) Jackson was a very respected and prominent senator. Jessie Jackson was a famous civil rights leader but in 1984 was still considered quite radical. I knew it would be controversial to have Jessie Jackson speak at a St. Albans commencement at that time. Before I had to make a decision, Senator Jackson died suddenly of a heart attack in the summer before his son was a senior. After consulting the chairman of the Governing Board, Vernon Holleman, I asked Jessie Jackson to speak. As spring came, Mr. Jackson entered the contest for the Democratic Party's nomination for president. He agreed to speak even though he would have to take the red-eye from the California primary.

A very large donor, who was also a strong Republican, had a grandson graduating. When he heard that Jesse Jackson was going to speak at his grandson's commencement he called me up and gave me half an hour of hell on the telephone. But he was also a gentleman. I saw him the next day at St. Albans Grandparents Day. He said in his gruff voice, "Mark, I get mad at you like I get mad at my own sons." The message was clear: "I'm mad. Make no mistake. But the relationship is not over."

Because Jessie Jackson was speaking, over two thousand people came to commencement in the Cathedral. There was also considerable press coverage. Of course, it would have been presumptuous for me to suggest to him to "take it easy." Mr. Jackson stepped into the Great Pulpit. The grandfather sat in the second row, arms folded over his chest, a frown on his face. Mr. Jackson stood silently for a moment facing the congregation. Then his powerful voice filled the Cathedral.

"Eighteen years ago I was in a civil rights march in the deep South. There was violence and hatred in the land. I got a message to call home."

Mr. Jackson turned to face the graduates.

"The message was that you were born, my son. Eighteen years later, you are graduating from one of the finest schools in the land, and I stand before you as a candidate for the president of the United States."

Mr. Jackson paused.

"You will never know. You will never know, my son, how far we've come."

THE BIRD COUNT

The great proclamation of Christianity is that God Almighty, who created all matter, took on the flesh of a particular human being. In theology this is called the Incarnation. This leads to a sacramental view of life: that the physical, mental, and spiritual are so interrelated that what affects one aspect of a person affects all aspects.

Episcopal schools believe in the education of the whole student. The spirit should be nurtured through chapel services, religion classes, and service to others. The mind is to be sharpened by rigorous academic work. The body is to be trained, whether aesthetically in the arts or athletically in sports.

The Duke of Wellington may or may not have been correct when he said, "The battle of Waterloo was won on the playing fields of Eton." However, the idea that competitive sports should be an integral part of a school's educational offerings was first developed in Church of England institutions, nor is it surprising that many Roman Catholic schools and universities in America have sought and achieved great athletic success. Roman Catholics are the most sacramental of Christians.

I certainly wanted St. Albans to be first rate academically. There were many indications, from college admissions to results on national examinations, that it was. I also wanted it to have a vigorous athletic program. During the twenty years I was there, St. Albans won the Founders' Cup eleven times. The Founders' Cup is given for overall excellence in all sports in the Interstate Athletic Conference.

Being the best athletic school in the conference more than half of the time while being anyone's equal academically was a credit to the coaches of St. Albans. Many were also classroom teachers. Whether they were teacher-coaches or full-time in athletics, they were the kind of people who were able to inspire young men to reach for new goals and to attain accomplishments that they had not thought possible.

Doug Boswell's West Virginia accent made his sense of humor even more delightful. But his real success as a coach came from the knowledge each of his athletes had of how much Doug cared for him as a young man in the process of growth, not just as an athlete who might contribute to a sporting win. What Doug was able to do for those he worked with gave me my best athletic day as a headmaster.

The year before Doug Boswell came to St. Albans as head coach of football, the St. Albans team had won only one league game. Doug did not have a chance to work with the players until the fall season began. Again, the team only won one league game. At the end of that season, the juniors and sophomores on the team pledged that they would work hard on personal conditioning and would dedicate the summer to preparing for the next season. Moreover, Doug inspired them to make personal sacrifices, such as playing in unfamiliar positions, for the good of the team.

The next season went well, and by the last game of the season, the team was undefeated in league play. That game was against Landon and would decide the league championship. However, Landon was heavily favored. Landon was the defending champion and had an eighteen-game winning streak going. Its defense was the best in the Washington area having given up only twenty-five points all season. The St. Albans team, however, was inspired by Doug Boswell and scored twenty-one points to Landon's fourteen to win the Interstate Athletic Conference championship. My own joy was doubled because, earlier that day, Skip Grant's runners had achieved unprecedented success in the Interstate Athletic Conference cross-country championships, winning all four races. The varsity, varsity B, fifteen and under, and the grade school teams defeated all the league competition.

Young coaches at St. Albans seemed to absorb that same caring for athletes as people. Malcolm Lester came to St. Albans as an English teacher. He had been an outstanding lacrosse player in college but was relatively young and inexperienced as a coach. It was every St. Albans lacrosse coach's dream to beat Landon, but it rarely happened. In 1994, early in his career, Malcolm's team had a real chance to beat Landon. However, they were unable to do so. In lacrosse, the goalie usually feels responsible for a loss because he had allowed the winning goals. When that 1994 game ended, I saw Malcolm run out to the St. Albans goalie, give him a big hug, and walk off the field with him. He was letting a young man know that he was valued and appreciated.

Although St. Albans had many highly successful coaches, only one St. Albans teacher during my tenure had an article written about him in *Sports Illustrated*. He was not a coach, nor an Upper School teacher. He was Bob Hahn, fifth-grade teacher for decades. Every year, Bob conducted the Christmas bird count on the lawn of the White House, recording how many species were spotted during daylight hours. One year, *Sports Illustrated* did a short article on Bob and the bird count.

Over the years, the Lower School had many fascinating characters on its faculty. One of the most successful was Alex Haslam, seventh-grade science teacher. His disregard for sartorial splendor reminded me of my brother, also a scientist. Alex was one of the kindest men I have known. If he passed a beggar on Wisconsin Avenue, he not only made a gift but also stopped to talk. He treated everyone as a person of value.

On many evenings, Alex would be with his students doing astronomical observations on the hill beside the Little Sanctuary. Most of us knew that, despite his urgings, the telescopes were as frequently trained on the sights of Washington as they were on the celestial splendors.

One problem for educators is that so much of the grading process involves negative rewards. Points are taken off for mistakes, thus sending the message that mistakes will brand you as a failure. Yet we all know that many times we learn most from mistakes. If you are taught that mistakes will be permanently held against you, that only perfection is acceptable, then you may not be willing to try the difficult or to take the risks that lead to growth.

Alex Haslam devised a grading system that did not penalize a student for mistakes. Only positive points were counted toward the grade. If you had enough positive points, no matter how many mistakes you had made, you could get an A.

In 1995 I wrote in the *St. Albans Bulletin,* "Alex Haslam's greatest accomplishment is that he has not only shared with boys his knowledge of science, but also the wonders of the created order. He sees the Creator's hand in all that he observes and no boy could pass through Alex Haslam's science class without getting some glimpse of God's creative purposes."

When Martha and I moved to the Casady School I soon came to know a Casady parent named David Albert. He had attended St. Albans while his father, Carl Albert, was Speaker of the U.S. House of Representatives. David went to Harvard College and then Harvard Medical School. He returned to his native Oklahoma and had been highly successful in medical technology. David talked to me about his St. Albans experience.

After we had been in Oklahoma two years, Alex Haslam stopped by to see us for a few days one summer. Alex, David Albert and his wife, and Martha and I all went out to dinner together. David spent the whole evening praising Alex.

"I came from a highly political family, and at first thought I would follow that path. But Alex Haslam turned me on to science, and it has been my great interest ever since."

A faculty made up of dedicated teachers and interesting characters does not happen by accident. The Lower School of St. Albans has been blessed by three outstanding leaders during its history.

Alfred True headed the Lower School for more than thirty-five years. He was a small man, but radiating from him was a powerful force. It was the force of graciousness. No one met him without realizing that here was a true gentleman. His whole manner spoke of civility and goodness. He was a lifelong bachelor, and I suspect that more than half of the Lower School mothers in those years carried a secret crush on him.

Mr. True loved to walk. After he retired, he could be seen almost every day, walking purposefully through northwest Washington. Yet, he was always ready to interrupt his walk for a pleasant chat with any of the hundreds of friends he had.

I remember one hot day when I left St. Albans to go to a funeral for a past St. Albans parent. Norman Farquhar may have set a record by paying thirty-six years of tuition to St. Albans. Moreover, two of his four sons had won the Headmaster's Prize, under two different headmasters. Norman's funeral was held at Christ Church, Georgetown. I was glad I was in an air-conditioned car to drive to the funeral. As I was parking my car, I saw Mr. True walking toward the service. He was in his nineties. He had walked from the Westchester to Georgetown, a distance of several miles. I knew it would be futile to offer him a ride after the service. He would walk home while the much younger headmaster drove back to school.

All that walking had its effect. Mr. True was born in the last month of the nineteenth century and lived to see the new millennium. He was the only man I have known who lived in three different centuries.

Pete Gordon, who succeeded Mr. True, projected a very different image. He had the broad-shouldered presence of someone who had grown up in Pittsburgh. His aura was enhanced by service in the U.S. Marine Corps. However, only Lower Schoolers were fooled by the toughness. Anyone who knew Pete at all well knew that he was a very kindhearted man. He felt it deeply on those rare occasions when he had to impose serious discipline on a boy.

Pete knew that grade school boys prefer idiosyncrasy to consistency. Boys were strictly forbidden to wear hats indoors, unless, of course, it was a Pittsburgh Pirates or Steelers cap.

Like all great teachers, Pete knew how to raise a young man's expectations. Once a student on scholarship came to see him.

"I'm thinking of dropping out of St. Albans, going to an easier school, and then into the army. I have an uncle who is a sergeant, and he has a good life."

Pete smiled, then asked gently, "Did you ever think that if you stay at St. Albans and go to a good college you could end up a general?"

Pete had such wisdom about schools that I often went to him to talk about Upper School problems. I knew I would receive thoughtful, experienced advice. When talking about people's behavior, he had a favorite saying. It was not original with him, but it became a mantra for me. "We cannot control what cards we are dealt, but we can control how we play them."

Following Mr. True and Pete Gordon was a tough challenge, but Paul Herman continued the tradition of strong leadership of the Lower School. I thought that Paul's greatest strength was getting teachers to improve. He helped them to get out of the ruts that some fall into. He was able to encourage them to reinvent themselves and find new methods of reaching students. Paul knew that the great schools must be places of growth for both students and teachers.

THE PRAYER WHEEL

I knew before I went to St. Albans that the students were bright, talented, and motivated. On several occasions during my first year, they also showed me their finer side. During the first month of the academic year, there was the usual number of opening functions for students, faculty, and parents, most of which Martha attended. There were also several receptions to give people a chance to meet the new headmaster and his wife. Martha was wonderful about greeting people but with some frequency would excuse herself to go to the ladies' room and throw up. People were pleased when they learned that the new headmaster's wife was pregnant, something to which St. Albans was not accustomed. In February, Kevin was born at Sibley Hospital. When I went to school, I found a large sign hanging stretched between several dormitory windows. "WELCOME KEVIN." I was even more touched a few days later when two students showed up at our house bringing gifts for our older children.

"We thought the baby would be getting all the attention and maybe Cara and Sean needed some presents." I was particularly impressed because both students were the youngest in their own families.

That same winter a student, Donnie McKnew, was badly hurt in an automobile accident. He was going to be immobilized on his back in a hospital bed for weeks. Three of his classmates came to see me.

"Would you like to put your name on the prayer wheel?"

"What prayer wheel?" I asked.

They had drawn a large circle on a bed sheet and divided it into twenty-four pie-shaped sections. "We will have one or two names and an hour of the day in each section. We'll put the sheet on the ceiling over Donnie's bed. That way he can look up there at any time of day or night and know who is praying for him at that hour."

IDENTIFICATION

Although St. Albans students often exhibited extraordinary thoughtfulness and decency, they were also subject to the same foibles and temptations as other adolescents. During the twenty years I was at St. Albans, two French men served successively as Dean of Students. I used to joke that they had not been raised on the Fifth Amendment. Actually, each was successful because he was able to maintain friendships with the students and at the same time be tough enough to stand for what was right. But there was one thing a French upbringing had not prepared them for: the American adolescent ritual of buying alcohol with fake identification.

When we decided to issue school identification cards so that St. Albans boys could get student discounts, the Dean of Students thought of a way to save his secretary the time-consuming work of looking up each birthday. The birth date line on the card was left blank. The dean told each student to fill in the line. Of course, as the rest of us learned this, we laughed and told the dean how this was every American teenage boy's dream. I was impressed, however, that on the recall of the ID cards, we found that less than 10 percent of the students had magically become twenty-one overnight.

Possessing a fake ID brought a moment of great embarrassment to one St. Albans student. A teacher found a wallet that a student had dropped in the gym. It held a fair amount of money. There was a real driver's license belonging to a junior. There was also a fake ID with the student's photograph and a birth date making him twenty-one. The name on the fake ID was "Mark H. Mullin."

I was confident that he did not have fake identification to get into meetings of headmasters. He just thought it would be funny to use my name when he tried to buy alcohol. I called the junior into my office. He looked puzzled when he came in because he had no idea that his wallet had been found.

"Tell me," I asked. "If my name is on something, then it belongs to me, doesn't it?"

"I guess so," he answered cautiously.

"I guess this is mine, then," I said as I pulled out his wallet and took the money out of it.

He looked even more puzzled. Then he remembered the fake ID with my name on it. The look of horror and embarrassment on his face showed me that he did not need a lecture about what he had done. I returned his wallet and money to him but kept the fake ID as a souvenir.

St. Albans students also engaged in normal moaning and groaning, particularly about work. One of the things I valued most about St. Albans was that it combined academic excellence with serious athletic competition. Of course, the students often felt they were being overworked in both academics and athletics.

One day the cross-country team was warming up beside the track. Their coach, Skip Grant, had made it clear that the team was going to have a tough workout that day. The runners began to complain.

"We've got term papers to do and an awful calculus assignment. Don't give us a killer workout today. Let us go early. We've got so much homework tonight."

Skip saw a jogger coming along the track. He was a mature man who lived a few blocks from the St. Albans track. Skip flagged the man down and addressed him so that the cross-country runners could hear.

"Excuse me, sir. I see you jogging here from time to time."

"Yes, I try to run whenever I get a chance."

"But you are a very busy man, aren't you."

"Well, I am pretty busy."

"But you still find time to run even though you are busy."

"Yes, I do."

"Thank you, Mr. Bush." The vice-president of the United States resumed his running. There was no more complaining from the cross-country team.

SNOW

Sometimes students were able to turn the table on the headmaster. For years St. Albans prided itself on never closing during snowstorms. All the rest of the city might be closed, but St. Albans would remain open and teach classes to whomever could get there. It was a point of great masculine pride to both students and alumni.

Of course, as Washington grew, traffic became heavier and more students lived further from the school. Getting to St. Albans in snow became more and more difficult. It was a particular hardship on the faculty. Housing prices in the District of Columbia became so high that teachers moving into the area had to live far from the school. During my first few years as headmaster, I maintained the policy of never closing for snow. In the winter of my fourth year there was a storm that dumped more than twenty inches of snow on Washington over a weekend. All Sunday afternoon there were announcements on radio and television of closings for Monday. Schools, the federal government, and most businesses were to be closed. About suppertime I got a call from John Walker, Bishop of Washington.

"Mark, I know it has been St. Albans policy never to close for snow, but I have just had a call from the mayor. He wants all cars off the streets tomorrow so they don't impede snow removal. Would you be willing to close St. Albans?"

I was not willing to argue with both the mayor and the bishop to defend a tradition that had outlived its time. Because we had never closed, we did not have a telephone chain to notify parents. I called the heads of the Upper and Lower Schools, and they agreed to get their teachers busy on the phone.

The next day, I walked over to St. Albans, as did some other people. By afternoon I decided that, although there was still a lot of snow on the roads, we should open the following day.

Quite awhile after supper that evening, I was at home when the phone rang.

"Headmaster Mullin?" It sounded like the voice of a mature man, probably one used to having authority.

"Yes?"

"This is the Mayor's Office. We want you to close that school again tomorrow."

I went ballistic and spoke angrily. "The snow had been on the ground almost thirty-six hours. Why couldn't you people in City Hall make up your minds earlier? Now it is so late it will be hard to reach all our families."

Then I heard the laughter in the background. Finally, the culprit himself began to laugh. It was an eleventh grader, surrounded by his friends, who had fooled me completely.

A few years later the faculty decided that the increased traffic and the greater distances people lived from St. Albans made the old policy obsolete. When I announced the faculty vote to the St. Albans community, I received more letters of complaint than I did on any other issue. It always interests an educator to know what issues his alumni think are really important. No present or past mothers objected to the change. So often they had been the ones actually doing the driving on the dangerous streets.

Several years later, I was granted a semester's sabbatical. Martha and I went to Europe. Although I was not in daily contact with St. Albans, I did receive the minutes of the monthly Board meeting. During the time we were staying on the coast of Brittany, our mail did not come until late in the afternoon. One day I received the minutes of the May Board meeting. The first item I read about was the snow policy. The Board had voted to return to the old policy of never closing for snow.

More than any ability to answer questions, my childhood lisp, which sounded cute on NBC Radio, made me a Quiz Kid. 1946. (Photo by Johnny Mack.)

My older brother, Mike, kept pet snakes in our Chicago apartment. Neither Smoky the cat nor I were quite sure about them. Mike went on to become a distinguished biologist. 1947. (Photo by Toivo Kaitlia.)

My parents, Joe and Alma Mullin, while Joe was
president of Shimer College. 1956. (Family photo.)

Chris Ohiri greets me at the finish of the mile at the Harvard versus Yale meet. 1961.
(Photo courtesy of Harvard University.)

A cartoon by Bill Robertson from the sports page of the *Boston Traveler*. 1962.

Bill McCurdy, Harvard track
coach, at a party Martha and I
gave in Washington when he
retired. Harvard runners from
four decades attended. 1984.
(Author photo.)

The finish of the mile in the Oxford versus AAA meet. 1963.
(Photo by E. D. Lacy.)

Martha and I are married at the Cathedral of St. John the Divine in New York City. 1966. (Photo by Ira L. Hill Studio.)

Traveling in a gypsy wagon in County Galway, Ireland. 1968. (Author photo.)

Seymour St. John, headmaster of the Choate School, gave me my first job in an independent school in 1968. Here he speaks with Choate alumnus, John F. Kennedy. 1958. (Photo courtesy of Choate Rosemary Hall Archives.)

Resting on the way to the top of Ireland's holy mountain, Croagh Patrick, with Choate students Art Warner, John Hoffman, and John Geoghegan. 1973. (Author photo.)

With Martha. 1974. (Author photo.)

A faculty party at Choate. 1974. (Author photo.)

Martha and I arrive at St. Albans with Cara and Sean.
1977. (Photo courtesy of St. Alban's.)

At prayer with Bishop Walker and Canon Martin. 1977. (Photo courtesy of St. Albans.)

Bob Strickland of Channel 9 interviews St. Albans astronauts Rick Hauck and Michael Collins. Doc Arnds, who taught mathematics to both of them, stands in between. 1984. (Photo courtesy of St. Albans.)

With the Rev. Jesse Jackson when he spoke at his son's graduation. 1984. (Photo courtesy of St. Albans.)

Kevin Mullin with St. Albans students at the Annual Pumpkin Carving Contest in our home. 1985. (Author photo.)

With Martha in front of the John Harvard statue when I was a Marshal at Harvard's 350th Anniversary. 1986. (Photo courtesy of St. Albans.)

Chairman of the Governing Board, Tillman Stirling surprises me with a gift as I complete ten years as headmaster. 1987. (Photo courtesy of St. Albans.)

Kuba Zelinski came from Poland to study at St. Albans. 1987. (Author photo.)

Mother and daughter just before Cara's wedding to King Milling in the Washington National Cathedral. 1993. (Author photo.)

Martha, Charlie Dunne, Irish author John B. Keane, Peggy Steuart, and I on a Flying Bulldog trip to Ireland. 1993. (Author photo.)

With Chris Brasher, Roger Bannister (in coat and tie), and Chris Chataway at the centennial of the world's oldest international track meet in Oxford. Forty-one years earlier, on the same track, Brasher and Chataway had set pace for Bannister when he ran the first four-minute mile. 1995. (Author photo.)

Speaking to the seniors minutes before they received their diplomas at my last St. Albans graduation. "You have become what we wanted you to become." 1997. (Photo courtesy of St. Albans.)

Kevin Mullin graduates from St. Albans. 1997. (Photo courtesy of St. Albans.)

Casady girls celebrate Halloween in our home. 1998. (Author photo.)

Running with Sean Mullin for a few hundred yards in the middle of the Boston Marathon. A spectator called out, "Who is the nut in the suit?" 1999. (Author photo.)

Holding the Woolsey Trophy; my last time on the sideline as a headmaster, Casady School. 2001. (Author photo.)

Our granddaughters, Sophie and Raina Milling. 2005. (Photo by Cara Milling.)

Our family gathered in our home in Charlottesville, Virginia. 2005. (Author photo.)

"Of course the Board has the right and the power to do that," I grumped to Martha, "but what cowards. They wait until I am out of the country and don't even let me know that they are considering the matter."

I threw the Board minutes down on the floor and did not pick them up again that evening. I was still muttering about my anger when I went to bed. The next morning Martha got tired of stepping over the papers on the floor. She picked them up and began to read them.

"Mark, what is this about seven teachers resigning? Their replacements have been found, and they will be ready for the classroom as soon as they complete courses in English as a second language."

"Let me see that." I read through the minutes and realized that every item was a joke. I could imagine what fun the secretary of the board and a couple of his friends had had writing them.

Once again, I had been snow-blinded.

OUTDOOR ART

St. Albans students were not immune from adolescent preoccupation with sexual organs. On two occasions that interest moved out-of-doors. Just south of the Cathedral, mounted on a high pedestal, there is a larger-than-life statue of George Washington on horseback. When I first came to St. Albans, both horse and rider were gilded with a bright gold that looked a little garish near the solemn gray limestone of the Cathedral. One morning I got an angry call from the Cathedral provost.

"Have you seen the George Washington statue? Did your boys do that?"

I hurried over to the statue. The private parts of the stallion had been painted a bright blue. As word spread at St. Albans about the gelding of the gilded horse, I let it be known that those responsible had better come see me soon. In a little while, two seniors came to my office. They were both fine young men.

"We did it. But it was all in fun. Don't worry. We used latex paint. It will wash right off."

I shook my head at the inexperience of my students with household maintenance. "Latex paint washes right off, if it is washed right off. That stuff has been on the horse for hours."

Indeed, when the offending blue was removed, the gold came off also. Now the private parts of the stallion were a dull metal color. Wisely, the Building Committee of the Cathedral decided that the duller color was more appropriate, and all the gold was removed from George Washington and his stallion. The students' prank ended up making both the first president and his horse look considerably more dignified.

A number of years later, I got a call at 2:00 A.M. from Donald Brown, one of the dormitory masters. I knew that he often worked very late at night, but he had never called me at that hour.

"Mark. You had better get over here right away. You need to see what is on the library roof."

I threw on a pair of jeans and a sweatshirt and drove to school. There on the library roof was a six-foot male organ, apparently made of papier-mâché, and pointed directly at the Cathedral.

The thought of the Cathedral authorities seeing that in the morning and the phone call I would get prompted me to immediate action. I found an extension ladder outside the Drama Department office. I carried it to the library and was soon on the roof. A couple of boarding students must have heard some noise because they came outside. Seeing who it was on the library roof, they retreated. They missed a wonderful chance to remove the ladder, leaving the headmaster with the object on the roof to face the sunrise.

I was able to get the object down the ladder and into the back of my station wagon. As I started up Wisconsin Avenue to return home, I had an awful thought.

"What if a D.C. cop pulls me over for some reason? I certainly am not dressed as a headmaster. If he looks in the back of the station wagon he will run me in as some kind of pervert. He will never believe why I am driving around at 2:30 A.M. with that six-foot object in my car." Fortunately, I made it home without incident.

St. Albans students were not the only ones to operate nocturnally on the Cathedral grounds. One morning, a few days before the Landon football game, we arrived at school to find that the word "Landon" had been written several times in brown letters on the sidewalk in front of the school. It was also written down the side of the ten-foot stone Peace Cross near the Little Sanctuary. I was reasonably certain that the

Landon students had not meant to deface a cross. They probably just saw a target of opportunity and in the dark did not realize what it was. I called the headmaster of Landon.

"We can clean up the sidewalks. Don't worry about it. But I think I will leave the word Landon on the side of the stone cross. That way people who are trying to decide between St. Albans and Landon can get some idea of what your students are like."

"I don't know who they are," he yelled into the phone, "but I will be there in two hours with the culprits."

An hour and a half later, the headmaster of Landon arrived with five shamefaced young men. I told the St. Albans students not to heckle the Landon lads while they spent the day on their hands and knees scrubbing the paint from the sidewalks and the Peace Cross. I was neither surprised nor disturbed when the St. Albans students did not follow my instructions.

THE HIDDEN SECRET

In the early 1990s I was asked to be on a panel at a national conference. All I was told was that the topic would be "Academe's Hidden Secret." Each panelist could approach the topic any way he or she chose. On the panel with me would be a university professor of the humanities, a member of a university education department, and two policy types from the federal government. The other panelists spoke thoughtfully about curriculum, national and state testing, organization of schools, and funding. Then it was my turn.

"After hearing the concerns raised by the other panelists, it appears that what I am going to tell you really is a hidden secret. None of the others mentioned it. The secret is about the most important thing in education. Try this experiment. Ask ten people about their education. Say to them, 'Don't tell me the names of the schools and universities you attended. Tell me about your *education*.' I am willing to make a bet that most of them will begin by talking about one or two teachers that had a significant impact on them. In most cases it will be a positive impact, but in some it will have been a negative experience. Teachers, individual teachers, are what make the most important difference in education. If you want to improve education, you must attract and retain quality teachers and then provide the circumstances that will make them effective."

I have no doubt that the most important responsibility of a headmaster is to be sure that the school has the very best teachers possible. If that is done well, everything else about the school (recruitment of new students, fund-raising, college placement) will fall into place.

Of course, providing a reasonable salary is the most important way to retain good teachers. That is essential if a school wants to be great. I would suggest three other aspects of school life that are important in keeping good teachers.

First, let them know that they are appreciated. Formal evaluations may be helpful, but I found that the spontaneous, unexpected note to a teacher about something well done was always very much appreciated. I was also pleased that over the years I was able to set up several awards for teachers that carried significant cash grants. That is always a nice way to say thank you.

Second, treat teachers as professionals. Give them the freedom to teach in the manner they find most effective. Of course, there was less danger of my telling a calculus teacher how to do his job than a religion or history teacher, but I was amused that Donald Brown frequently proclaimed, "Mark Mullin may be emperor of this school, but in this classroom, I am king."

Third, consider their families. I learned that from Seymour St. John at Choate. It does not make sense to ask a teacher to make sacrifices for other people's children if the school does not care for the teacher's family. I encouraged faculty to take time off to attend events in which their children were participating. "How can we ask busy St. Albans parents to leave their jobs and come to St. Albans events if we do not do the same for our own children?" I loved playing Santa Claus at the Christmas party for faculty children that Martha started and for which Jeanne Richards did so much by finding an age-appropriate gift for each child. Unfortunately, a child had to be a true believer not to see the black eyebrows and five o'clock shadow beneath Santa's beard. Members of the school family also helped. The Parents Club set up a system by which parents could give unused tickets to concerts or professional sporting events to teachers. Bill Manger, who served on the Governing Board longer than anyone in the history of St. Albans, made his house in lovely Woodstock, Vermont, available to some faculty families in the summer.

While retaining good teachers is the most important job, hiring promising new ones is also essential. Of course, it is a subjective art, an inexact science if there ever was one. Once in awhile it is obvious that a person is a natural teacher. Ted Eagles taught history at St. Albans for more than two decades. During this time, fate placed him on the jury in the trial of Marion Barry, the Washington, D.C., mayor arrested on a drug offense. Ted's fellow jurors recognized his qualities and elected him foreman. A reporter did a profile of each of the jurors. One sentence caught Ted perfectly, "One did not have to attend St. Albans to smell the chalk dust on his jacket."

In the November 1981 issue of the *Washingtonian*, Howard Means wrote that the faculty of a great school should be a "bedlam of eccentricities and passions." Certainly, that fortuitous phrase applied to many of my colleagues at St. Albans. When I was interviewing teacher candidates, if I could not find eccentricity, I looked for interesting people. If they intrigued me, maybe they would be interesting to their students. I also liked candidates who were interested, who asked good questions and had the self-confidence to show their curiosity. I wanted teachers who were both interesting and interested.

Mariano Munoz-Lopez was raised and educated in Spain. However, what intrigued me about him was when he told me during the interview that he owned a live-in cave in Spain.

"You know, I don't have any heating or cooling to pay."

Because Bob Morse was a Cornell trained physicist, I assumed, correctly, that he knew his subject. What made him unusual was that he and his wife had sailed around the world. There were just the two of them on their sailboat until they stopped in Australia. There his wife gave birth to their first child. They put the child on the boat and sailed the rest of the way back to America.

Bob introduced the great egg drop to St. Albans. His physics students were given precise requirements about materials and overall dimensions. Then they had to design and build a protective case in which a raw egg could survive a four-story drop from the roof of the True-Lucas

Building. On the day of the drop, shouts of excitement and moans of disappointment echoed around the campus.

Peter Kelley also had a nautical background. He had been a math major at Princeton. However, in a time when few of our students were going into the military, his years of service as an officer on a nuclear submarine brought something different to his classroom.

Of course, knowing how to motivate young people is very important in a teacher. When the True-Lucas Building was renovated, a new and larger Lower School library was created. After the books had been shelved, Edie Ching, the librarian, showed me around. Edie understood Lower School boys.

"I've put the books on sex-ed in this little alcove that is away from the librarian's desk. No thirteen-year-old boy wants to admit he needs information on sex. The boys can look at the books without the librarian seeing them. Besides, if they think they are getting away with something, they are more likely to open the books. In these times, I want to encourage them to be well informed about sex and its potential consequences."

Sandy Larson clearly understood that many adolescent boys need a time in the day for a little relief from pressure. This is particularly true in a school with high academic demands and competitive athletics. Because of his quiet manner and slight frame, few students knew that Sandy had been an outstanding athlete at St. Albans in the 1950s. During those years, he appreciated the sanctuary he found in Dean Stambaugh's art room. When Sandy succeeded Dean in the 1980s, he continued the tradition of having the art room be a place where students could work at their own pace. In art, this encouraged them to produce more, and certainly better, work than if he had always been pushing them. Sandy had an intuitive ability to know which boys needed direction and instruction and which would flourish more by being allowed to experiment and try their own things. The art studio was flooded with sunlight. It was filled with plants and the music of Sandy's great record collection.

Sandy's approach to watching his students in athletics was much like his teaching. He attended every home football game and most basketball games. During the fall, he did not sit in the stands with the cheering fans. He took his own folding chair and sat by himself beyond the far end zone. However, his students certainly knew he was there supporting them.

Brian O'Connor taught English and coached soccer at St. Albans for a few years between college and working for the Kennedy political machine. When he was asked to teach an Upper School course in public speaking, he understood the fear many adolescents have of speaking before strangers. However, the only audience he could provide his students was the others in the public speaking class, hardly a representative group. Brian's solution was to have the class board a Wisconsin Avenue public bus. Brian would secure the driver's permission and then a St. Albans student would deliver a speech to an amused collection of commuters and shoppers. They, in turn, were asked to respond as one would for an applause meter. Brian not only cured his teenage charges of any fear of speaking in front of strangers, but he also provided an entertaining divergence for those using Washington's public transportation.

Unlike some adolescent boys, the willingness or desire to perform in front of others motivates many teachers. I suspect that many good teachers are frustrated actors. Being a teacher means that they have a guaranteed audience to play to every day.

I often asked teacher candidates, "Why teaching?" The most honest answer I got was from a young woman, Sally Higginson.

"They pay you to talk."

I hired her on the spot.

During an interview I always tried to find out if the candidate had a sense of humor. It is so important in relating to young people and in surviving the stress of school life.

Doc Arnds taught mathematics at St. Albans for most of his career. He had the distinction of having taught the essential subject of math to two young men who later became astronauts, Michael Collins and Rick Hauck. Doc's sense of humor added much to what some students found to be a dry subject. He retired at the end of my first year at St. Albans. Then he took a job teaching in Iran. After he had been there but a short time, riots began that led to the ouster of the shah. When he got back to America I asked him if he ever felt danger.

"Oh, the Iranian people were so nice. If we were on the street and there was a radical demonstration, people would recognize us as Americans and pull us into their houses and hide us until the radicals left."

"Was there a lot of disturbance?"

"Oh, yes. The school was closed more than it was open."

"That's too bad."

"What do you mean, bad? Best job I ever had. Worked three months and got paid for twelve."

John Davison has taught at St. Albans for many years. When he first arrived there, he was a young bachelor and very handsome. Housing was expensive in Washington, but John found a way to get free room and board. John Warner (later Senator Warner) had just married Elizabeth Taylor. He had a son from his first marriage to one of the Mellon heirs. Because John Warner and Elizabeth Taylor led very active social lives, John Davison was hired to live at the Warner house. In exchange for room and board, he was to look after John Warner's son and provide some tutoring.

One day Elizabeth Taylor was in bed with a cold. She was taking care of herself but was not terribly sick. When John Davison came home from school, he went to her bedroom to get some instructions about the son's schedule. He found Elizabeth Taylor, who was feeling better, sitting up in bed eating caviar and drinking champagne.

"Would you like something to eat or drink?" she asked. "Here, have a seat and try these." She handed him a full plate and glass. John Davison looked around for a place to sit. There were only two chairs in the room and Elizabeth Taylor had thrown clothes and a bathrobe on them. She motioned to the end of the bed. John sat down.

At that moment the phone rang. Elizabeth Taylor picked up the receiver and listened. "Just a moment please. He's right here." She handed the phone to John.

The caller was a college friend whom John had not seen in a couple of years. "Hey, old Buddy. How ya doin'? I called your home and your mother gave me this number but didn't say where it is. What's up? What are you doing?"

"You are not going believe what I am doing. . . ."

GOD'S LOVE LETTERS

It is wonderful when a teacher is also a practitioner of the material being presented to the students. Donna Denize came to St. Albans after teaching in a boarding school for girls. Part of her success at a school for boys is that she not only teaches poetry but is also a poet in her own right. Her poems have appeared in a number of anthologies. In 2005, a collection of her poetry appeared with the title *Broken Like Job*. Soon after we left St. Albans in 1997, she sent us a poem.

God's Love Letters

For Mark and Martha Mullin

The Divine is all paradox.
In silencing my voice, I hear
That Unknowable, Speak,
speak through ages in which
I have never lived, never even
drawn breath or spoken one
syllable.

So, How is it I know the love of David
or hear the harper's melody in strings
quivering by Spirit that moves
fingers and heart, saying simply, "Play"?
How is it I know the comforting
of Naomi's voice to Ruth
or taste the sweet waters Naomi drew
from a dry well and a dry sky
in the insufferable desert of human hearts?

And how can I *hear* and *know* the accent
of gentle Nightingales' in hidden
words of love which Muhammad spoke
to his daughter, Fatimah—nightingales
singing sweetly to her chaste heart singing
love's melody, same one that brought
the weeping Abraham with Isaac and
readied sword to sacred spot
where he heard one word, "Stop"?

(A) Voice that beckoned Moses
"*Retreat*" to a mountain where,
standing in eternal solitude

the Sinai of his heart heard even the bushes
voice the enchanting melody
of Divine Glory: "felicity in fidelity to
the music of the soul;
So With fire We test the gold,
(and) with treasures of dust
We test the soul."

In the beginning was the word
but in the end, the deed is all,
deeds not words be your adorning,
So Saul becomes Paul, and a wooden cross
the King's throne, where love's calling
is heard, and they follow
for they *know* the Shepherd's Voice.

Oh, sons and daughters of Dust,
The Divine is all paradox.
where it is in letters, sent through human voice,
and the works of all His yesterdays
in love's letters of Divinity to humanity,
mine
is merely lover's words arriving
in a soiled, crushed envelope
a letter, a voice reaching
the hand of the Beloved,
yet no less precious
because of its condition!

KISSES

Passion for the subject, ability to communicate with young people, a
sense of humor, and a touch of eccentricity were the most important
characteristics that I looked for in a teacher. Some of the best faculty
members I have worked with did not have fancy educational background themselves. I did not mind, however, if a teacher candidate had
been exposed at some time to quality education. We had a good per-
centage of teachers who had attended first-rate schools or universities.

I was proud of the fact that at one time there were three members of the small St. Albans faculty who were graduates of Oxford.

Jim Billington served on the Governing Board of St. Albans during my first six years there. He was head of the Woodrow Wilson Center at the Smithsonian and later Librarian of Congress. Jim had been a Rhodes Scholar. His daughter won a Rhodes Scholarship a year or two after the program began to accept women. I knew that there had been some father-son Rhodes Scholars. I suspected that the Billingtons were the first father-daughter Rhodes Scholars.

Before the daughter left for Oxford, I was at the Billington house on some school business. I happened to mention to Jim's wife, Marjorie, that there were three faculty members (including myself) at St. Albans who had first kissed our future spouse at Oxford.

A few days later, Marjorie called me and said, "Everybody else has talked to our daughter about the Oxford tutorial system or the Bodleian Library. When I repeated your remark about first kissing a future spouse she really got interested."

Four years later, I was obnoxious about saying, "I told you so," when the daughter married a man she met at Oxford.

The rest of the story happened two years later. Martha and I were on sabbatical and stayed a few days with our friend, Jane Hare, in Oxford. I was asked to speak at the English St. Albans School north of London. Later, during the sabbatical we would spend a month in the headmaster's house.

After I spoke at the English St. Albans School, we drove back to Oxford. As we came through the center of town, we happened to see Jim Billington and his son standing in front of the bus terminal. Even from our car I could see that they looked confused. This was strange, as Jim had lived in Oxford as a Rhodes Scholar. Surely, he knew his way around the city. I pulled up in front of them and said, "Your ride is here." To my surprise, they got right in our car. Then they explained what had happened.

The Billington daughter (the former Rhodes Scholar) had continued to live in Oxford after she married. She was ready to have her first baby. Her mother, Marjorie, had flown over from Washington a few days earlier. Jim and his son had just arrived from Moscow where Jim had been interpreting for Ronald Reagan on the president's trip to Russia.

"We've called the house but there is no answer. I suspect that they've gone to the hospital, but we don't know which hospital. We can't get into the house until someone returns from the hospital and that could be hours. We don't quite know what to do."

"Well, we are staying with a friend in north Oxford, and I'm sure she'll welcome you until you can get someone to answer at your daughter's house. But I'll bet she can find where your daughter is. She was head of all British nurses in Germany right after World War II. She'll know how to get an answer from any hospital."

Indeed, in her typical fashion, Jane Hare made the two Billington men feel right at home. And it took her only a few minutes on the phone to learn in which hospital Jim Billington's granddaughter was happily beginning her life.

HALLOWEEN

I do not know if people considered me an eccentric, but most people knew that I am a Halloween junkie. Early in my career as a headmaster, I began the custom of putting on an outrageous costume and going from classroom to classroom. If a teacher had his back to the door I would mimic him until the fact that all the students were looking at the door and laughing would make the teacher turn around. Sometimes I would just barge into a classroom, disrupt things, and then run off as though I were a student.

After a few years of this, the students and the experienced teachers knew that if a monster had the nerve to interrupt a class, it was probably the headmaster. However, it usually took new faculty members a year or two to figure out.

One year we had a very earnest new teacher. He was fresh out of Yale, where he had been a math major. When I arrived at his classroom on Halloween, he was busy doing a complicated equation on the board. His back was to the door. I stood there, a misshapen creature in black, imitating his moves as he wrote the equation. As student after student noticed me, a ripple of laughter began to run around the classroom. The teacher sensed he was losing his audience. He spun around from the board and saw the creature in the doorway to his classroom.

"Goddamn it. Get the hell out of here."

As I flew down the hallway I could hear the burst of laughter from the students, and one of them shouted to the teacher, "Do you know who that was?"

The tables were turned on me a couple of years later. I was rambling down the halls in a gorilla suit one Halloween when I saw the head of the Upper School coming toward me. He had with him a group of German school principals who were visiting Washington. They seemed a serious lot. I hoped to go on past them, but the head of the Upper stopped me and insisted on introducing each of the visitors to the headmaster. I hate to think what they told their colleagues in Germany about American education.

By the time we got to Casady School in Oklahoma I owned two gorilla suits. There was an experienced English teacher at Casady who always taught by round table discussion. Therefore, he was very upset when his class was interrupted because it broke up the discussion. On Halloween two gorillas burst into his classroom. The shorter gorilla threw a banana toward a student, but the banana fell to the floor.

"Pick that up."

The shorter gorilla was having trouble seeing through the mask and could not find the banana on the floor. The teacher grabbed the gorilla by the arm.

"Pick up that banana!"

Again, the gorilla disobeyed. It was bad enough to have his class discussion disrupted but to be flatly disobeyed in front of his class was more than the teacher could stand. He was a large man and he began to shake the gorilla vigorously.

"*Pick up that banana!*"

Fortunately, at that moment a student picked up the banana and handed it to the shorter gorilla. The teacher released his captive and both gorillas fled.

The next day the teacher came to see me.

"Tell me that wasn't you in the gorilla suit yesterday. Tell me that wasn't you."

"What makes you think it was?"

"The students think it was you."

"Well, let me put it this way. The shorter gorilla, the one you shook, that wasn't me."

"Oh my God. Oh no! How can I make it up to her? I'll send her flowers."

"You don't get it. If you had recognized us, it would have spoiled all the fun. Martha and I laughed about it all night."

TWO PRINTS

The day before classes began in the fall of 1987, Vaughn Keith came to see me. He was a Latin teacher. We exchanged a few pleasantries and then Vaughn said, "I have been diagnosed as HIV positive." He sat there waiting for my response. Into my mind flashed the image of a photograph I had seen in a newspaper a few months before. It was a photograph of the pope holding an AIDS child in his arms. With that picture still in my mind, I got up, walked over to Vaughn, and hugged him. As we embraced I realized that we had started down a path that would have a significant effect on St. Albans and well beyond.

I knew that just two months before, the good people of a town in Florida had burned down the house of an AIDS child to force the family to leave town and the local school. Fear of AIDS was rampant in the country in 1987. I am embarrassed to admit it, but after Vaughn left my office I washed my hands fifteen times in the next forty-five minutes. My rational mind told me that I was unlikely to contract AIDS just by hugging Vaughn, and if I had any exposure, washing with regular soap and tap water was unlikely to do any good. But I said to myself, "If it makes you feel any better, go ahead and wash. Easing your emotions won't hurt anything."

The path St. Albans took was to be public about Vaughn's condition. We knew of no other independent school that had been public about an AIDS teacher. Of course, in an independent school parents have the option to withdraw their children. I did not know whether or not in a few months many of us on the faculty would be unemployed. Going down that path was so much easier because of the wisdom and support of Tillman Stirling, chairman of the Governing Board. With Vaughn's permission and approval, I met with the faculty and then the students to tell them that a popular teacher was HIV positive and would continue teaching. I sent a letter to all the parents. I ended it by saying, "How we all respond to this situation is very much a measure of St. Albans School and each of us as individuals. I ask your prayers for Mr. Keith, for St. Albans School, and for our students that God may use this tragic situation as a vehicle for growth in understanding and compassion."

More than two hundred parents took the time to write in response to my letter. I did not try to count the number of people who spoke to me about the matter. Only three people expressed any reservation to me. No student withdrew from school. No student asked to be reassigned to the other Latin teacher. In fact, a couple of weeks later, a student asked me, "I have a bad cold. Should I go to Latin class today? My teacher has no immune system."

Both print and television media reported the story. I understand that my letter was circulated among school heads in Germany. Six months later the *Washington Post* reported that the federal government's Office of Personnel Management was changing its position on AIDS, "because the director of the Office had been influenced by her son's Latin teacher."

Vaughn taught for two more years until spring vacation, 1990. He died a week later. A few months after that, a package arrived in my office. It was from Vaughn Keith's father. It contained beautiful prints of the two universities I had attended. The American print was made in 1874. The English one dates from 1782. I treasure them dearly.

WALKING THE WALL

Being a parent is as important as any challenge we have in life. Yet we learn it by on-the-job training and the example (usually mixed) of our own parents. It has always been hard. As John Silber, former president of Boston University, has pointed out, it is so difficult that thirty-three hundred years ago child-parent relationships had to be included in the Ten Commandments. Being a good parent is particularly difficult for busy professionals and even more so in a city as social as Washington. Even the most conscientious parents feel that there is not enough time to spend with their children. Sometimes they try to compensate for absence by inappropriate involvement. Once a Washington parent called me at home two nights in a row. The calls were made from two different cities west of the Mississippi River where the parent was traveling on business. The issue that was so important: election of fifth grade homeroom officers.

It is good for a headmaster to be a parent himself. It helps him understand the experiences his students' parents are having. I was certainly not immune from the foibles of parenthood. It was my practice to stand on the sideline with the football team during varsity games. In all those years (and many close games) on the sideline at St. Albans and Casady, only once did I start out on to the field to tell a referee that he was a blind idiot. Of course, it was when my son, Sean, was playing against Georgetown Prep. The game would decide the league championship. Fortunately, by the grace of God (and I mean that literally), Skip Grant, the athletic director, was standing near me. He grabbed my arm.

"I don't think that is a good idea."

"Skip," I said, turning back to the sideline, "you are right." He saved me from embarrassing myself, my school, and, most of all, my son.

Like many busy parents, I was not immune from having to be out of the house too many evenings. I frequently had school functions four or five evenings a week. I remember one stretch when I was out on school business for twenty-one evenings in a row. On a majority of those evenings Martha was with me also. That kind of pace can be hard on family life. However, how a child views it is a matter of age and perspective. One time, after we had been out for several evenings, fourth grader Kevin asked wistfully, "Dad, are you going out again tonight?"

A few minutes later, twelfth grader Sean came into the room where I was getting dressed. He asked hopefully, "Are you going out tonight, Dad?"

With time, Kevin's perspective changed on how much time with Dad was a good thing. For a number of years we attended Renaissance Weekends. These were gatherings originally held at Hilton Head Island for families. Instead of just partying at New Year's, there were panels to discuss important policy and personal issues. Everyone was expected to participate, adults and children.

Our second year at Renaissance, Kevin, who was then thirteen years old, was assigned to a panel with other children. The topic was a good one for children to discuss, "How Can Grade A Professionals Avoid Getting an F as Parents?"

The most famous child on the panel was Chelsea Clinton. Her father had been elected president just two months before, following a long and demanding campaign. The other children on the panel also had highly successful and influential parents. Child after child spoke of how his or her parents were working long hours at important jobs but also tried to carve out "quality time" with their children.

Kevin brought the house down with a different response. "I don't know about these other kids. I have the opposite problem. I can't get away from my dad. Even when I go to school he is there."

Headmasters are also not immune from the worries of other parents. When Kevin was in the eighth grade at St. Albans, Chelsea Clinton was in the eighth grade at Sidwell Friends, and Sarah Gore was in the eighth grade at National Cathedral School. One night, Sidwell Friends sponsored a dance for eighth-grade students from all three schools. Knowing when the dance was scheduled to end, I gave Kevin a curfew half an hour later.

Kevin did not come home until about forty-five minutes after the curfew. I went into a routine typical of fathers: "Dangerous city"; "murder capital of the world"; "your mother and I were worried sick."

Kevin gave me the sort of withering look that only an eighth grader can give his father. "Dad, I came home in a bulletproof car with two men holding machine guns. I think I was safe."

"Which girl?"

"I'm not telling."

That was enough to silence me. Mothers, however, never believe their child is safe enough.

"What if there had been a kidnapping attempt?" asked Martha.

Being the child of a headmaster has its difficult moments. I am sure there were many times something I said or did embarrassed my children. Once, however, a wall helped my children get a moment of sweet revenge. When I was in grade school my father taught at the University of Chicago. We lived on the west side of the campus. My grade school was on the east side. In those gentler days, at quite a young age I was allowed to walk alone the mile to grade school through the campus of the University of Chicago. Along the way I passed the Biological Sciences Building. It was in this building that my father worked in his physiology laboratory. In front of the building a wall separated the sidewalk from a window well that allowed light into the windows of the basement labs. The wall and the window well ran for half a block, stopped for a gateway, and then ran for another half a block. On the sidewalk side, the wall was only three feet high. On the other side, it was ten feet down to the bottom of the window well. That was high enough to scare a grade school boy. Of course, every day walking to or from school, I walked on top of the wall. I looked down at the safety of the sidewalk on one side and the danger of the window well on the other.

When Kevin was a student at the School of the Art Institute of Chicago, Sean joined us when we visited him there. I insisted that they come out to the University of Chicago campus and see the scenes of my youth. Both boys were smart enough to act interested. We walked by the apartment building where my family had lived and then headed for my school. As we came to the wall in front of the Biological Sciences Building, I explained how I use to walk on that wall.

"Come on, Dad. Let's see you do it now."

I jumped up on the wall and began to walk. I felt like a ten-year-old showing off for his friends instead of a mature man with adult sons. When I had walked about twenty feet, a whistle began to blow behind me.

"Hey, Bud. Get off the wall!"

I turned and saw a uniformed University of Chicago security guard gesturing angrily. I jumped down to the sidewalk accompanied by loud laughter from Sean and Kevin. You can imagine their delight at seeing their father, the headmaster, get busted by campus security.

Sean and Kevin were aware that I had successfully avoided a similar fate from the Washington Cathedral Security. There is a wall that runs on the north side of the Bishop's Garden on the Cathedral Close. In the Bishop's Garden is a giant spotlight that illuminates the Cathedral tower at night. If one stands on the wall in just the right spot, one can cast a giant shadow on the tower. When we had visitors from out of town, I enjoyed taking them to the Cathedral Close at night. I would ask them to watch the tower. After I got on the wall behind them and started my pantomime, they could see a twenty-foot King Kong shadow climbing the Cathedral Tower. Fortunately, all the years we were in Washington my luck held, and I never had to explain to Cathedral Security what the headmaster of St. Albans was doing on the wall of the Bishop's Garden in the dark.

For all the years I was at St. Albans, Martha and I had children in Cathedral schools. For the last seventeen years we had sons at St. Albans. The departure of the last child for college is something that parents look forward to and also dread. Long before it happened to us, the wife of a former chairman of the board came to see me.

"Mark, you really should speak to the parents of seniors, especially those whose senior is the youngest child in the family. Talk to them about the empty nest syndrome. Be sure to tell the fathers that they need to be particularly sensitive to their wives at that time. It has been very hard on me to have our last one go off to college."

Five years later the same woman hailed me across Wisconsin Avenue. She ran across the street to speak to me. "Mark, Mark. Forget about the empty nest syndrome. Tell them about the full nest syndrome. Both of mine have graduated from college and have come back to live with us. It's driving me crazy."

DANGER

I have done something as a parent that no father would want to do or should do. On two occasions I have taken my children into mortal danger. We moved to Washington from rural Virginia with some trepidation. It was then a crime-ridden city with a high murder rate. Even though St. Albans and the headmaster's home are in a lovely and relatively safe part of the city, we wondered if this move would be safe for our children.

When the first spring vacation came, we decided to go to Colonial Williamsburg to enjoy the history and have a few days in a less urban setting. Our neighbor recommended an inexpensive motel on the edge of town. After a happy day of wandering among the Colonial buildings, we decided to grab a quick supper at a fast food place. As we were driving back to our motel a heavy rain began to fall through the darkness. When we parked, I said that I would run in and get an umbrella. Cara and Sean went with me as each one wanted to have a say about which channel would be on the TV. Martha sat in the passenger seat of our car holding six-week-old Kevin in her arms.

There was a knock on her window. A man stood there. Martha looked straight into the barrel of a pistol. It was not a Colonial flintlock.

"Roll down your window."

She obeyed.

"Let me have your money."

"Honest to God, I don't have any. I would give it to you if I did. It's in the motel."

"Get out of the car."

She opened the door and stood up. She knew that at any moment I would be returning carrying an umbrella. I might scare the man. Would he react by shooting me, or perhaps her? We suspect that it was not until she stood up that he saw that she was holding a baby.

"Get back in the car."

The man disappeared into the dark night. A second later I came out of the motel. When she told me what had happened, my first reaction was anger. We ran into the lobby of the motel. I felt a desire to embarrass the motel that did not provide enough light in its parking lot.

"Man with a gun. Man with a gun," I began to shout over and over again in the lobby. Within seconds, the manager whisked us into his office. He called the state police who took our statements. Even though I did not think that the gunman would return, we wanted out of there. I told the manager and the state policeman, "We are leaving right now. We are going back to the District of Columbia where it is safe at night."

In fact, we did not go back to Washington that night. We called our friends Debbie and Bill Davis at the Blue Ridge School. "We will be there in two hours. Have lots of hugs and daiquiris ready."

Two years later, I held Kevin in front of a Committee of the U.S. Congress. "Before this little boy was two months old," I testified, "a man put a gun to his head. Are you going to let this happen again?" Sadly, our leaders have not found a good answer to that question.

In 1979, Martha and I took a group of St. Albans students to Ireland. Our two older children, Cara, age ten, and Sean, age eight, were with us. As part of the trip, we had arranged for an old Irish fisherman, Dermot Walsh, to take us in his open fishing boat to Skellig Michael, a small island (now uninhabited) about six miles off the coast of Kerry. It is a stone slab rising 750 feet straight out of the Atlantic Ocean. In the early Middle Ages, when Danish raiders were attacking Ireland, monks built a monastery of stone beehive huts at the top of Skellig Michael. They cut stone steps into the side of the cliff that could easily be defended. Climbing those steps is still a breathtaking experience. Although the monks are gone, it is still sacred ground and the most spectacular place I have ever been. Only the distant coast of Kerry interrupts the view of the ocean in every direction. Far, far below, the waves crash endlessly against the cliffs. The gray rocks of the monks' huts and the chapel are a sharp contrast to the rich green grass on the little level area where the monastery was built.

We had made a couple of other trips to Skellig Michael with Dermot, when we took Choate students to Ireland. No Hollywood casting director could have found a better Irish fisherman than Dermot Walsh. He was tall and in his hand-knit Irish sweater he looked strong and lean. His high cheekbones made him handsome, but the lines in his face told of the decades of fierce winds and salt water he had faced. Like many Irish fisherman, he carried no life preservers.

The first half hour of our trip in 1979 was very calm. We boarded Dermot's thirty-foot boat in Portmagee and followed a smooth inland passage that separated the Kerry mainland from Valentia Island. Before we could see the open ocean we could hear a mighty roar. When we cleared the headland we could see that the sea was agitated and great waves were rolling in to the shore. The little boat pitched violently as it entered the open ocean and then began to roll precipitously with each wave. The farther we got from shore the greater the roll became. At times we were at the top of a wave and could see that land in any direction was far away. Most of the time the waves were towering above us.

We, who were not sailors, became seriously frightened that a wave would tip the boat over or just enter the boat and cause it to founder. The wind howled across the water. We looked up at the walls of water above our heads. We held onto the wooden seats and sides of the boat as we lurched from side to side, leaning at what seemed impossible angles. Eight-year-old Sean got down between our legs and began to moan, "We are going to die. We are going to die." That certainly did nothing for the nerves of the others. I noticed that one student was on his knees, his lips moving in what was surely earnest prayer. I truly believed that there was a very good chance that the boat would founder and we would all die.

When we were about three-fourths of the way between the mainland and Skellig Michael, Dermot Walsh said, "We are going to turn back. Even if we got to Skellig Michael the waves would crush us against the cliffs when we tried to dock. And we certainly don't want to stay out here." I knew that turning a boat around in high seas can be particularly dangerous, but Dermot managed it well. We all felt better as the coast of Kerry grew larger in front of us. There was a great sense of relief as we rode the last waves and entered the calm waters of the inland passage for the last half hour of the trip.

I am not a sailor. That night I wondered if I had been foolish to think we were in such a difficult situation. Perhaps the danger had not been as great as I had imagined.

The next morning we found headlines in all the papers that screamed, "FASTNET TRAGEDY: 17 MEN LOST AT SEA."

The Fastnet Race was a world-class yacht race, attracting top sailors from around the world. It went from the west coast of England around the Fastnet rocks off the coast of Ireland and back to England. The storm had come up suddenly. Because they were in a race, few of the competitors had been willing to turn back. Their yachts were built for speed not strength. Thirty yachts had been demasted. The papers had pictures of helicopters plucking yachtsmen off the decks of racing ships in tremendous waves. Others had gone down with their yachts before rescuers in helicopters or lifeboats could get to them. Some of their bodies were recovered. Others were not.

We had been in the same waters in the same storm. We had been with an old Irish fisherman. That is how he got to be an *old* fisherman. He knew when to respect the power of the sea.

The trip to Skellig Michael was not the first time we had been on the ocean when lives were lost. The first time we did not have our children with us. In the early 1970s we took a cruise ship from New York to the Bahamas during spring vacation. On the return voyage the Bermuda Triangle lived up to its reputation with a vicious storm. While our ship rolled mightily, we got no indication from the crew that we were in particular danger. However, about noon an announcement was made that we were going off course to look for an oil tanker that had sent a distress signal that it was splitting in two.

Several hours later our ship spotted the stern section of the tanker. It was wallowing in the heavy waves. That large an object being tossed randomly by wind and waves is an awesome sight. Our ship circled it twice looking for survivors. None were seen. Before we got back to New York it was announced that one man, who had been in the bow section, had been rescued by a helicopter as he clung to a hatch cover. The rest of the crew was lost.

Three years before that we had seen a successful rescue. We were crossing the Atlantic from New York to Ireland on the Queen Elizabeth II. An announcement was made that we were going off course because a Russian trawler had hit and sunk a Canadian fishing boat. The Russians had not stopped to offer assistance. Several hours later we could see, off the port side of our ship, a small rubber raft with four men in it. The Queen Elizabeth II started to lower a lifeboat, but then a Royal Canadian Air Force helicopter roared in. It picked the men up one by one. As it started back to Newfoundland, it circled the Queen Elizabeth II and all the passengers cheered.

FATHER OF THE BRIDE

They made movies about it, but nothing can really prepare a man for the experience of his daughter's wedding. This is particularly true if she is his first child to get married. I had performed a fair number of weddings, but how different it was when it was my little girl who had overnight blossomed into a beautiful, confident woman.

Cara was in the third class of women at Washington and Lee University, which had been all male for two hundred years. There she met King Milling, a third-generation Washington and Lee student from New Orleans. As Martha and I got to know King, we easily understood why Cara loved him. Indeed, he is a third son to us and another brother to Sean and Kevin.

Cara and King strengthen a pet theory of mine. My parents met in college. Martha and I did not attend the same college, but my college roommate introduced us. Now, our daughter was to marry a man she met in college. I used to tell seniors, "Roughly half of the adults I know married someone *because* of where they went to college. So, for half of you, the way college will most influence your future happiness or unhappiness will not be classes, facilities, or even reputation. It will be the spouse you meet because of your college." It was advice that usually fell on totally deaf ears.

From the beginning of the engagement, both Cara and Martha said that I would be father of the bride—not clergyman. It was a very wise decision.

Early on, the father of the bride discovers that numbers assume the same unreality they have in matters of astronomy or the national debt. I, who in those days did not like to spend more than ten dollars on a bottle of wine, found myself saying, "Oh, if having standing rib roast at the reception only adds five hundred dollars, let's do it."

The hours spent on the details of all the arrangements somehow kept the reality of what was happening at bay. But then there were moments when the knowledge came crashing in on me that the child, whom I held in my arms minutes after she was born, was now a woman. Cara had been living in Cleveland. She bought her wedding dress there. She brought it to Washington when she returned two months before the wedding. The first time she tried it on for us I began to cry; she was so beautiful.

Cara's wedding was at the High Altar of Washington Cathedral and was performed by my good friend and colleague, Will Billow. John Kraus, the verger, gave us special permission to have the bride come in from the west end and walk the entire length of the nave.

As the service began, I stood at the west end of the Cathedral, Cara on my arm, watching Martha walk down the nave with Sean and Kevin on either side of her. It was a moment of such intense love that I do not expect to exceed it in this life. Then I began to walk with Cara toward the man she loved.

Of course, my eyes overflowed, and I continued to cry until we reached the altar. For everyone who knew me, the fact that I was crying was a sure sign of how happy I was about Cara's marriage to King.

The ceremony, the reception, the dancing, and Cara and King's departure all passed in a cloud of joy. An hour or so after the bride and groom left, the dancing ended. Then a moment occurred that did not appear in the movie versions of *Father of the Bride*. Nor did it appear in our video of Cara's wedding because I neglected to ask Chuck Hurley,

Martha's cousin who did a great job of videoing everything else, to record the scene.

While I had opinions about many aspects of the wedding, I had said from the beginning that the choice of a band should be Cara's. My taste in music might not exactly coincide with hers. The band Cara chose asked for half the money up front and the other half the night of wedding. That seemed fair. I dutifully sent off a check. At the reception it was soon apparent that Cara had made a great choice. The band was so good that the kitchen staff came out and danced.

The band stopped playing at midnight as planned and began to pack up. I walked over with my checkbook in hand.

"Oh no," the leader said. "The contract called for the first payment by check and the second in cash. I have to distribute it among the band members."

I had gotten some money from the ATM that morning. Martha also had some cash. But I was still short. Fortunately, it was now past midnight. A new day! I could make another withdrawal. So, at 12:30 A.M., in white tie and tails, I stood in front of the ATM on Wisconsin Avenue, the perfect picture of the father of the bride. However, there was no one there to take my picture.

Martha and I got home some time after that. As we were getting into bed the phone rang.

"Dad? It's Cara."

Getting a phone call from his daughter on her wedding night can make a man anxious. But I thought she sounded serene.

"Dad. I just wanted Mom and you to know the whole wedding was exactly the way I wanted it to be."

"That's wonderful. You are so sweet to call. Now you get back to whatever you two were doing. I love you."

I went to sleep the happiest of men.

DESSERT

Our daughter had her wedding reception in the St. Albans refectory. One of the reasons the wedding was such a success was the wonderful work of Charlie Dunne. He and the kitchen staff provided food and service that were exceptional. St. Albans had great success with the Marriott Food Service. However, on one occasion, I allowed my own expectations to get the better of me. Bill Marriott was a St. Albans graduate and parent. When he moved the Marriott Corporate Office into suburban Maryland, he invited me to an opening reception. I had a prior commitment but called him to ask if I could visit the new headquarters another time. Bill invited me to come out in two weeks. "I'll give you a tour and then we'll have lunch."

I said to Martha, "Lunch at the Marriott Corporate Office. This should really be something. You don't have to have much dinner for me that night."

Bill Marriott was gracious with his time. Most impressive to me was the computer room. Just by pushing a couple of buttons, Bill could find out what the restaurant in any Marriott Hotel in the country paid for a pound of chicken that day. Since this was in the 1980s, it was new for me to see a large room filled with nothing but computers. Bill said, "My father thinks I'm crazy but I'm having fun." I knew that Bill's father had started with one small root beer stand in Washington. Then Bill added, "Now, let's get some lunch."

I began to anticipate lunch in the executive suite of Marriott Headquarters. As we stepped into an elevator, Bill did not push the top button. Instead, he hit the basement button. We stepped into a large room where a couple dozen people were eating at plastic tables. Bill walked to a serving counter. "This is where we train all our newest employees. I eat here so I can see how they are doing. Do you want fries with your burger?"

When Charlie Dunne took charge of the Marriott Food Service at St. Albans, he soon charmed us all. His sense of humor and great ability to provide the appropriate food for any occasion made him a very valued member of the school. I had such faith in him that for any special event I would only give him a rough idea of what I wanted, and he would produce just the right menu. Perhaps the fact that he is from Ireland and I am of Irish descent helped him to know what I would like. However, there was one time that Irish connection got us in trouble.

One year, four men came from Hazelden to talk about a program they might present at St. Albans. Hazelden is one of the oldest and best-known alcohol treatment centers in the United States. Almost everyone who works for Hazelden is a recovering alcoholic. I invited the Hazelden visitors for a special lunch in the Burling Lounge. I asked the Dean of Students and the heads of the Upper and Lower Schools to join us. I told Charlie Dunne that we were having special visitors, and I would like a nice luncheon.

"It will be all adults, some from outside and some from the school. Don't have anything too heavy."

Charlie produced beautifully decorated chef salads in individual bowls. As we ate, we had a good discussion of the alcohol problems of adolescents. The salad dishes were cleared and the representatives of Hazelden began to describe the presentation that they had made to other schools.

At that point, Charlie proudly came into the Burling Lounge carrying a tray of desserts. He announced the dessert, with its high alcohol content, in his lovely Irish lilt.

"Grasshoppers."

ADMISSIONS

Greg and Marie Wood came to Washington for the first time when he was appointed the number-two person at the Australian Embassy. It was unusual for someone in such an important position to have children as young as the Woods did, but all three of their children were in grade school. Their friends in Australia told them that they would like Washington but warned them that the public schools were academically weak and sometimes dangerous. Because the Woods arrived in the middle of the winter, every private school they called said that it would be happy to consider their children for fall admissions but not before. Their residence was a couple of blocks east of the Cathedral. That meant that they were in the area for the public grade school, John Eaton. Reluctantly, Marie took the boys up to register them at John Eaton. They walked so they could get a sense of the time it would take to get to school in the morning. Marie was pleasantly surprised by the school. The building, though old, was cleanly renovated and brightly decorated. The children seemed well behaved, and the principal, Pat Greer, was an impressive woman. Still, Marie kept worrying about the warnings of her friends in Australia.

As they walked on Thirty-fourth Street toward home, Marie suggested that they detour through the Cathedral because they had not been inside it yet. It was a gray winter day. As they entered it, the Cathedral was gloomy with shadows. Marie and the boys stood looking up at the great columns disappearing into the darkness of the ceiling. Walking between the columns came an elderly priest, a small man wearing a black cassock. He said, "Hello." Then, in a way that was interested rather than challenging, he asked the boys, "Why aren't you in school?"

"Oh," explained Marie, "we've just moved here from Australia, and I've taken the boys up to John Eaton to register them. Do you know anything about that school? Is it any good?"

The elderly priest smiled. "I don't know it well. But I was headmaster of St. Albans School here on the Cathedral Close for twenty-seven years. I do know that the present headmaster sends his youngest child there. So he must think it is good."

To this day, Marie believes that Canon Martin was sent to her by God.

Her boys started John Eaton the next day. On the way home, Marie asked each boy about his day.

"I have a friend already," said the youngest. "His name is Kevin."

"That's wonderful," replied Marie, happy that her child felt accepted in this foreign land.

The next day at the close of school, Marie met Kevin and his mother. A few days later, Kevin's mother called to invite Marie and Greg to dinner. As she was giving directions to their home, it came out that it was the headmaster's residence for St. Albans.

We soon became close friends with Greg and Marie. They are highly intelligent but also very down-to-earth and fun. We saw them as often as we saw any couple in Washington in those years.

Two years later, their oldest son was in sixth grade, which is the last grade at John Eaton. One day I asked Greg and Marie if that son would be continuing in the public system. They said, "Well, he's applying to Sidwell Friends, Georgetown Day, and Landon. But, of course, we don't know what will happen."

I was a little taken aback. "I don't mean to be nosy or defensive, but is there a reason he did not apply to St. Albans?"

"Oh yes. We were afraid that if he were not qualified it would put you in an embarrassing position. And we did not want to presume on our friendship with you."

One could not describe the Woods as typical Washingtonians. Fortunately, there was still time for their son to take the admissions test. He was well qualified. A number of St. Albans faculty expressed real regret two years later when the boy left St. Albans because his father returned to Canberra to head the Australian civil service.

THAT MAN

One of the important responsibilities of a headmaster is fund-raising. At most independent schools, tuition does not cover the entire operating budget. All headmasters worry about raising tuition too high. All things, however, are relative. One time I looked up the price of a standard midsized Chevrolet in 1977, my first year at St. Albans. It was very close to St. Albans tuition. Eighteen years later, tuition was still close to the price of a 1995 Chevrolet. I like to think that a St. Albans education lasts longer than a Chevrolet.

I never met a headmaster who felt his teachers were being paid as much as they should be. One time, when we were seeking permission from the Cathedral Chapter for a tuition increase, someone raised the old adage about the middle class. "The rich can afford St. Albans, and the poor can get scholarships. But if you keep raising tuition you'll squeeze out the middle class."

I asked the speaker to define "middle class." He gave a range of incomes. "Well," I replied, "the lower number you gave is higher than our median faculty salary. Don't you think our first responsibility should be to get those who spend their lives caring for other people's children *into* the middle class?"

I got a different viewpoint on money from a new St. Albans board member. I had chatted with Brendan Sullivan occasionally at parent functions but did not feel I knew him well when he was elected to the board. I did know that he was one of the toughest and most respected attorneys in Washington. I went to see him just to get better acquainted.

"Mark," he began, "I have one complaint with St. Albans."

I waited apprehensively to learn what was upsetting him.

"You don't pay your teachers enough." I almost jumped up and hugged him. With his leadership we were able to make some real progress, in several years giving 10 percent raises.

If a headmaster cares for the future of the school, he raises money for improvements to the physical plant and for endowment. Most great academic institutions have great endowments. For example, the *income* from Harvard's endowment is greater than the *principal* of the endowments of all but five other universities.

I liked raising money. First, it meant that I got to know some very interesting people. In the intimate world of the independent school, it is very hard to raise significant money unless you have a personal relationship with the donor. Second, raising money means that you are encouraging people to respond to their better, more caring, selves. It is a pleasure to be involved in that process. Third, asking for a big gift gave me an adrenaline rush. I have experienced the same rush in athletic contests. One prepares carefully for it. Then the day of decision arrives, and one goes for it. Fourth, money raised is measurable. So much of what we do in schools is not measurable. Oh yes, there are test results and college admissions. But the things that really matter are not measurable and may not be known for years: What sort of person will this student become? What sort of contribution will he make to others? With fund-raising you can measure the results.

Finally, I liked raising money because I like spending it. I like spending it to improve the educational experience of students. I like spending it on scholarships to make it possible for a good student to come the school. I like spending it on teachers, to try to provide a decent living for them and their families. I like spending it on buildings that will be used by students born long after I am dead. I had many happy experiences fund-raising. I had only one bad experience. It nearly caused me cardiac arrest. Curiously, it involved one of St. Albans most generous donors.

Admiral Frank Jones had always been very generous to St. Albans. He was an alumnus, parent, grandparent, and former chairman of the board. When we started the campaign for a $6,000,000 renovation of the True-Lucas Building, we showed him the plans in the early stages of development. His engineering background and experience building U.S. Navy ships allowed him to ask some pertinent and useful questions that produced design improvements. We did not, however, ask him to make a gift. He had been so generous in the past that we wanted to raise part of the cost to show the commitments of others before we approached him.

However, Frank Jones was not a man to wait around. Early in the fund-raising campaign I got a letter from him. It said that he was making a very large pledge. It was much bigger than anything he had given before and would take us a significant way toward our goal. Typically, Frank's note said, "Mark, don't bother writing a thank you note. You have other things to do." Without even calling him, I jumped in my car and drove to his house to thank him. He welcomed me into his living room. Before I could say anything, Frank yelled upstairs, "Margaret, Mark Mullin is here."

Margaret Jones was a strong woman. She had been an admiral's wife for many years. When she was old enough to have a grandson in high school, she had ridden her bicycle from northwest Washington to southern Alexandria to watch her grandson in a cross-country meet. That is over thirty miles round trip.

I heard Margaret Jones come running down the stairs. Her face indicated that she was upset. She came up to me but pointed a finger at Frank.

"Do you know what that man has done? Do you know what that man has done?"

My heart stopped beating. Frank's pledge had been large enough to have a significant impact on the amount of money he could leave his children and grandchildren. Margaret Jones, of course, had not attended St. Albans. It was obvious to me that, by going to their house unannounced, I had stirred up a family fight about this very large gift. Now I was in the middle of the fight. I stood there speechless, frozen with embarrassment and fear.

Margaret continued, "That man has agreed that we should go to an Annapolis reunion on the same day as St. Albans Grandparents Day. I would rather be at St. Albans."

Having expressed her frustration with Frank and her love for St. Albans, she offered me a cup of tea and waited to hear why I had come to visit them.

My hands were still shaking so much that the teacup rattled as I thanked them both for their wonderful gift.

There were many people like Frank and Margaret Jones connected with St. Albans and later Casady that made fund-raising easy. People who give serious money to a school are usually gracious and thoughtful. Much as I enjoyed fund-raising, I did have one spectacularly missed opportunity. A couple of years after Martha and I arrived at St. Albans, we were able to spend a little time one summer in Europe. One day we were visiting a museum and enjoying the great works of art. Toward the end of our visit, Martha went to the ladies' room. I waited outside. Suddenly, coming toward me was a St. Albans father. Draped on his arm was an attractive young woman. I estimated her to be halfway in age between his wife and his St. Albans son. Unfortunately, before I could look away, our eyes met. We could not pretend that we had not seen each other. The St. Albans father came over to me, and we each said, "Hello."

Then he asked, "What are you doing here?"

"I am waiting for *Martha*, who is in the ladies room."

Soon he drifted away. He did not introduce or even mention the young lady who still clung to him.

We came back from Europe and at the end of the summer went down to visit friends at the Blue Ridge School near Charlottesville, where I had been before going to St. Albans. The headmaster at the time was Hatcher Williams, a wise old fox with more than twenty years of experience as a headmaster. He asked me about our trip to Europe, and I began to tell him about meeting the St. Albans father in the museum. Of course, I was careful not to mention any names. When I had finished the story, the headmaster of Blue Ridge gave me a quizzical glance.

"Mark, I assume that when you got back to Washington the first thing you did was call that man up and say, 'It was great to see you in Europe. Now I'd like to discuss your becoming the largest donor to this year's annual giving fund.'"

Unfortunately for St. Albans, I never did make that call.

MR. NORTH

One of the reasons I enjoyed raising money was that it helped fund scholarships. Actually, almost every student is on a sort of financial aid. Tuition usually does not cover the cost of an independent school education. Therefore, unless parents make a significant financial contribution, someone else's money is helping with their child's education. In any good school, there are students who receive specific scholarships. These are usually based on the parents' financial situation. Of course, a scholarship may be life changing for the individual who receives it. It is important to remember also that all students benefit from a scholarship program that brings in a more interesting, more diverse, more talented student body.

I cannot write about scholarships without thinking of William Stanley North. Mr. North was a successful Chicago businessman whose son attended Harvard in the 1950s. One Christmas vacation the son was driving back to Chicago and was killed in a car crash. I remember hearing about the accident when I was in high school. It had been given some press coverage because the son of Illinois governor and Democratic presidential nominee Adlai Stevenson had been in the car. A scholarship was established in memory of William Stanley North II. It would go to a freshman at Harvard who came from anywhere in Illinois. When I was informed that I had been given that scholarship, I was also asked if I would be willing to travel the 130 miles from my home to Chicago to meet William Stanley North, father of the deceased student.

We met in his impressive office in downtown Chicago. Mr. North was clearly a very successful man but also a kindly one. I do not remember anything of our conversation. What I do remember is the impression the meeting made on me. I had been proud that I was a Harvard National Scholar. However, the scholarship itself meant little more to me than a paper transaction between my father and the Harvard business office. Now it took on a new meaning. Mr. North had lost a son. That tragedy had resulted in there being a scholarship available to help me go to Harvard. I had an obligation to use my time there well.

I am embarrassed to say that I thought little more about Mr. North after my freshman year. Fifteen years after graduating from college, I became a headmaster and began raising money for scholarships. Occasionally, I would tell a potential donor how a scholarship changed my life. At such times I would remember Mr. North. After I had been at St. Albans for a number of years, I was glancing through the *Harvard Alumni Magazine*. There was report on a class preparing for its fiftieth reunion. Accompanying the article was a picture of William Stanley North, who was heading up the fund-raising for his class. I tracked down his address and wrote to him. "The scholarship in your son's name made it possible for me to attend Harvard. I want you to know what I have done with my life." I told him that I was an Episcopal priest and headmaster of St. Albans School. "The opportunity you gave me made all the difference. Now I'm spending my time preparing young men for Harvard and other fine colleges. Thank you for changing my life all those years ago."

It takes little imagination to know the reply William Stanley North sent me.

One of the strengths of a good independent school is that sometimes a headmaster can act for the welfare of the school without consulting any committee or getting permission from the board. A headmaster should not do that too often, but once in a while decisive and immediate action can be valuable. While St. Albans had admissions and scholarship committees, it was understood that, from time to time, I could act independently of those committees.

During my last two years in college, one of my roommates was John Valentine. John's father was a factory warehouse foreman in Detroit who sent two sons to Harvard College. The elder son became a research doctor while John eventually earned a Ph.D. Immediately after graduating from college, John worked in the coal mines of Appalachia because he was interested in the people who had migrated from there to the factories of Detroit. When John was called up by the draft, he decided to become a Marine officer. Early in the Vietnam War, he was sent there to head a rifle platoon. After some months in Vietnam, his platoon was ambushed. Seven men were killed. John was wounded seriously and lay under a bush for several hours thinking that he was going to bleed to death. Fortunately, the medics were finally able to get to him, and he was helicoptered out. He was soon on his way to the hospital at Great Lakes Naval Base, Illinois.

John visited us several times in Washington after the Vietnam Memorial had been built. At first, he refused to go the Memorial, saying, "My mistake put seven of those names on there." He is the kind of person who would be hard on himself.

I used to urge him to go, saying, "When they take someone from the streets of Detroit, send him to Harvard, and then drop him into the jungles of Vietnam, he can only do the best he can, knowing that very bad things may happen. Don't blame yourself." Finally, he did go to the Vietnam Memorial. He rubbed his hand over each of those seven names. That was a wonderfully healing experience. Touching the wall has been helpful for so many people.

When I was asked to preach at the memorial service for deceased classmates at my twenty-fifth Harvard reunion, Martha reminded me of John's experience. At the service, I told my classmates of going to the Vietnam Memorial myself and running my fingers over the name of a classmate who had died in Vietnam. The magic of the Memorial is that as you touch a name, you see yourself reflected in the dark stone of the wall. I suggested to the twenty-fifth reunioners that as we remember our classmates who have died, we should look at ourselves and reflect on what we have done with our lives and what we hope to do in the years we still have ahead.

After he got his Ph.D., John Valentine taught for a while at the New School in New York City. I performed his wedding in a field in his brother's summer place near Poughkeepsie. The following winter Martha and I were in New York for a St. Albans alumni gathering. We met John and his bride for a late night drink. John began to talk about a letter he had received recently.

"You know, while I was working on my Ph.D., I spent some time in Poland at the University of Warsaw. I met a fascinating family there. The father is a doctor. The mother was the first member of the Philosophy Faculty at the University of Warsaw to join Solidarity. They have two sons. The Zelinskis just wrote to me about the older son, Kuba. They were wishing that he could have the experience of living in freedom for a year at the impressionable age of sixteen. But we just have a little apartment in Brooklyn and he'd have to go to a New York public school. Do you think I should invite him over?"

I thought a moment and then asked, "How bright is he?"

"Very bright. I got to know the boy really well when I was in Poland. He is really sharp."

"How's his English?"

"He has an accent. But he is pretty fluent. He's studied English for quite a few years, and both his parents speak it."

"I'll take him at St. Albans for a year."

"What, are you kidding?"

"No, I'll take him."

"Well, his parents are comfortable by Polish standards. But they are not allowed to send any money out of the country. They couldn't pay anything."

"I would like the St. Albans students to have the opportunity to get to know a young person who has had to live under communism. If you can take him during vacations when our dormitory is closed and give him a little spending money, I'll give him a full scholarship for room, board, and tuition."

"Don't you have to test him?"

"I trust you when you say he is very bright. Of course he'll have to struggle awfully hard because of the language problem. But it's not as if we have to get him ready for college admissions. He can be a junior and then go back to Poland. I'm sure he'll gain a lot from the experience, and so will St. Albans."

At the end of the first semester Kuba came to see me in my office. He was very nervous.

"Mr. Mullin. It has been so wonderful to have this time in America. But I have been wondering, is there any possibility, any way that I could stay and graduate from St. Albans?"

I laughed out loud. "Kuba, you are getting all As. You are even getting an A in English. If the faculty knew that you wanted to stay and I didn't let you, they'd hang me."

At Prize Day the following year I presented Kuba with an American flag that had flown over the Capitol of the United States. I said to the audience, "All of you who are parents have made sacrifices to send your son to St. Albans. I want to tell you of the sacrifice Kuba's parents made. They have not seen him for two years. He

was unable to go home last summer because the communist government might not have let him leave the country again. His parents are
not here today, and they will not see him graduate tomorrow, because the whole family is not allowed out of the country at the same
time. They made that sacrifice so that Kuba could get a St. Albans
education."

Stanford University gave Kuba a full scholarship. He went on to
get a Ph.D. and teach at an American university.

Kuba used to tell me about his little brother. "He's the smart one
in the family."

"Oh no, Kuba. He couldn't be."

When the younger brother turned sixteen, he came to St. Albans
on a scholarship, although by now the family could contribute a little
toward his expenses. It turned out that Kuba was right about who was
the brightest one in the family.

In the early 1990s, there was a young man who grew up in a very
small southern town. His mother had only an eighth-grade education.
He had not seen his father in five years. He had never left the state
where he was born. The rector of the local Episcopal Church got to
know him. The rector spotted his high intelligence even though it had
been underdeveloped by the rural school system. The good priest, having once spent a week at the College of Preachers, knew that there was
a school called St. Albans on the grounds of Washington Cathedral. He
knew the school had a small boarding department. The rector arranged
to have the youngster tested. St. Albans gave him a full scholarship. In
September, the young man's mother drove him up to Washington. To
save money on the trip north, they spent the night in the car.

Martha and I had him to our home with the other boarders. A
couple of times, I took him with me when I did Saturday errands in
Washington. He seemed to need adult male attention. He made decent
grades, but we all knew he would do better as his academic skills continued to develop.

At the start of his second year, his mother again drove him to
Washington. Once again, they slept in the car. That year the dormitory
masters had arranged a cookout for the parents of the boarders on the
day the parents brought them to the dormitory. In the late afternoon I

ran into the young man and his mother in front of the school. She told me she was about to start driving home.

"Oh, why don't you stay for the cookout?"

"No. I think I'll get going."

It did not occur to me that she might be avoiding the cookout because she was afraid she would be socially ill at ease with the other St. Albans parents. I was just trying to be welcoming, but I said something to her that was very insensitive.

"You really ought to stay for dinner. After all, you've paid for it."

She stared down at the ground. "No, I haven't paid for it. My son is on full scholarship."

"Oh yes, that's right. Well you know I went to college and graduate school on scholarships."

I have never seen an expression change so fast. She went from embarrassment to astonishment to radiance in just a few seconds. With her limited experience, she had never imagined that anybody who had once been a scholarship student could become headmaster of St. Albans School.

"Do you hear that, my son? Do you hear that? Mr. Mullin went to school on scholarships. Maybe someday you can be a headmaster."

THE PACKAGE

Raising money for scholarships or any other purpose requires a headmaster to spend considerable time with alumni. They usually have a more permanent affection for the school than parents. Almost always, alumni activities are fun. People come to alumni events to renew old friendships and to be, for a short time, eighteen again. They are usually accomplished people, and getting to know them is a pleasure. One time, however, it caused us considerable distress.

In 1996 I was invited to give two lectures at universities in Estonia. Martha and I were excited to visit this small country that had just separated from the Soviet Union. We also arranged to visit some secondary schools there. We visited schools that taught in Estonian and schools that taught in Russian, reflecting the difficult legacy of a half-century of Soviet rule over the Baltic States. My impression was that the Estonian language schools encouraged much more critical thinking in their students.

Kevin was a junior at St. Albans. A bachelor teacher agreed to live in our house with him while we were gone. We left an emergency number where we could be reached but did not encourage Kevin to call that far just to chat.

At about 3:00 A.M. in Estonia, the phone rang. I sleepily answered it.

"Dad? It's Kevin."

I realized that it was only 8:00 P.M. in Washington, but I was still nervous to hear his voice.

"Yes. How are you?"

"I'm fine. I'll tell you why I called. The *Washington Post* is bugging me. They think they've caught the Unabomber, or they are about to catch him. I'm not sure which. He was a Harvard classmate of yours."

"What's his name?"

"I don't remember. It's unusual. The *Post* wants your yearbook and your *Harvard 25th Anniversary Report*. But I didn't want to give them anything without checking with you. What should I do?"

I remembered that the *Washington Post* and the *New York Times* had worked with the FBI and had published the Unabomber's manifesto. "Go ahead and give them what they want. Just be sure to tell them I need it back."

When one is four thousand miles away from one's child, there is a tendency to worry a bit. Kevin was unsure whether the Unabomber was in custody or whether the authorities wanted my Harvard books in an effort to catch him. I knew also that the Unabomber did not like academic administrators.

When we got back to the United States, we learned that the Unabomber was safely in jail. The *Washington Post* did report that his last known address was in Afghanistan. That came from my *Harvard 25th Anniversary Report*. Later, it turned out that the street in the address did not even exist.

Two months went by. Then a package arrived at my office. It was addressed to Martha but sent to my office. It was lumpy and wrapped in brown paper. It had a return address from Montana, but the name meant nothing to me. Who had sent it? Could it be connected with the

Unabomber who had been living as a hermit in Montana when he was arrested?

Of course, being a good husband I do not open my wife's mail. I took the package home, carrying it carefully. Maybe Martha knew the name on the package.

She did not. I was about to call the police. Martha remembered the project she had done for the Black Student Fund. She had located over a thousand former students.

"We've got a name and an address. Call Directory Assistance and see if you can get a phone number."

Directory Assistance gave me a phone number in Montana. I called it. A male voice answered. I asked for the name on the package.

"He's not here right now. I don't know when he'll be back. It could be quite a while."

I felt like asking, "Quite a while? You mean like thirty years to life?"

Now we were really worried and ready to call the police. Suddenly, Martha remembered. She did know the name on the package.

Six months earlier we had attended a St. Albans reunion at the home of Jacque and Bob Alvord. Some years before, a member of that class had died. Because he was dead, his name was not on my radar screen. However, the class invited his widow to attend the reunion. She had come with her grown son who had not attended St. Albans. Not knowing many of his late father's classmates, he was standing by himself. Typically, Martha went over to talk with him. He was on Public Radio in Montana. When Martha expressed interest in his shows, he promised to send her some tapes. It had taken him six months to get around to it and thus had given us a good scare.

THE HEIGHTS AND THE DEPTHS

St. Albans alumni have had great success in many different fields. The school is justly proud of their accomplishments. Three alumni, however, have been modern day explorers, going where few other humans have ever gone. Michael Collins was the pilot of the Command Module for Apollo 11. He was orbiting the moon when the first man set foot on it. At times he was orbiting alone above the dark side of the moon. Someone called him the loneliest man since Adam.

Shep Jenks was the navigator on the first submarine to go under the North Pole and realize the long-held dream of a water passage between the Atlantic and the Pacific. Under the polar ice cap he could use neither radio nor celestial navigation. The currents made dead reckoning very difficult, yet Shep plotted the sub's course with remarkable accuracy. I liked to tell visitors that St. Albans men had been to the heights and the depths.

Rick Hauck flew in the space shuttle three times. His first trip, on which he served as pilot, was also the first trip by an American woman, Sally Ride. He piloted another trip. Then, from Cape Kennedy, he watched his friends die in the Challenger disaster.

When America went back into space, Rick was chosen to command the flight of Discovery. All went well, and he brought his spacecraft and crew safely back to earth. After Rick had been debriefed and had returned to Washington, we invited Rick and his wife out to dinner to celebrate. During dinner Rick said that he would be leaving NASA and talked a little about the career options open to him.

Martha asked, "But what are you going to do for your next thrill?"

"Oh, I want to go skiing this winter. When we are in training for a space flight we are not allowed to ski. Even a sprained ankle would put us off schedule."

Just as he said this, his wife pointed at the next table. "That man is choking." A waiter rushed over and began ineffectually patting the man on the back.

Of course, as an astronaut, Rick was highly trained in emergency first aid. He went behind the choking man and performed the Heimlich maneuver. Nothing happened. Then Rick tried again, this time putting all his strength into it. A whole shrimp popped out of the man's mouth.

In a couple of minutes, when he had regained his composure, the man came to our table. He offered his thanks. I could not resist adding to the drama.

"Do you know who just saved your life? This is Rick Hauck who just took America back into space as commander of the Discovery."

"Is that right? I was a navy pilot myself." He and Rick spent a happy time reminiscing about their pilot days.

A few years later we had to move out of the headmaster's house for a summer because it was being renovated. We looked at several houses that were available for short-term rentals. At one house, the woman showing us her home kept looking at us as though she knew us. Finally, she asked, "Weren't you at the Phoenix Park restaurant a few years ago? Your friend saved my husband when he was choking."

"Yes, that's right."

"He left me. That's why I'm having to vacate this house. I wish your friend had let the son of a bitch die."

Rick Hauck's flight as commander of Discovery had been in the late fall. Near the end of Christmas vacation, Rick called me at home late one afternoon.

"Mark, do you have a slide projector I could borrow? I just got my personal slides back from the Discovery trip."

"No, you cannot borrow my slide projector. But you can bring the slides and your wife and come for dinner. Then we will all watch them together."

While Martha straightened up the house, I went up to the grocery store to get something nice for dinner. While I was there I ran into our good friends Greg and Marie Wood. They were at the Australian Embassy and were St. Albans parents. They told me that they had just returned to Washington from vacation. They had driven three hundred miles that day with their three grade school–age sons in the back seat. They were also getting some food for dinner.

"Why don't you come to our house for dinner?" I asked. "I've already bought enough food."

"We're awfully tired. How about another time?" Greg apologized.

"Oh, come on. A friend has just returned from a trip. He and his wife are coming for dinner. He is bringing the slides from his trip."

Out of friendship for us, not a desire to see someone's travel slides, Marie said, "OK. We'll be over as soon as we feed the boys." Greg shot her a withering look but said nothing.

Rick had his slides organized and ready to go by the time Greg and Marie arrived. I introduced the two couples, but the name Rick Hauck did not register with the Woods.

I said, "Let's see the slides before we eat." Greg's frown grew deeper. He slouched on the sofa.

When the first slide came on, it was looking down on the Florida coast. The next one was shot across the Himalayas. I watched Greg almost rise out of the sofa as he tried to figure out what we were looking at. When a slide showed an astronaut floating inside the space shuttle he realized that I had been having fun with him. A delighted Australian settled back to relish the rest of the slides.

While these modern explorers were educated under my predecessors, Canons Lucas and Martin, I am proud of the accomplishments of students who were at St. Albans in my time. Yet I need to be careful about letting the school take too much credit. One never knows what talents lie latent until after a student has finished school. I think about some of the students from my years. Two have been elected to the U.S. Congress. Only one of them was involved in student government. Two have received the Emmy award for work in television. Neither took part in drama at St. Albans. One was a member of the University of Miami football team that won the National Championship. He did not play football at St. Albans. Another was on the U.S. Olympic Crew team. He did not row at St. Albans.

Half of me wants to laugh at myself and ask, "Just what were you doing as an educator?" The other half of me draws a lesson against overspecialization at too young an age. Moreover, I believe that St. Albans gave these young men the skills and self-discipline to be successful in whatever they undertook.

THE BICYCLE

While many alumni have visited us in our home, one visitor was particularly meaningful for us. It happened after I had left schoolwork and we were living in Charlottesville.

John Keating was in my third graduating class at St. Albans. While he was in college, his father was posted to Sweden with the U.S. Air Force. John visited his parents over Christmas vacation. He was out one night with a group of friends. It was a beautiful night, the moon and stars lighting up the snow. As they passed a railroad station, John decided to climb on a stationary tank car to enjoy the view from on high. From the top of the tank car, he waved to his friends. His left hand hit the electric power line used by the Swedish railroad. The line carried 16,000 volts.

John lived, but he lost his left arm and his left leg. Perhaps a letter I wrote to John while he was in the Swedish hospital caught the spirit of both John and St. Albans.

Dear John:

How wonderful to have your great letter arrive today! Of course, I am terribly touched and pleased that you have felt the concern and love that so many at St. Albans are sending your way. The bond you spoke of between graduates and the whole community is the most wonderful thing anyone could say about the school. But I am even more thrilled to hear of your progress and to read between the lines the courage, the determination, and the optimism with which you have faced this accident. I knew you would—but it is still good to hear it in your words.

As a matter of fact, when word of your accident spread at school, several people said to me that there was no one in the Class of '80 who would be stronger or better able to bounce back from such an ordeal than John Keating. The other thing being said around school is that you are already flirting with the Swedish nurses! That doesn't surprise me either, and I worry more about them than about you if you are, indeed, in the hospital two more months.

As you know we have two new lacrosse coaches and, until they ran into a very tough Landon team, they had the spring season going extremely well. That reminds me to tell you that when I first spoke to the student body about your accident, I told them that my most vivid image of you was you charging down the lacrosse field with a feather in your helmet, looking absolutely ferocious and terrifying. Then you walked over to the sidelines where you were as gentle and kind to two-year-old Kevin Mullin as any person could be.

Do give my best to your parents. Thank you for the wonderful thoughts you expressed in your letter. I did have to laugh at your concern about your spelling! I guess one can never escape from the influence of the St. Albans English Department. Hang in there, and do know that you continue to be supported by the love and prayers of so many people at St. Albans, and very much mine.

Sincerely yours,
Mark H. Mullin
Headmaster

Soon after we moved to Charlottesville we had a call from John who was now forty years old. He said he wanted to come see us in late July. He would then tell us why he was in Virginia. John arrived with Melynda, whom he had married in 1988, and their three sons. He explained that they were on their way home to Alabama from Jamestown, Virginia. On June 8, John and two older amputees had set out from Newport Beach, California. In forty-four days they had ridden specially constructed bicycles over thirty-five hundred miles. They had stopped at fifteen rehabilitation hospitals along the way to say to recent amputees, particularly older people, "Look, if we can do this, you, too, can recover. Life is not over after amputation, even beyond the age of forty."

PONCE DE LEÓN

I was standing in the main hallway of St. Albans one day talking to an alumnus who was back in town. Although still relatively young, he was now a professor at a leading law school. Suddenly, he pushed past me and grabbed the arm of the chief custodian who happened to be walking past us.

"Hey, Leroy. How are you?"

Leroy Weaver laughed, poked the alumnus in the stomach, and answered, "I'm great. But you've put on a little weight since your tennis playing days."

I was delighted to have an alumnus eager to talk with Leroy, who could remember him as a student. I only knew him as an adult.

Ponce de León searched futilely for the fountain of youth. Coming back to your school or college reunion splashes a little water from that fountain on you. You see people who knew you when you were young. They knew you when you had a head full of hair and a heart full of hopes. Being with classmates can do this, but sometimes it is even nicer to be remembered by a teacher or staff member who knew you in the flowering of your youth. If staff members are well treated they are sometimes more likely than teachers to be at a school for many years.

My predecessor, Canon Charles Martin, certainly set a tone that everyone—including those who provide clerical services, maintain the buildings, and prepare the meals—is a part of the school community. He also understood that students, particularly those from privileged backgrounds, need to see that the contributions of all adults at a school are important and valued. I tried to carry on his tradition.

One time I asked Bob Oldham, Superintendent of Buildings and Grounds, to send Pearley Harmon to the Burling Lounge at 2:30 P.M. so that I could show him an electrical problem. Pearley was the chief engineer at St. Albans, but when he was growing up he had had little opportunity for formal education. When he stuck his head in the Burling Lounge he saw that an Upper School faculty meeting was in session.

"Oh, excuse me. I'm sorry. I'll come back."

I stopped him. "No, wait a minute. Please come in." Pearley reluctantly stepped into the lounge. I continued, "Pearley, all of us on the faculty know you as a man who can fix anything. You have helped all of us so many times. I understand that recently you completed by correspondence the requirements for your high school diploma equivalent. St. Albans values the education of anyone, whether it is a teenager or an adult. We want to give you this certificate of admiration for earning your diploma and our appreciation for all you do for us." All the teachers were immediately on their feet, giving Pearley a loud standing ovation.

In the mid-1990s, the Cathedral proposed a plan to create a unified maintenance service that would bring all maintenance workers on the Cathedral Close under one central authority. That authority would then dispatch them as needed to any of the six institutions on the Cathedral Close. There were also significant issues about billing procedures for the services that were already shared, such as grounds maintenance. I believed that the Cathedral plan to include our maintenance workers would significantly decrease their sense of identity with St. Albans and their job satisfaction. It would certainly dramatically reduce interaction between maintenance staff and students.

I was pleased that the Governing Board of St. Albans shared my views. The situation got so complicated that the Cathedral and St. Albans went to binding arbitration, a sad state of affairs for two Christian institutions that are supposed to be working together. Brendan Sullivan, who was then on the St. Albans Board, represented the school. Although not all the financial details were exactly as we wanted, Brendan won the most important issues and our maintenance people remained part of St. Albans.

GENTLEMEN

During the twenty-five years I was a headmaster I came to know many other headmasters. It always struck me that very different sorts of people become headmasters. Perhaps that reflects how different independent schools are from each other. After all, that is part of the benefit of being independent. The school can shape its own identity. Two headmasters, a Southern gentleman and an English gentleman, gave me stories I enjoyed telling.

John Tucker served for many years as headmaster of Norfolk Academy. He was very much the Virginia gentleman, tall, stately, and invariably polite.

In the fall of 1989, Norfolk Academy announced that it was holding a symposium on educating affluent children. I decided that it would be valuable to attend. After I registered, John Tucker wrote saying that he was glad I would be attending. He and his wife, Barbara, were having some people to their house for dinner on the first night of the symposium, and they hoped that Martha and I could join them.

When we arrived at the Tucker home, John made a point of introducing us to the other guests. Most of them were local and knew each other. As far as I could tell, we were the only ones not from Virginia. After drinks we went through the elegant buffet line. Martha and I took our plates into the living room but found that all the seats were taken. We went into the study, which was empty, and sat down. John saw us alone in there.

"Oh, I'll get some other guests to come and join you."

"That's alright, John. It's nice for Martha and me to have dinner together, just the two of us. We don't get that often enough."

John turned without a word. In a minute he was back. He had brought a beautiful silver candelabrum from the dining room. He placed it before us and said, "Have a romantic dinner."

I must confess that I was not as polite to an English headmaster. We were friends with Vivian Anthony, headmaster of Colfe's School. The school, which is hundreds of years old, is a day school for boys south of London. Vivian had come on a tour of American schools and spent several days staying with us in Washington. In 1984 he let us stay in his house in England while he and his family were on August vacation in Wales. Another time his whole family visited us in Washington.

In the early 1990s, Vivian left Colfe's and became permanent secretary of the British Headmaster's Association. In 1993 the National Association of Independent Schools (NAIS) met in New York City. We had heard from Vivian that he was going to be there, representing the British schools. When we got to New York, I called his hotel room and left a message. Life is hectic at these big conferences. Usually several thousand attend. It is not always easy to make contact with someone. When Vivian finally reached us by phone, he said that he was leaving that night for London, but he could stop by our room at 11:00 A.M. for a few minutes. I told him that I had to interview a teacher candidate at that time but that Martha would be happy to see him if he could come by the room. Our oldest son, Sean, was also in the room because he had come to the conference to interview as he sought to enter teaching.

When I came back to the room after interviewing the teacher candidate, Martha said that Vivian had left about fifteen minutes before. She told me that she had been crying when he arrived because she had just finished reading *The Bridges of Madison County*. Seeing her crying had upset him, and it had taken her a few minutes to convince him that nothing was wrong. The book had just moved her.

After I had been in the room for awhile, the phone rang.

"Vivian Anthony here. Hello, Mark. How are you?"

"I'm fine, but sorry I missed you."

"Well, it was good to see Martha and Sean. Say, Mark, I am in a bit of a fix. I have to give a speech in ten minutes, but I left my notes in your room."

"What floor are you on?"

"Twenty-eight."

"No problem. Come down the elevator. Stop at our floor. I'll meet the elevator and give you your notes. Then you can go on to the meeting room and your speech."

I gathered up his notes and went to the elevators. A down elevator stopped. Vivian was not on it. Another stopped. The door opened. There stood Vivian in the front of the crowded elevator. Most of the other passengers had badges indicating that they were also attending the NAIS Conference.

Temptation overcame me. I scowled, thrust his notes into Vivian's hands, and said in a loud voice, "The next time you are in my wife's room don't leave your possessions." The doors of the elevator shut, blocking my view of a very embarrassed and flustered English headmaster and a crowd of educators staring at him. I never did have the nerve to ask him how his speech went.

THE GRAND BAZAAR

Chris Wadsworth was my college classmate and also a Class Marshal. He has been a headmaster of three schools. He served two American schools, Nichols and Belmont Hill. His last assignment was at Robert College, the leading secondary school in Istanbul, Turkey. It is, however, operated by an American Board. When Chris got the job, his son said, "Dad, that's the ideal job for you. The board is three thousand miles away, and the parents won't be able to understand a word you say."

Martha and I visited Chris and his wife, Lori, at Robert College. The school is located a bit south of the center of Istanbul. The headmaster's house is on a high bluff overlooking the Bosporus. One evening before dinner we sat outside, having drinks and looking down on the Bosporus. The boat traffic on it is like the vehicle traffic on I-95. Chris said, "Mark, do you see those boats on the Bosporus? The big tankers, carrying thousand of gallons of oil from the Black Sea to the Mediterranean, glide silently along. But that little outboard motor boat with three people in it makes such a whine that you can hear it all the way up here. It's just like a faculty meeting. The people with real influence keep quiet and the others buzz."

After learning of the Bosporus theory of faculty meetings, I've always had a hard time keeping a straight face while I was conducting meetings.

During that visit with the Wadsworths, I had a lesson in communication problems. Lori showed us how to get from their house to downtown Istanbul by waterbus along the Bosporus. She also took us to sit on piles of rugs and have a meal with her friend, the rug merchant. After that, because both Chris and Lori worked at the school, Martha and I took the waterbus each day to the center of Istanbul. Even though we spoke no Turkish, we got along fine. My problems began when we got back to the Wadsworth's home. One night I slipped in the guest room shower, grabbed the shower curtain, and broke three of the rings that held it to the curtain rod. The next night, I somehow cracked the plastic toilet seat. I was determined to replace these fixtures without causing the Wadsworths any inconvenience. As far as I knew, Istanbul had no nearby Lowe's or Home Depot where I could pick up such items. Martha said she remembered seeing toilet seats on display somewhere as we passed a stall in a market. I hoped that wherever there were toilet seats for sale there would also be shower curtain rings. We decided that we would spend the next day finding that stall.

The problem was that the Grand Bazaar in Istanbul has four thousand stalls. We could find no map, directions, or logical plan to the Grand Bazaar. We wandered but found nothing that looked like plumbing supplies. I tried asking. I spoke no Turkish, and most of the merchants in the Grand Bazaar had very little English. "Toilet" is a fairly universal word so I tried using it. Those I asked wanted to be helpful but assumed that I wanted to go to the toilet, not buy one. They gave me directions in Turkish with much pointing, but I found no toilet seats for sale. Then I tried demonstrating a curtain rod and ring with my hands, but that produced a very different reaction, and I immediately gave it up. We continued to wander, trying to figure out a way to follow a pattern that would take us past every stall. We found no plumbing supplies. Martha continued to insist that on another day she had seen toilet seats for sale in a stall. Finally, it was time to head home to meet the Wadsworths for dinner and an admission that I had broken the guest room fixtures and had been unable to replace them.

We left the Grand Bazaar and walked down the hill toward the waterbus stop. As we got near the water, we passed the much smaller spice market. Suddenly, improbably, there a stall was with a row of toilet seats outside. I stuck my head in the stall and saw shower curtain rods and rings. One had to buy the complete set of rod and rings, rather than just rings, but I was so triumphant that I did not care. The owner of the stall offered no wrapping as I bought the needed items. I brought them, unwrapped, on the waterbus back along the Bosporus to the Robert College campus. As we walked up the hill to the Wadsworth's house, they came out to meet us. I carried my newly purchased shower curtain rod and toilet seat as proudly as Don Quixote carried his sword and shield.

CAN YOU DO THAT?

In the spring of 1997, Canon Charles Martin, my predecessor as headmaster of St. Albans, died at age ninety. I preached at his memorial service in the Cathedral. I told several Canon Martin stories.

After I had been offered the position of headmaster of St. Albans in 1977, Canon Martin showed Martha and me the headmaster's residence. He showed us the interior and then took us out to see the backyard and garage. There was a metal pipe sticking out from the side of the house. I was pretty sure what it was but asked anyway. Canon Martin, then seventy years old, jumped up and did a series of pull-ups. "Can you do that?" he asked.

Canon Martin was famous for never closing St. Albans no matter how deep the snow. The first time I closed the school for snow, at the request of the mayor and the bishop, I decided to walk over to the school just to be sure that no student was dropped off by a parent who had not gotten the word. I was the only person walking across the Cathedral Close in the early morning snow. Then I saw a figure coming toward me. It was Canon Martin, walking in from Westmoreland Circle to take the early service at the Cathedral. I wanted to dive into a snowdrift. Canon Martin, ever the gentleman, uttered not a word of reprimand. He just greeted me with a friendly, "Good morning," and strode on through the snow.

Canon Martin was famous as a hospital visitor. If he knew that anyone connected with St. Albans was in the hospital, he would try hard to make a call. In fact, when our youngest child, Kevin, was born,

Canon Martin was his first visitor. No doubt a conspiratorial doctor tipped him off. When the terrible lightning strike occurred, killing a Landon student and putting seven people in the hospital, he must have been eager to go to the hospital. He knew, however, that I, as the priest-headmaster, should do the visiting. In his wonderful way he did find someone who needed visiting. While I was visiting the lightning victims in the hospital, Martha was at home, worried about all that had happened and concerned about what I was going through. She was touched and grateful for Canon Martin's visit to her.

Canon Martin's last visit to St. Albans occurred just a month or so before his death. One of his great contributions to St. Albans was starting and supporting the Voyageur Program that introduced urban and suburban young people to the joys and challenges of wilderness activities. When Voyageur celebrated its twenty-fifth year with a festive dinner, the Voyageur leaders, Syl Mathis and Mark Moore wanted to present Canon Martin with a plaque of gratitude. They knew, however, that his memory was slipping badly. They told me that when it came time to give him the plaque, they would come down to where he was sitting so that he could not get near the microphone. During dinner I felt their fears were justified when I heard Canon Martin ask his son, Charlie, "Why are we here?"

After dinner, an appropriate speech was made about Canon Martin's contributions to the Voyageur Program. Syl took the plaque and headed to where Canon Martin was seated. He accepted the plaque and walked straight to the microphone. His son and I exchanged a worried glance. For the next seven minutes, Canon Martin gave a lucid and entertaining account of the early Voyageur years. Then he said, "I have to go home now," and walked out of the room and away from St. Albans for the last time.

ROYALTY

For six years I served on the Mid-Atlantic Selection Committee for the Marshall Scholarship. It provides two years of study at a British university for Americans who have just graduated from college. The Marshall Scholarship program was set up to express British thanks for the Marshall Aid and is funded by the British government. We always met in the British Embassy in Washington. We would spend a long day discussing which candidates to interview. A month later there were two even longer days of interviews and final decisions. The last night our spouses would join us for a dinner at a nice restaurant. The length of the meetings and the intensity of the discussions meant that all of us on the committee got to know each other well. On the committee were four of us who were former Marshall Scholars, a former Rhodes Scholar, and a senior representative from the British Embassy.

One year, about two months after our last meeting, I got a call from the representative of the British Embassy.

"Mark, you may know we have some out-of-town guests at the Ambassador's Residence."

"Yes, I saw that in the newspaper."

"You know one of them really likes to swim."

"Yes, I've heard that she does."

"St. Albans has the closest indoor pool to the Ambassador's Residence. Is there any chance she could use it very early tomorrow morning? It would have to be when no one else was there, and it would have to be kept absolutely secret until after she has been there. She does not want any press about so early in the morning."

"We have a group called the Early Birds who come at 6:30 A.M. But if she will come before that she can use our pool, and we can keep it secret."

"Great, she will be there at 5:30. Can she have the pool all to herself? Of course, her security people will be there."

"If she is going to use our pool I have to have one of my own lifeguards there for the protection of the school."

"OK."

"Now if she comes to an institution, isn't the head of the institution supposed to greet her?"

"Only if it is an official visit. I am afraid you are out of luck, Mark."

"Oh well, I tried. Have her there at 5:30. Our lifeguard will be there, and there will be no leaks to the press."

I waited until he was home for the evening to call Rob Green, head of St. Albans aquatics.

"Rob, would you be willing to open the pool tomorrow at 5:30 A.M.?"

"Why? Does Princess Diana want to swim? Ha! Ha!"

"Yes. . . ."

There was a long pause on the other end of the line. Then, "I'll be there."

"This has to be kept absolutely secret."

Our daughter, Cara, was fourteen years old at the time. Like most fourteen-year-old girls then, she was crazy about Diana. She was thrilled that the princess was even in the same city. It was a Friday night. Cara had her friend, Seanna, at our house for a sleepover. Both girls liked to sleep late in the morning and were always slow about getting dressed. I said nothing to them that night for fear they would let something slip to a friend on the telephone. However, at 5:10 the next morning, I woke the two very sleepy girls.

"If you can be dressed in ten minutes I can get you within fifteen feet of Princess Diana."

Cara and Seanna moved like lightning bolts. We drove to the pool, got out of the car, and situated ourselves at a respectful distance from the door to the pool. In a few minutes, two large black cars pulled up. Diana stepped out of one, wearing a white warm-up suit. She smiled at the girls and disappeared into the doorway.

On the way home, the two excited girls made it clear that I was definitely father of the year.

Of course, after Diana left Washington, it did not matter who knew of the royal swimmer. One week later, *People* magazine reported, "Headmaster Mark Mullin of St. Albans School denies reports that the school is selling bottled water from its pool."

Once in a while we experience moments that have a special magic, that lift us from our ordinary lives to something that is sparklingly, joyfully different. There are also the awful times when we are face-to-face with terrible tragedy and plunged into deep pain. We meet the reality that the human condition inevitably means suffering, loss, and death. On one Friday in May 1991, I experienced both magic and tragedy.

For all our belief in democracy, Americans still find monarchy, particularly the British royalty, fascinating. Some of it is just the interest that celebrities hold for so many people. Part of it is that we were raised on stories of British kings and queens. We heard these stories in

"Once upon a time" tales, in Shakespearean intrigues, and in history lessons. In a country as young as ours, the British royal family, with its thousand-year lineage and great traditions, does carry a little magic dust with it.

It was a beautiful May morning—warm, but not too hot. A Washington spring is a glorious thing, and this was spring at its best. To make the day extra special, the Queen of England was coming to Washington Cathedral. Three or four thousand people gathered inside and outside the Cathedral to see Queen Elizabeth II. I am not sure I have ever seen a better-spirited crowd. Everyone was in a holiday mood. A crowd at a sporting event is inevitably a partisan one. Some will be for one team and others for the other team. This was a crowd unanimous in its joyful sharing of royal magic. Those who did not find the monarchy exciting stayed away.

Security for the Cathedral was very tight. Martha's Irish face made the guards look her over carefully as she stepped through the metal detector. The ceremony was impressive but not too long. The huge crowd streamed out of the Cathedral into a wonderful May morning.

For some of us, there was another exciting event ahead. Both Landon and St. Albans were undefeated in conference play in lacrosse. This would not only be the final game of the season but would also determine the championship. And this year, unlike many years, St. Albans had a reasonable chance of beating Landon. The game was to be played on Satterlee-Henderson Field, just a few hundred yards down the hill from the Cathedral that the queen had visited five hours before.

Kevin, then age thirteen, and I left home early for the lacrosse game to support the team during the warm-ups. Martha said she would come later, in time for the second half. The afternoon was still beautifully warm, and Kevin was wearing shorts. As the game began, however, dark clouds started to form. There is a common weather pattern in Washington in the spring. A warm day can be cloudless until late afternoon. Then dark clouds rush in, and a brief thunderstorm brings heavy rain. Within an hour, the sky has cleared again. Halfway through the second quarter I turned to Will Billow, the St. Albans chaplain, and said, "The sky looks really bad. I wonder if we'll be able to get through the whole game."

As the first half ended, rain began to pelt down, and there was a distant flash of lightning. The announcement was made that the game would be postponed until after the storm had passed. Both teams went to their locker rooms in the gym. Will and I went to the little wooden shack where refreshments were sold. It was crowded with spectators escaping the storm. I did not know where Kevin was, but I figured that he and his grade school buddies would seek shelter somewhere.

The rain came down in sheets, and we heard a couple of thunderclaps that sounded close. Then there was a tremendous explosion of thunder that made all of us in the refreshment shed jump. We looked around, realized that we were all right, and felt a little foolish for being scared.

The rain continued to lash the shed. In less than a minute a young student appeared at the door of the shed. "The lightning caused a fire in the tennis shack!" Will and I ran out into the rain.

When we got to the tennis shack, we found no fire. But on the ground near the shack we saw bodies. What appeared to be about a dozen people lay on the ground. My impression was that the feet all pointed toward a central point. Already, teachers, students, and parents were bent over the bodies; some were giving mouth-to-mouth resuscitation. I knew that I had to summon help, but I was desperate to know where Kevin was. I was torn between my instincts as a parent and my duty as a headmaster. The heavy rain and the helpers bending over the victims made it impossible to see who had been hit. I took a quick scan of those on the ground, looking for the long, thin, bare legs of a pre-adolescent Kevin, but I did not look carefully. I knew it was my responsibility to get help. I was pretty sure the lightning had knocked out the telephone in the tennis shack, and this was before people carried cell phones.

I dashed across Garfield Street and burst into a house. I must have been an awful sight: hair matted by the rain, clothing soaked, a frantic look on my face. A young boy stood in the living room staring in disbelief at the wild stranger who had come unbidden into his home. "Where is your phone?" Wordlessly, he pointed to the kitchen. I pushed 911. "I've got ten people hit by lightning at St. Albans School, Garfield and Thirty-fourth. We need help," I shouted. With assurances that help was coming, I started back across Garfield Street.

It was not long before several ambulances arrived, and the injured were loaded and rushed away. We learned later that on the way to St. Albans one ambulance had skidded on the wet pavement and crashed. There were no injuries, but that ambulance never made it. Fortunately, enough others did. I still had not seen Kevin but thought that if he had been hurt someone would have told me.

Martha had been ready to go to the game when the storm hit. She decided to stay home. After a while she heard all the ambulances and wondered if it might be related to the game. Then Peter Barrett called. He was a Lower School teacher who had found a working phone at school. With his typical thoughtfulness, he knew that Martha would be worried. He called to say that he had Kevin in tow and would bring him home. He told her that I was all right but would probably not be home for a while. Kevin had been standing in the tennis shack only twenty feet from the lightning strike. He had seen the people fall to the ground.

When I got to the hospital, a nurse told me that one teenager was dead. She did not know his name or which school he was from. I asked if I could see him. She took me into a small room and pulled down the blanket that was covering his face. I did not recognize him. Later, I learned that he was Noah Eig. He had been a sophomore at Landon but had been accepted as a transfer to Sidwell Friends for the next year. The headmaster of Landon arrived. He told me that Noah's parents were on their way to the hospital. They had been told that Noah was hurt. They did not know he was dead. I asked if he wanted me to be with him when he told them, but he thought it should be someone they knew.

Several St. Albans parents had been struck by the lightning. They were also at the hospital. As I visited them I was relieved to learn that, although a few would be kept overnight for observation, no one was in critical condition. Several did have some minor burns. There had been four or five people who had stopped breathing, but CPR saved all but Noah.

The morning after the lightning, I called Brendan Sullivan to ask if St. Albans had a legal problem. After all, Noah had been killed while attending a function on campus.

"No Mark, you do not have a legal problem. But you have a hell of a theological problem when you speak to your students about this."

I found I also had a psychological problem. I did not feel guilty for the way the game had been handled. The game had been postponed before the lightning hit. Nonetheless, I felt responsible. At the time of Noah's death, I had had fourteen years of being responsible for anything that happened on the St. Albans campus. Noah's death haunted me. Fifteen years have now passed since the lightning. Yet, even as I write these words, that same feeling of being both responsible and helpless returns to me. I did call on Noah's parents several times and rejoiced to send a note of congratulations when, a year and a half later, they had a baby girl.

I worried also about the possible effects on Kevin. He had been so close to the strike and had seen all the people hit and a boy killed. I knew that for several weeks he hid in a closet whenever there was a thunderstorm. Anytime visitors came to our house I got them aside to suggest that they ask Kevin about the lightning strike so that he would have another chance to express his feelings.

A memorial service for Noah was held at Landon School. All of the St. Albans lacrosse team attended. The Landon headmaster, Damon Bradley, was gracious enough to invite Earl Harrison, headmaster of Sidwell Friends, and me to speak. Earl read from the letters of recommendation written by Landon teachers for Noah in his application to transfer to Sidwell. Later, a number of people told me how touched the Eig family was when I said, "I will never walk on to Satterlee-Henderson Field without thinking of Noah." That prediction proved to be true.

THE PET

One of the pleasures of living in Washington was the number of people from other countries who lived there or who came to visit. St. Albans had a more cosmopolitan student body than many schools because of the sons of diplomats and World Bank employees. School heads from around the world take tours of American schools. Most want to see Washington, so they were likely to contact St. Albans. Whenever possible, Martha and I invited them to stay with us.

Life at St. Albans brought other foreign guests to our home. Solomon Hapte-Selassie was a young boy when the communist takeover of

Ethiopia moved his father from a government cabinet position to prison. Many of Solomon's relatives were put under house arrest. His mother escaped from Ethiopia on foot taking her three preadolescent children with her. Somehow, she made her way to Washington. She was working as a nanny when a St. Albans alumnus, who had been stationed in Ethiopia, spotted her in a playground. He arranged for Solomon to be tested at St. Albans. The results were good, and Solomon came to the school. We loved having this gracious Ethiopian in our home, and he spent a lot of time with us. Even after he graduated and went to Dartmouth, he came to see us during vacations.

One summer night while he was in college he stopped by our home. The headmaster's house did not have central air-conditioning in those days, and we often left windows and doors open. We were in the living room talking, and Solomon wanted a refill of his soft drink. We knew him so well that I said, "Go out to the kitchen and help yourself."

"Hey, Mr. Mullin. I like your new pet."

"What pet?"

"The one in the kitchen. What is it?"

I went to the kitchen to see what he was talking about. There, sitting on the counter beside the sink, was an opossum. It had wandered in through the open back door. Having never seen an opossum, Solomon assumed that if it was in our kitchen, it must be a pet. Naturalists may not forgive me for saying this, but I think the opossum is the ugliest animal God ever created. If one is frightened, as this one was, it is truly an awful sight.

I knew that opossums do not usually attack humans. But any wild animal may bite if it feels threatened. A bite from any mammal means that one has to have rabies shots if the animal cannot be caught and tested. I wanted the opossum out of my kitchen, but I did not want to get close enough to be bitten. Solomon and I donned heavy gloves to protect our hands. We each took a broom, shut the doors from the kitchen to the rest of the house, and prepared to drive the beast out through the back door. I swung at the opossum, missed, and hit the light switch. The kitchen was plunged into darkness. I knew that the opossum, with its excellent night vision, could probably see us, but we could not see it. Solomon and I ran screaming into the dining room. Martha and our children howled with laughter at the sight of the two of us frightened by a little opossum. We let half an hour go by and then cautiously opened the door from the dining room into the kitchen. I reached into the kitchen and flipped the light switch. Indeed, the beast was not there. I suspect that our screams had driven it out the back door.

As the inefficient communist government of Ethiopia had more and more economic problems it realized that it needed foreign currency and tourists. To attract affluent tourists, it needed someone who understood the West. Solomon's father was taken from jail and put back in the cabinet. It is a lesson in third-world power politics that a person can go from the cabinet to jail then back to the cabinet without passing Go. Eventually, Solomon's father was allowed to make a brief visit to Washington. We felt very honored to be present when he was united with his family.

We tried not to scare all our guests as we had Solomon. Martha has a wonderful way of making even complete strangers feel that our house is their home. Paul McKeown was the headmaster of a school in Canberra that enjoys the same reputation in the Australian capital that St. Albans has in Washington. He is tall and rugged, just what one would imagine an Australian headmaster to be. He was also one of the most senior headmasters in Australia. Paul visited us several times. In 1990 he wrote in our guest book, "If there is one place on this earth, where you can come and be certain that your joy in life will be restored, it is the Mullins!"

Many of us have had the experience of admiring someone from afar and then finding on closer inspection that the person has feet of clay. With the really great people, however, all is consistent.

When I was a student at Oxford in the early 1960s, I heard Bishop Trevor Huddleston give a series of lectures. He had grown up in England, but after ordination in the Church of England he was sent to South Africa. While he was there, a young black man was so impressed that a white man would be kind to a black that he decided to investigate Christianity more closely. That young black man was Desmond Tutu who went on to be Archbishop of Cape Town, chairman of South Africa's Truth and Reconciliation Commission, and winner of the Nobel Peace Prize.

Trevor Huddleston was one of the first people actively to protest the racial policies of the South African government, long before it became fashionable to do so. Eventually, he was expelled from the country. I well remember his speech at Oxford forty years ago. This man, who had seen so much suffering and cruelty, emphasized the potential for goodness in all of creation. He frequently quoted the great phrase, "And God saw everything that he had made, and behold, it was very good."

Some years after I became headmaster of St. Albans, the Cathedral hosted a gathering of all the archbishops in the Anglican Communion around the world. They asked for people to offer housing for archbishops who came from regions where the price of American hotels would be a difficulty. I volunteered our guest room and asked for Trevor Huddleston, who was now Archbishop of Mauritius and the Indian Ocean. Before he came, I began to get a little nervous. I had so long admired this man but had never met him. What would he be like in person? What would he be like as a houseguest? I should not have worried. He was not only a gracious guest, but also he had something about him that let you know this was a man of prayer and deep concern for others. He was equally at ease talking with our children as he was talking with Walter Mondale. They met at a neighborhood party to which we took the archbishop. We also took him to a picnic given by St. Albans parents on an island in the Potomac. The thing that impressed him most about his visit to Washington was finding a large snake on the island. He wrote in his archbishop's newsletter about his surprise in finding such a large snake in the capital of the United States. When Huddleston died, seventeen years later, Desmond Tutu said, "The world is a better place for having had a Trevor Huddleston. Thanks be to God for this incredible stalwart."

RUSSIANS

We had another guest who set a very different tone than Trevor Huddleston. Jim Billington, director of the Woodrow Wilson Center and now Librarian of Congress, who was also on the St. Albans Governing Board, brought this guest to us. In 1980 Jim was escorting Yevgeny Yevtushenko on a visit to Washington. Many people would say that Yevgeny Yevtushenko was the greatest Russian poet of his generation.

Jim asked me if he could show St. Albans to Yevtushenko. I agreed and took them on a short tour. We looked in on an English class that was reading poetry. Yevtushenko could not resist, and he began to recite some of his poetry in English. The students were spellbound. Before he left St. Albans, I asked him if he would consider giving a more public reading. He said he would if he could do it in the Cathedral. He was going on to other places in the United States, but he would be in Washington on his way back to Russia.

The Cathedral was cooperative. Invitations were sent to the whole St. Albans family. We also planned a dinner party at our home after the reading. At the dinner there would be Yevtushenko, his translator, the Billingtons, the chairman of the board and his wife, and a number of other guests. One guest offered to bring half a case of high quality champagne. That was a lifesaver for me. Jim had told me that Yevtushenko expected to drink a lot of good champagne after he read publicly.

I asked a couple of students to save seats in the front row for our dinner guests. However, two imposing men walked up to them and said, "Ve are sitting zer." Somehow, my polite, blue-blazered students knew these were not men to be argued with. They decided to save the second row for the dinner guests.

Yevtushenko was magnificent. His great Slavic voice echoed through the Cathedral. Sometimes he read in English and sometimes in Russian. His translator would then repeat the poem in English. Whether his words were cosmic and powerful or heartbreaking and sorrowful, their imagery filled the great spaces of the Cathedral.

As we were walking back to our house he said, "Did you notice those two men in the front row? That is the head of the North American KGB and his buddy. They usually come to my readings to be sure I am not too far out of line."

The dinner party was also a success. The champagne flowed. The talk was lively and stimulating. Toasts were given in English and Russian. It must be true that a Russian poet can get away with things that mere mortals would not dare. I learned the next day that during dessert Yevtushenko turned to the wife of the chairman of the St. Albans Board and said, "Your breasts are small, but they are very provocative."

In 1990, I was invited to visit the Soviet Union with a group from the National Association of Secondary School Principals. We saw schools in Moscow and Leningrad. I was particularly glad to visit the school in Moscow with which St. Albans had just established an exchange relationship. This was at the time of the Gorbachev reforms. In fact, Gorbachev was awarded the Nobel Peace Prize while we were there.

The other six members of our group were all public secondary school superintendents or principals. They were all good educators, and the group got along well together. I got some kidding about running a "private, elitist school," but it was all done in a good-natured way.

Toward the end of the trip we visited the Leningrad Pedagogical Institute. It was the leading training facility for teachers in northern Russia. In our meeting with the dean of the Institute, he told us of many educational reforms being introduced in Russia. He spoke particularly about wanting education that would make students more independent thinkers. He also discussed the need to instill moral values in students. He said that one way they were trying to implement these goals was to move away from so much centralization.

"Just a week ago, a law was passed that will allow for the establishment of schools that will not be under the control of the government."

The other members of our group were all good Americans who believed in free enterprise and as much freedom from government as possible. They broke into spontaneous applause.

"You hypocrites!" I laughed. "You tease me for running an independent school, yet you applaud when Russia decides to have them."

While all of this was done in friendly kidding, I have always been saddened by the attitude of some Americans who somehow consider independent schools to be un-American. Nothing could be more capitalist than an independent school. It receives no money or subsidies from the government. It is at the mercy of market forces. If it provides a service that people value, it will flourish. If it does not, people will not pay to send their children there, and the school will close. I find the opinion that independent schools are contrary to the American way particularly odd in view of the American university system. It is the envy of the world. Many more foreign students come here to university than Americans go abroad. Our university system is a wonderful mix of public and private institutions. Does anyone think it is un-American to go to a college that is not run by the government? Our precollegiate education, on the other hand, does not match that of many other industrial nations. The government runs 90 percent of it.

Unfortunately, spouses had not been invited on this trip. That was a shame because it was Martha, not I, who had always wanted to visit Russia. She knew that both coming and going our group would be changing planes in Helsinki, Finland. On the way home we had a night there before catching an afternoon flight to New York.

Before I left the United States, Martha had asked, "Since you are going to Russia and I am not, please bring me back a Lapp coat from Finland." I said I would try. When I had driven the length of Finland as a college student, I had seen Lapps (now called Sami) above the Arctic Circle in their beautiful coats. Mostly, it was the men wearing the striking blue coats with the red and yellow trim. They wore them as naturally as an American from the West might wear denim.

After spending the last night of our trip in Helsinki, I set off from the hotel as soon as the stores were open. I had to be back by 1:00 P.M. to get the bus to the airport. I had seen an ad for a shop that specialized in "objects of Lapland." After asking enough people for directions (of course I had no Finnish), I found the shop. It had Lapland objects and clothing but only for children. I wandered the streets looking in any likely shop. No luck. I began to realize that looking for a Lapp coat in Helsinki was like looking for an American Indian outfit in New York City. You could find children's costumes but nothing for adults.

It was getting close to the time I had to be back at our hotel for the bus to the airport. No Lapp coat for Martha. Then I realized that I had only been trying small shops. What about a department store? Fortunately, I was in downtown Helsinki and soon found a large department store. The directory said something about gifts and Lapland on the second floor. Up I went. There it was: a beautiful, colorful, adult Lapp coat. But would it fit? The coat was too expensive to purchase and bring home if Martha could not wear it. A salesgirl came over to me. She had no English. I had no Finnish. The girl tried to help, but we were not getting far about the size.

Then across the floor, in another section, I saw a salesgirl who was taller than the one waiting on me. I motioned her over. I handed her the coat to try on; she understood. In sign language I asked her to stand near me. I measured from the top of her head to my eyes. She came to just the level Martha did. I bought the coat.

Lapp coats are very colorful and are made of heavy wool. They are only worn above the Arctic Circle. Although she was very pleased that I had brought her the coat, there were few times she could wear it in Washington. The most common occasion was the outdoor picnic she insisted on having every December 31st. There was one time, however, when she wore it on a hot June day.

Each year, a different embassy sponsored the Cathedral Flower Mart. Martha always worked as a volunteer in one capacity or another. The year Finland was the sponsor she wore her Lapp coat. She roasted but was rewarded when a couple of times Finnish people assumed she was a fellow Finn and spoke to her in Finnish. They could not believe that an American would own a Lapp coat.

I am happy to report that when we were above the Arctic Circle in Norway in 2005, we visited a Sami camp and Martha was able to get a colorful hat to match her Lapp coat.

On that educators' trip to Russia, the Superintendent of Schools of Loudon County, Virginia, Dave Thomas, and I hit it off immediately. He was a few years older than I and had been a football player at West Point.

On the third day of the trip Dave told me that one of the reasons he had come on this trip was because of his son, Michael. During his junior year in high school, Michael had become quite interested in Russia. He asked his parents to let him visit there during the summer after his junior year. They had said that he should wait a year and then they would give him a trip to Russia as a high school graduation present.

At the start of his senior year, Michael was driving to football practice when he ran out of gas. He coasted to the shoulder of the road. Then his car was struck from behind by a dump truck. Michael was brain dead for two days before his heart stopped.

"I am going on this trip that Michael wanted to take but never will."

We visited several schools in Moscow, but our last day in the city was reserved for sightseeing. The highlight, of course, was the Kremlin, which has not only government buildings but also several cathedrals remaining from Czarist days. When we got back on the bus to return to our hotel, Dave was missing. When he was fifteen minutes late we began to worry that he had gotten in trouble with the police or the KGB. Finally, after we had been waiting for more than thirty minutes, Dave arrived. Several people asked what had happened, but he mumbled a quick "sorry" and sat down next to me toward the back of the bus. As the bus started he quietly explained to me. "I wasn't lost. I was in St. Michael's Cathedral. My son, Michael, not only played football, but he also ran track. In the spring before he was killed, he won a medal he was very proud of. I brought Michael's medal with me. I hid it in St. Michael's Cathedral. I hid it so well that they can clean that place every day for one hundred years, and they'll never find it. There will always be something of Michael in Russia."

A few weeks after we got back to the United States, we invited Dave and his wife to our house for dinner. He had told me that they liked to dance. The four of us had dinner and then headed to a place we knew in Washington where there was dancing. After we had been dancing for a while we switched partners. Dave danced with Martha and I with his wife.

I said to her, "I love to dance. In fact, I expect to spend the first thousand years I am in heaven dancing with Martha."

Dave's wife gave me a very strange look that I could not interpret and said nothing more until we switched back to our own spouses at the end of the song.

A few days later we got a note from her. She thanked Martha for the dinner and then went on,

> Mark, you may have wondered why I was so strange at the end of the time we danced together. Let me explain. My favorite picture of my son, Michael, was at the Prom in the spring before he died. Because Dave is superintendent, we always attend the Prom. That year was Michael's first time at a Prom. Someone took a picture of the three of us. Michael looked so handsome in a tuxedo. After we had our picture taken, Michael asked me to dance with him. When you said that about dancing in heaven, I realized for the first time . . . I will dance with Michael again.

LIFETIME DANCING

In 1995, Margaret Meyers published her first novel, *Swimming in the Congo*, based on her childhood in Africa. When she was Writer in Residence at St. Albans, she heard me tell the story of Michael's medal being hidden in the Kremlin and his mother's response when I said I expected to dance with Martha in eternity. In 1997 she sent me a poem she had written.

Lifetime Dancing

A snowy night in Moscow:
the count in uniform, dark, desirable
the lemon-oiled, glistening sweep of ballroom floor
and Anna,
tiny-wristed Anna,
be-pearled, with a black velvet décolletage and a pansy wreath
resting purple upon her upswept hair.

Purple for passion, so they say, and
we bow to the cliché as the waltzing begins and
the passion flares,
passion lasting and inevitable, her
slender fingers trembling upon a gold-braid shoulder, his
strong hand pressing warm,
warmer,
against her waist.

The wise know that dancing need not be so doomed,
                                    so short,
                                            so Russian.

The wise know there are ways to
            extend the dance, to
                    spin it out, to
                            relish it with a long, slow savor.

Remember the ugly gray tiles on the
smaller-than-small

kitchen floor that first year,
dancing closer-than-close from necessity,
and above all, from
inclination.

Remember dancing barefoot
on the slippery blue bathroom rug while
brushing your teeth,
laughing.

And later,
remember dancing on the living room rug
(that Sear's fake Oriental for fifty-nine dollars that
you weren't sure you could afford)
swinging the baby high, an awkward threesome.
You glanced down at all your shoes—the polished black wingtips
                                    the elegant Jackie O. pumps
                            the tiny white leather lace-up
                                    booties
                                and then the baby giggled.
You laughed in a silly rush of joy.

Remember the proms,
            weddings,
                    christenings.
The inessentials have dimmed in significance
        (You weren't crazy about her first date, if you recall,
        the flowers were delivered to the wrong church,
        and someone's toddler threw a tantrum during the pastoral
        prayer)
But the essentials live on
as palpable,
as sturdy,
as the radio in the corner,
        the CD player and tape deck,
        the rack of scratchy old records you can't bear to throw away:

a mutual and interior music
a sacred habit of love
a vocation for a lifetime of dancing—and beyond.

THE GREAT DRUID

In the fall of 1989 I got a message that John Walker, Bishop of Washington, had gone into the hospital for tests. I went to see him even though I knew that he would be inundated with visitors. He was much loved in the Diocese of Washington.

John Walker began his ministry in schoolwork, serving as a religion teacher at St. Paul's School in New Hampshire. He moved to Washington as a canon of the Cathedral and in 1977 was elected bishop, the first African American bishop of the Episcopal Diocese of Washington.

He was a caring pastor to the clergy and parishes of the diocese. He had the daunting challenge of paying off the high construction debt the Cathedral had acquired. With his leadership, the debt was eliminated and the final phase of construction begun. John's breadth of vision made him a leader in the efforts to make America conscious of the evils of apartheid. He cared for people everywhere.

Shortly after I saw John in the hospital, it was announced that he would have cardiac surgery. It seemed to go well. After he was out of intensive care, Martha and I went to see him. He was weak, but his wife, Maria, and he greeted us warmly. We chatted for a while about our families. As we started to leave the hospital, Maria walked us to the elevator. Before the elevator arrived at our floor, a doctor came up to Maria.

"We've lost him."

We returned to his room. We said prayers. Martha and I each held his lifeless hand for a few moments.

Just a year and a half before, we had spent several delightful days with Maria and John in England. While I was on sabbatical, Martha, Kevin, and I had spent a month at the home of the headmaster of the English St. Albans School.

One day's march north of Londinium, the Roman occupiers of Britain had built a city and named it Verulamium. Alban lived there toward the end of the third century. Legend has it that he was a soldier in the Roman army. During the Diocletian persecutions, a Christian priest was being hunted by the authorities. Alban hid the priest and was so moved by the man's faith that he converted to Christianity. When the priest was about to be discovered, Alban put on the priest's clothes and offered himself in his place. Alban refused the demands of the authorities that he renounce Christianity. He was beheaded on the hill above Verulamium, thus becoming the first Christian martyr in Britain. Later a shrine developed at the spot of execution. St. Albans Abbey was founded in 948. Sometime in the next one hundred years, a school, also called St. Albans, was begun. The town of St. Albans grew up around the abbey. When the abbey was destroyed during the Reformation, the school also closed. A generation later it reopened in 1570 under a charter from Queen Elizabeth I.

Sometimes, people would say to me, "You think you run such an academic school, but you don't know enough to use the possessive apostrophe in the school's name."

I would answer, "St. Albans existed before the apostrophe." And it is indeed true that the town of St. Albans, the abbey, and the English St. Albans School existed before the apostrophe came into use in the English language.

Today, the Cathedral of St. Albans stands impressively at the top of the hill. On the hillside, St. Albans School remains a first-rate academic institution. At the base of the hill, on a large grassy plain, the ruins of Verulamium stretch for hundreds of yards. They are among the largest and best-preserved Roman ruins in England.

During the month we were living at St. Albans in England, John and Maria Walker came to stay with us for a few days. Nine-year-old Kevin Mullin had devised some sort of game involving hiding and running around the Roman ruins. John joined in. Kevin played the part of the Brave Celtic Warrior, and the Bishop of Washington was the Great Druid.

When John Walker died a year later, his funeral was held in an overflowing Washington Cathedral. His good friend, Desmond Tutu, administered the sacrament. I remember wondering if, when John was born into a black family in Detroit in the 1920s, his mother ever dreamed that he would accomplish so much that at his death the President of the United States would attend his funeral.

My first day on the job as headmaster of St. Albans had been on July 1, 1977. When I arrived on the Cathedral Close, I did not go directly to the school. Instead, I attended the early morning Holy Communion Service in Bethlehem Chapel of Washington Cathedral. Because it was a weekday the congregation was very small. But among the worshippers was John Walker. It was his first official day as Bishop of Washington. He was not conducting the service. He was there to pray and receive the sacrament. On that day, I could not anticipate the close working relationship we would develop or the friendship our families would have. But as we greeted each other after the service, we both sensed a spiritual connection—the bond of two men taking up new responsibilities and beginning the day by receiving the body and blood of Christ.

THE FLAG

In March of 1997, the leadership of the Governing Board of St. Albans told me that it wanted me to step down as headmaster. I felt a variety of emotions.

The first strong emotion was fear, fear for my family's well-being. We had no inheritance and no sources of outside income. Our youngest son, Kevin, was set to enter the School of the Art Institute of Chicago in the fall. There were four years of college tuition ahead of us. Because we had always lived in school housing, we had no equity in a home. In a few months, I would turn fifty-seven. I did not know if I could get another headmastership at that age. Except for internal appointments, it is also rare for someone in his late fifties to be hired as a middle-level administrator or teacher.

That fear was about the future. The emotion about the present was confusion. I did not know how to proceed. I knew how to be a headmaster, how to develop support for the school. I did not know how to defend myself, nor did I know how to rally support. Fortunately, Brendan Sullivan, who had just completed a six-year term on the St. Albans Board, soon learned of the situation. He was extremely generous with his time and wise advice. He was not my lawyer, but he was a good and trusted friend. Talking things over with him frequently and listening to his thoughtful suggestions were both comforting and helpful.

The best advice I got was from Martha. "Do what's right and we'll live with the consequences."

We decided that, above all else, I must be truthful. I would not say, "It is my choice to leave. I am leaving because I want to do so." I would not use that overworked phrase, "I have resigned so that I may seek new opportunities." If an academic institution or its head is not committed to the truth, what does it stand for?

I also believed that it is unprofessional and damaging to a school for a head to criticize the board in public. Of course, I would not do it on those occasions when I spoke to parent or alumni groups. It was harder to say "no comment" to the press when others were telling their side of the story.

I wish that I could say that I was a good enough person not to have felt anger. That would not be true. I was irate at times. I was angry about what was happening at St. Albans and how some people were acting. I was distressed about what it was doing to my family then and what the long-range effects on them might be. Martha and I found that we often woke in the middle of the night and were unable to go back to sleep. My solution was to watch all three parts of the *Godfather* series. I guess there was some sublimation going on. I certainly enjoyed watching the Corleone family handle its problems in ways that were not open to me. Fortunately, the anger never dominated me. There were too many other emotions.

One of the strongest emotions I felt was frustration. I was frustrated that it was so hard to get an answer to "why?" Months after I left St. Albans, the *St. Albans Bulletin*, under a new school administration, reported on the events of 1997.

> News of the board's "flagging confidence" came as a surprise to Mark Mullin, who had received no prior warning that the board was actively dissatisfied with his work, much less ready for new leadership. Mullin had received annual raises and regular praise for his accomplishments, including a laudatory letter (from the chairman of the board) in June 1996. "We couldn't have been guided by a better person these years." That St. Albans had flourished under Mullin's leadership would be conceded by most observers. During his tenure, St. Albans solidified its position as one of the country's top college preparatory schools.

The reasons the leadership of the board eventually gave me seemed to me to fall into three categories. First, there were complaints that had never before been mentioned to me. Second, there were complaints about events that occurred after the move to oust me began. Third, there were complaints based on statements that were inaccurate. I found myself thinking, "Am I wrong? Is there more substance to these complaints than I understand?" Self-doubt is often a part of a situation such as this one.

My doubts, but not my frustrations, were somewhat relieved when nine former chairmen of the Governing Board wrote a letter to the current Governing Board. The letter, which the past chairmen wrote on their own initiative, said, "When the grounds for dismissing the headmaster that have been articulated to us stand revealed, they will seem to be trivial or pretextual, wholly disproportionate to the decision taken."

I was aware of only one specific issue on which I differed from some members of the board. I want to describe it in some detail because it was a genuine area of disagreement and because it points to a situation that I mishandled.

Before I came to St. Albans, the school used people who were also classroom teachers as college advisors. I continued the practice. I knew from my experience working with college placement at the Choate School that I could write more thoughtfully about the intellectual strengths of students that I had taught in the classroom than about students I only knew in my office. Before I came to St. Albans and all the time I was there, the school had an excellent college placement record. Of course, there were always individual students who were disappointed. However, St. Albans achieved college placement results that were the equal of any school.

In the spring of 1996, some board members made it clear that they wanted a change in the system. They wanted a full-time college advisor. However, they said it was my decision.

To me it was an educational issue: will a student be better served by someone who has actually taught him and knows his academic abilities as only a teacher can? Or will he be better served by someone who has more time to spend on college admissions officers, in effect, a lobbyist? Is the goal of college admissions to find the best match for the student or to provide what he or his parents want as a "first choice"? I decided that the students would be best served by retaining the present system while providing more clerical help to the college advisors to give them more time to work with college admissions officers.

In retrospect, I think I mishandled it in two ways. First, when I saw that some members of the board and I were in disagreement, I should have asked for a vote of the full board. Then, whichever way it went, it would be a decision made by all the people at the highest level. Second, I did not practice enough subtlety or humility. It seemed to me that I knew more about the matter than those board members who were seeking a change. Personally, I had had three of my children apply to college. Professionally, I had worked on college admissions at the Choate School and had kept a close eye on it for twenty years at St. Albans. I talked often with our college advisors and met frequently with college admissions officers. When a reporter from the *Wall Street Journal* wrote a book on college admissions, he quoted me twice. I know that I did not hide my belief that I knew more about college admissions than those who wanted a change. That is not a good way to handle board members, to say the least.

One strong emotion I felt was gratitude. Several hundred people, alumni and parents, wrote to the board supporting me. Many others wrote me letters, called me on the phone, or spoke to me in person. Many went to meetings to express their belief in me. Like Tom Sawyer, I experienced what it would be like to read my own obituary and attend my own wake. I was, and remain, grateful to all these people. I was particularly moved by the teachers and students of St. Albans. Their support was what I found the most meaningful. While I felt deep gratitude for such support, the board must have had other feelings. Shortly after I was finally dismissed, the entire Governing Board of St. Albans resigned. An alumnus who had served as chairman of the board before I came to St. Albans was brought in to form and lead a new board.

Along with the gratitude I felt, however, went another emotion. I do not know what to call it except "painful ambivalence." When I read or heard good things about my service as headmaster, I was grateful. But I also experienced pain. It was the pain of saying to myself, "If half of the nice things this person is saying about me are true, why is this happening?" Curiously, the more good things I heard, the more pain I felt.

The strongest and most persistent emotion I felt was sadness. I was sad for St. Albans. I had always wanted it to be better than other places, to set the standard of integrity, openness, and how people should treat each other. I believed that St. Albans was such a school.

The *Washingtonian* article on the events of that spring said, "One of the saddest aspects of the spectacle was the damage done to the values that St. Albans, as a Christian school serving polite Washington society, had always professed." An article in *Capitol Style* ended,

> In fact, what happened at St. Albans could prove very instructive for the future leaders of this city's corporations, law firms, universities, and federal agencies, where only the toughest and shrewdest of them will survive, where it's not about how you play the game, as Canon Martin used to say, but rather about who wins. Whatever innocence Mullin's young charges once harbored about the way the world works, it was surely lost in the fight for the soul of St. Albans.

I also felt a deep sadness for Sean and Kevin. Both had loved St. Albans and had been very active in its life while they were students. I had always worked hard to keep alumni connected with the school. Now, my own sons would always feel a shadow between themselves and their school.

Finally, I felt sadness for Martha and me. We had given twenty years of our lives to St. Albans. I had expected to retire from St. Albans and, perhaps, someday have my ashes in the Little Sanctuary. A headmaster's wife is involved in his work in ways that are true of few professions. Now that chapter of our lives was ending abruptly and painfully.

Not surprisingly, it was those three life dreams, which had been part of my life for so long, that helped get me through the troubles at St. Albans and started the healing process.

Running track teaches many lessons. It teaches one to continue functioning even while experiencing pain. It teaches that one should never quit, even when winning looks doubtful. Most of all, it teaches that one defeat is not the end. As soon as one race is over, whether it has been won or lost, it is time to start preparing for the next one.

Some of the teachers at St. Albans knew how important track had been to me. The faculty of St. Albans did not find out that the board wanted to terminate me until just before the May board meeting. I was utterly amazed when the entire faculty of St. Albans formed two lines outside the room where the board would be meeting. Walking between those two lines was deeply moving for me. To some board members it must have felt like a gauntlet. Skip Grant, the athletic director, yelled to me, "Remember you are a McCurdy runner." Skip knew that Bill McCurdy, my Harvard track coach, valued courage above all else, even speed, in his runners. He taught us that courage is not the absence of fear. It is the overcoming of fear.

What moved me most deeply was finding the teachers still waiting at 3:00 A.M. when the meeting finally ended. I expressed my gratitude, and was answered, "You didn't think we'd leave you, did you?"

The lessons of running track were also helpful in the healing process. Knowing that the best way to get over a lost race is to prepare for the next one, I decided to seek another headmastership. There was a "get back on the horse" aspect to it. I wanted to run again.

Certainly, the faith that led me to the Episcopal priesthood was very helpful during this time. Christianity does not promise a painless life. It does promise the eventual victory of God's love. Believing this helped me accept what I could not change.

More difficult for me was the question of forgiveness. Christians are enjoined to forgive those who hurt them, to love those who persecute them. I also knew that letting go of anger is necessary for good mental health. I did not find it easy. It was most difficult to forgive those who hurt the ones I love. The forgiving I have been able to do has been through God's grace.

Some years after I left St. Albans, I read Desmond Tutu's book *No Future without Forgiveness*. It describes his work as the chairman of the Truth and Reconciliation Commission of South Africa. That book helped me increase the level of my forgiving. It also states Tutu's conviction that, while one can and should forgive, there cannot be reconciliation by denying or ignoring the past.

"It is not dealing with the past to say facilely, 'Let bygones be bygones.' For then they won't be bygones."

Of immense help to me was my belief that God has a purpose for every human life. I think that He will use us for His purposes, if we will allow Him to do so. I wanted to stay at St. Albans. If that were not to be, then God would use me somewhere else.

While I have always prayed daily, I had never used books of daily readings or meditations. Sometime that spring, the father of a St. Albans senior gave me a copy of A. J. Russell's book, *God Calling*. It contains daily thoughts that constantly stress how much God cares for us and that He has a purpose for each of us. Over and over that spring, I felt that the daily readings had been written especially for me on that very day.

When I became headmaster of Casady School, I was delighted to have the opportunity to serve a school community again. I felt fortunate to be able to help individual students and teachers. Believing that I was doing God's work was wonderfully healing.

What happened to me at St. Albans and afterward brought me further along a path that I had started so many years ago in England. It is the path to the realization that there is only one quintessential prayer: "Thy will be done." Saying that prayer expresses both trust in God's loving care and a desire to be an instrument of his purposes in this world. The hard part, of course, is not saying, "Thy will be done," but meaning it. I still have far to go along that path, but the events of which I have written moved me in the right direction.

I cannot imagine getting through that spring or beginning the healing process without the love I received from Martha and our children. Cara and Sean were wonderfully supportive. Kevin had the heartbreaking predicament of being a senior in a school he loved while his father came into conflict with its board. He handled it with such grace that the full Upper School faculty voted to give him the Vaughn Keith Award for "fortitude in adversity." Knowing what he had been through that spring, no award at Prize Day ever gave me such joy. Best of all was Martha's love: constant, confirming, and always keeping me fixed on what really mattered to us. Moreover, she insisted that we continue to celebrate the joys, laughter, and love of friends. All during our years in Washington, no matter how hectic life at school was, we had found time to be with friends. It often meant late nights, but sharing good conversation and wine with friends always enriched and enlivened us. Now, Martha made sure we did not lose that. Years before, I had been blessed with the right redhead.

Martha and I had planned to drive to New Orleans to visit Cara and her family at the end of the academic year. When the June board meeting was moved from early in the month to the end, I left Martha in New Orleans and flew back to Washington. At that board meeting my service as headmaster was terminated by a vote of fourteen to ten. The next day, I flew back to New Orleans. Twenty-four hours after I was dismissed, I was walking down Bourbon Street with our grand-daughter, Raina, in one hand and a margarita in the other. Thanks to my family, my healing had begun.

While we were in New Orleans I called Sean and Kevin, who were in Washington. They told me that someone had lowered the American flag in front of St. Albans to half-mast. Martha and I spent a few days in New Orleans and then two more days driving back to Washington. The next day, Sean, Kevin, and I drove over to St. Albans to clean out my office. I was surprised to see that the flag was still at half-mast. It took us three trips to bring my books and papers from St. Albans to our home. As we loaded the car for the last time, I noticed that a teacher and a coach were doing something with the flag. Mark Wilkerson had been a marine in the Middle East during Desert Storm. Now he taught in the Lower School. Buddy Burkhead was a retired member of the U.S. Capitol Police, who now coached part-time. I assumed that they were raising the flag to its top position, now that my office was cleared out. As I finished loading the car, I saw that instead of raising the flag they had lowered it. They folded it triangularly, military style. Mark Wilkerson, the former marine, walked over to the car window. He snapped to attention, handed me the folded flag, saluted, and said, "The commander always takes his flag." Holding that American flag to my chest, I drove away from St. Albans.

CHAIRS

In July 1997, I turned fifty-seven years old. I had no job, and our youngest son was about to begin his freshman year of college. That fall I interviewed for headmasterships at a number of schools. They were spread geographically from southern California to Massachusetts.

Inevitably, the search committee of each school asked me about what had happened at St. Albans. I tried to give an accurate but brief description of the events. However, I could hardly claim to be an unbiased observer. I usually find it easy to read an audience to which I am speaking, but it was difficult to get a feel for how members of search committees reacted. Usually, there was little comment. The one exception was the Casady School in Oklahoma City. One member of the search committee blurted out, "It's perfectly obvious what happened. You were done in by a bunch of goddamn politicians, the sons of bitches." The rest of committee sat in stunned silence. In Oklahoma one does not use that sort of language in front of a clergyman.

I, on the other hand, burst into laughter. "My wife is going to love you."

I was on a two-day visit. That evening, I called Martha to report on the first day. I told her about the school and what the member of the search committee had said. Before I could tell her how I responded, she exclaimed, "I love him." Indeed, he and his wife became two of our favorite people in Oklahoma City.

By January, I had signed on as headmaster of Casady School. I was excited about the opportunity to lead another Episcopal school. I wanted to work in a school that saw its purpose as serving God by educating young people.

I believed that having regular required chapel services added much to a school. The form of worship at both St. Albans and Casady was unashamedly Christian and Episcopalian. It was not watered down in fear of offending someone. We prayed to the God revealed in Christ. All students had to attend chapel but were free to form their own belief systems. The goal was exposure, not indoctrination.

Moreover, I thought that the attitude of the Episcopal Church toward knowledge was appropriate for an academic institution. The academic enterprise is the search for truth. The best scholars recognize that it is a never-ending search. In our human frailty, we never arrive at the final, absolute truth but must always be open to new ideas and understandings.

The Episcopal Church has taught that there is no single source of religious truth. Instead, it has looked to three sources—the Bible, tradition, and human reason—to lead us toward the truth. No one source, whether written document or church authority, possesses absolute truth.

This is not the relativism that says all opinions are equally valid. There is a difference between true and false, reality and unreality, and right and wrong. However, we recognize human imperfection in our striving for the truth. To claim absolute certainty about any truth is at best arrogance and at worst the blasphemy of saying that human beings can be Godlike in their understanding of the truth. Even St. Paul said, "For now we see through a glass darkly." A realistic humility toward our own capabilities for knowledge is a sound basis for intellectual growth and the academic pursuit of truth.

We went to Oklahoma City three years after the bombing of the Murrah Building. Casady School is seven miles from where the building stood. The force of the blast had been so great that the Dean of Students rushed from his office thinking that an explosion had occurred in a Casady chemistry laboratory. By good luck, no Casady parent or alumnus was killed that day, although some were injured. However, half the people in central Oklahoma knew someone who died. That was certainly true for many people at Casady.

In our second year at Casady, we attended the dedication of the Oklahoma City Memorial. There is now a beautiful reflecting pool where the street on which the Ryder truck was parked used to be. The 168 lighted chairs, each with the name of a victim, stand silently reminding visitors of those who died here. Most moving are the small chairs for the children who were killed.

A year and a half later, I was leaving the morning service at Casady's Chapel of St. Edward the Confessor. The admissions director stopped me.

"A plane has hit the World Trade Center."

I went on to my office and began a scheduled meeting of administrators. After awhile, Gladys Creek, my administrative assistant, interrupted the meeting. She told me that a second plane had hit the other tower. I told the Dean of Students to bring the Upper School back to the chapel in half an hour. At that service, I told the students what had happened and then led them in prayer. Once again, I was glad I was in a church school. The chapel was the place to share such awful news. After the service, I walked around campus talking with students, listening to what they were thinking and feeling. Several students talked about where they had been and what they had thought when the Murrah Building was bombed. A tenth-grade girl came up to me.

"Mr. Mullin. Mrs. Creek sent me to find you. Your daughter in New York City called your office. She, her husband, and your grandchildren are all OK."

I made the sign of the cross in silent thanks.

In many ways, Casady was much like St. Albans: a day school committed to Episcopal education and offering a strong academic program, a vigorous athletic tradition, and a variety of extracurricular activities. Casady was larger, with a thousand students and twenty buildings. Of course, location matters, and Oklahoma City is a very different place than Washington, D.C. Moreover, Casady is the only independent school I know with a producing oil well on the campus.

The greatest difference, however, was that Casady had been coed since its founding. Every school where I had worked before had been only for boys, although two of them had coordinate relationships with a girls' school. In many ways the girls added greatly to Casady. In general, the girls were more conscientious and hard working than the boys. They were also easier to read; when they were happy they showed it, and when they were unhappy they also made it clear. At Casady, the girls had more athletic success than the boys. During my last year at Casady, there were three Casady graduates on the field at the same time when Yale played Virginia in field hockey.

However, girls did present some problems for which I was not prepared. My first year, a delegation of female swimmers came to see me to complain that the winter formal dance was the evening of the championship swim meet. I pointed out that the meet would be over in plenty of time to get to the dance. "But there won't be time to get our toes done," they howled.

As I look back on my four years at Casady, the thing I am proudest of was the introduction of a social learning requirement. Twenty years earlier I had introduced a similar requirement at St. Albans. I was surprised when I got to Casady to learn that it did not have a requirement. Many students worked in service to others without being required to do so. But it seemed to me to be wrong to call yourself a church school, where students have required chapel, and then allow students to graduate without ever having done anything for others.

Through her involvement in a community project, Martha found a wonderful woman, Carmen Clay, to direct the program. I asked her to visit with Bryan Leithauser who had directed the St. Albans social service program for twenty years. Within a few years, other schools were using the Casady social learning program as a model. What mattered most to me was the impact on individual students. I think of a student who came from a wealthy family. Although neither of his parents attended Casady, they were very generous to the school. They lived in a beautiful home, well maintained by professional workmen, and located in the richest section of Oklahoma City. Because of the social learning program, their son spent a day with classmates restoring the run-down home of a crippled woman in a depressed part of the city. They even built a ramp so that she did not have to struggle up the stairs. That student saw how the woman, because of poverty and her physical disability, could not help herself. For the first time in his life, he had the experience of working with tools to repair a house. Best of all, the young man himself, not his parents or their money, had made a significant difference in someone else's life.

I do, however, have sympathy for that student's lack of experience with tools. From the time I was born until we left Casady, I had never lived in a building that was not owned by an academic institution, the church, or the U.S. Army. There had always been a maintenance service. Others sensed that about me. When we were leaving Casady, all the coaches took us to eat at the oldest saloon in Oklahoma. They thanked me for my support and interest in Casady's sports teams and then presented me with a very fine tool kit. "From now on you are not going to have Randy to call." Randy, of course, was the head of Casady's maintenance department.

BLOOD RITES

The roads got smaller and smaller as we left Oklahoma City and moved onto the rolling plains. The last few hundred yards were a gravel lane. We parked where we saw other cars and walked down the dirt path. The first thing we saw was a large teepee. Beyond it was a rambling ranch house with a fenced pasture behind it. A little ravine ran near the house. Between it and the house a dozen tables awaited the celebration. We greeted some of the guests we knew, were introduced to others, and stood wondering what was to happen. We had never attended an American Indian wedding. We felt privileged to be among the one hundred or so guests. We knew the groom but had only met the bride once.

An American Indian beating a drum produces a steady, monotonous sound. As the sound becomes part of one, the effect can be almost hypnotic, deadening the senses to other sounds.

Two men appeared on the other side of the ravine. One was beating a drum. The other carried a large pipe. From time to time he puffed on it, and that produced a significant quantity of smoke.

The bride and groom came out of the teepee. They held hands as they walked across a small bridge over the ravine to join the two men. We guests watched from the house side of the ravine. The sound of the drum remained constant all during the ceremony. It neither increased nor decreased in tempo or volume.

The man with the pipe stood in front of the couple. He began to chant. Again the chant had a certain hypnotic effect, but it did vary in volume and tempo. From time to time he would cup the smoke from the pipe in his hand and pour it over the groom and then the bride. A little later, the groom cupped smoke, poured it over himself and then the bride. She repeated the gesture, first purifying herself and then purifying the groom.

The man with the pipe produced a knife and a rawhide thong. He made a small incision in the wrist of the groom. Then he made a similar cut in the bride's wrist. He tied their wrists together with the rawhide so that their blood intermingled.

When the couple had been untied, the groom invited all the guests to come forward and drink a small amount of cherry juice and eat a piece of buffalo meat. We formed a line in silence, crossed the ravine, and received the cherry juice and buffalo meat. Although the juice and meat have other meanings for American Indians, the similarity to lining up to receive bread and wine in a Christian church was obvious to all.

The drum stopped beating, and animated conversation began as we took our places at the tables for a wonderful barbeque dinner. There were, however, no toasts or speeches, and no alcohol was served.

We drove back to Oklahoma City at dusk. As we left the prairie and started passing shopping centers and car dealers, we felt very much that we had moved from one world into another.

Oklahoma City is in the middle of the state. In an attempt to get to know the state, we made it a point to spend at least one night in each of its four quadrants. When we went to the northeast quadrant, I was particularly eager to visit the Cherokee museum in Tahlequah. My great-great-great-great-grandmother was a full-blooded Cherokee with the lovely name of Spring Flower. We know that she married a white man named Alvin Dark, but we do not know the dates of her life. Therefore, we do not know if she walked the Trail of Tears. However, the fact that Spring Flower's descendents ended up in Arkansas, through which the Trail of Tears passed, may indicate some connection.

When gold was discovered in the Appalachians, the U.S. government rounded up the Cherokee in 1838 and placed them in guarded camps. Even though the Cherokee were then a peaceful tribe with a high rate of literacy, the government forced them to walk during the winter from North Carolina to the Indian Territory, which later became the State of Oklahoma. Because the Cherokee were compelled to leave land that had been theirs for centuries, and because so many died on the long march, it became known as the Trail of Tears. The museum in Tahlequah movingly tells that story.

When we arrived in Tahlequah, we saw posters advertising a gathering at the local college honoring the actor Tommy Lee Jones, who is part Cherokee. Unfortunately, it had been the night before we arrived. We were sorry that we had not known about it, for we would have liked to attend. He has always been one of Martha's favorite actors.

As we were visiting the museum, Martha and I separated because we like to view and read exhibits at our own pace. Suddenly, I realized that I could not find her. I looked in several exhibit halls. No Martha. Could she have gone outside? I walked to the entrance hall, and there she was. I asked where she had gone.

"Did you see him? Tommy Lee Jones came into the museum. So of course, I had to go into the ladies room to fix my hair."

The museum also has an outdoor exhibit showing the life of the Cherokee in the ancient days. Cherokee guides explain farming methods, home life, and hunting techniques. One of the guides gave a demonstration of a native bow and arrows. He told us that he had actually used them to hunt bear.

"Do you know how to be safe while you are hunting bear with a bow and arrow?" he asked. His audience had no suggestions.

"You make sure you have a hunting partner who cannot run as fast as you can!"

Europeans are fascinated by cowboys and American Indians because they have neither. Newman and Trevena Vincent are from a small town on the coast of Wales. They had spent a year at St. Albans on a Fulbright exchange during the 1980s. When they came to visit us in Oklahoma, we took them to the old town of Guthrie, thirty miles north of Oklahoma City. Many of the buildings in Guthrie are unchanged from 1907 when it was the first capital of Oklahoma. It did not remain the capital long. A group of men (including the grandfather of a Casady board member) removed the state seal at gunpoint and set it up in Oklahoma City.

We walked around Guthrie with our Welsh friends. As we were getting back in our car, men started walking down the street from both directions. Suddenly, shots rang out. Three men fell to the street.

We had not known that every Sunday afternoon there is a re-enactment of a cowboy shootout in downtown Guthrie. Happily, our friend from Wales got his video camera working in time to record the action and then be photographed himself with the "gunmen."

We also took Newman and Trevena to the Wichita National Wildlife Refuge in the southwestern part of the state. Buffalo roam freely there, but one can never be sure of seeing the herd because most of the area is not accessible by car. We saw no buffalo as we drove through most of the refuge to the picnic area we like. We ate our lunch and apologized that they would probably not get to see any buffalo. Just then a herd of dozens of buffalo came into the picnic ground. They moved slowly, certainly not a stampede. But a buffalo is a very large beast, and one does not argue with a herd. The Welshman got some great video shots as he (and all of us) stood on a picnic table while massive heads and humps passed just a foot or two on either side of us. His videos of cowboys and buffalo made a great hit in his little fishing village in Wales.

POLITICS

While we were in Oklahoma, Martha accepted an invitation to be a member of the State Board of Planned Parenthood. It is not a popular organization in Oklahoma. Its employees are trained to use caution when opening the mail. At one board meeting someone joked, "Well, all the liberals in Oklahoma are now gathered in one place."

Martha always emphasized that while Planned Parenthood was pro-choice, it actually worked hard to decrease the number of abortions. It hoped that by increasing the knowledge and availability of birth control, many women could be spared the painful choice of considering abortion.

At Martha's suggestion, I had the education director of Planned Parenthood speak to groups of ninth graders at Casady. He began by randomly distributing colored poker chips. Each student got four chips. He asked each student to trade one or two chips with the person on either side of them. Then he explained. "Each trade represents a sexual encounter. Those with a blue chip have a sexual disease. Those with a red chip are pregnant. Those with a black chip have contracted AIDS. Those with all green chips, of which there were more than any other, have had sex with no physical consequences." Of course, there was always at least one student who had a blue, red, and black chip.

Then he asked the students to trade chips two more times. This time, some students hid the color of the chips they were trading. Some, with all green chips, refused to trade at all. "Do you see how knowledge affects your behavior? It should."

One year, Martha hosted a party for donors to Planned Parenthood at our home. In May of our last year at Casady, she was asked to host a fund-raising party for a pro-choice candidate for lieutenant governor. The incumbent lieutenant governor, who was running for re-election, had a child at Casady. Martha agreed to host the party, but I asked her to confine it to our personal part of the house, not the more public "Casady Wing" that was attached to our house. About a week after the party, the chairman of the Casady Board called me. "Mark, the lieutenant governor has called me. She says that you had a fund-raiser for her opponent on campus. Is that so?"

Knowing that we were leaving for Virginia soon, I laughed and said, "Oh, tell her that you'll have me run off the campus right after graduation." Then I got serious. I explained that we had been careful to keep the party only in the part of the building where we actually lived, "But this does raise a difficult issue. If a headmaster or his wife takes any sort of political position they are sure to anger some members of the school community. On the other hand, if they never take any political position, what sort of example are they setting about the sort of citizens we want our students to become? It would be wrong if a headmaster used his position to propagandize students. But is there a way for a headmaster to set an example of being an active and concerned citizen?"

Of course, this could have been a problem while I was at St. Albans in a city as political as Washington. The only time I did take a political position while I was at St. Albans, other than voting, was to testify to a congressional committee in favor of regulation of handguns. In retrospect, I wonder if I should have set a better example to my students about involvement in important public issues.

BURIAL AT SEA

Four miles away, Point Loma, on the coast of southern California, was still visible but seemed quite distant. In every other direction nothing but the sea sparkled in the brilliant sunlight. In January of my third year at Casady, we stood on the deck of a large, ocean-going marine research vessel owned by the Scripps Institute of Oceanographic Research in La Jolla. It was the first time the Institute had allowed one of its major research vessels to be used for a private purpose. The ship was about 150 feet long and in the calm sea rode very steadily.

The captain turned the engines to idle when we reached the spot where my brother, Mike, had always taken his new graduate students to introduce them to the use of dragnets in research. My brother's unexpected death at age sixty-three had brought us there on this beautiful Sunday morning. I joined his widow, Connie, and his son Steve at the edge of the stern deck. Because nets are lowered into the ocean from the stern, we were only a foot or so above the water. Mike's other children,

Keith and Laura, and his granddaughter Alex stood close behind us. The other thirty guests, including Martha and our children, formed a semicircle around us.

I said some prayers, committing the ashes to the sea and Mike to eternal life in God. Steve held the old fishing knife that Mike had used since he and I fished together as boys in Wisconsin. Steve cut open the cardboard box. Connie poured the ashes into the sea. I had expected them to sink immediately, but they ballooned upward in a great green cloud just under the surface. The cloud slowly disappeared. I remember thinking how visually beautiful it was. Someone handed Connie a basket containing sprigs of flowers. Each guest took a sprig and threw it into the sea.

When the flowers were all gone, the captain revved up the powerful engines and turned back toward shore. For a while no one spoke. Almost everyone found someone to hug. Most stood quietly, with their arms around one another.

Later, on the trip back to port, people talked, and we got to know some of the other guests. The most interesting guest was from Japan. He and Mike had been friends and scientific colleagues for many years. He himself had done underwater research at considerable depths. He had also climbed some very high peaks in the Himalayas. When I pressed him, he admitted that he believed that no one had covered greater vertical distance on this planet than he had. After he heard of Mike's death he had flown from Tokyo to California just to be at this service. He returned to Japan the next day. His physical presence matched the messages of grief and sympathy that had come from scientists on every continent on earth, including Antarctica.

In my prayers that day, I prayed that Mike would have eternal life. What does that mean? For one thing, it means that his organic material became part of the ocean and thus a part of the food chain he spent his life studying. Certainly, it means that he will live in the lives of all of us who knew and loved him. It means that he will live in the scientific lives of those he taught. Some of them will, in turn, teach scientists who are yet unborn. While he was still alive, a species of marine copepod was named for him (a copepod is a tiny crustacean that is abundant in plankton and thus important to the food chain). Thus, his name will live as long as humans study the creatures of the sea. I, as a Christian, believe that he will live on in a real way in God's kingdom of love.

· 7 ·

The Return

THE WRISTWATCH

$\mathcal{M}$y brother's untimely death was one of several reasons that I decided that twenty-five years of being a headmaster were enough. In June of 2001, I told the Casady Board that the following academic year would be my last one. After the Class of 2002 graduated from Casady, we moved to Charlottesville, Virginia. We do not live far from Thomas Jefferson's "academical village," which has grown into the University of Virginia. That choice involved us in a process that was new for us. Except for the six months I had been on active duty with the U.S. Army and the four months we lived in a church-owned log cabin in Alaska, I had never lived in a building that was not owned by an academic institution. Even the apartment I lived in as a very young child was in a building owned by the University of Chicago. Moreover, I had never really had a choice of where I lived. My parents, my college and graduate schools, the army, and the headmasters of the boarding schools where I worked had the final say. Then for twenty-five years we lived in houses designated as the "Headmaster's Residence." I am sure that several real estate agents were surprised by how inexperienced a man in his early sixties could be about house hunting.

From the beginning, Martha and I decided we wanted to live in an academic town. We wanted to be near a college or university and knew that we could not afford a house with guest rooms in a large urban area. We looked at Hanover, New Hampshire, Santa Fe, New Mexico, and

Charlottesville, Virginia. We chose Charlottesville because of its proximity to so many people we care about and because we already knew the area from our time at the Blue Ridge School and the cabin we leased for seventeen years in Orange County.

We had hoped for an old charming Virginia house. However, the ones we looked at were either too expensive or in need of serious repairs. I had always lived in housing that had been maintained by a school. I was reminded of what my classmate, Chris Wadsworth, said when he gave up being a headmaster. "The scariest thing about retirement is that when Lori calls the Maintenance Department, I'll answer." And so we became the first occupants of a brand new house. I have hopes that its plumbing will last longer than mine.

What do I miss most now that I am not in schools? Being around young people. I find that whenever I am with high school or college age students, or even young adults, I am refreshed by their readiness for the new, their sense of humor, and their belief that so many possibilities are open to them. I am reminded of the old adage, "If you want to stay young, be around young people. If you want to die young, try to keep up with them."

One morning in late August of the year I left schoolwork, I saw, for the first time, a school bus pull up in front of the house across the street from us in Charlottesville. It was a bittersweet moment. I was looking forward to my new life, yet I was sorry that I would not be greeting the excited faces of young people ready to tackle the adventures of a new day.

Despite the problems school snow days had caused me, I was a little sad the first time the Charlottesville schools had a snow day. Instead of being a day to have a little more time with my family and to get caught up on neglected work, it was now just the same as any other day for me. The sense of it being a special gift was no longer there.

I believe that a good schoolman has to be a creature of the clock. Second period begins at 8:50 A.M., and you need to be ready to start your class. And you have to end it precisely at 9:35 or you will make your students late for third period. I had always tried to be punctual in my office. It bothered me if I kept people waiting more than five minutes. They had more important things to do than sit in my outer office waiting for me. It is not surprising that John Cleese's spoof of a British headmaster is entitled *Clockwise*. To counteract my own obsession with time, I almost never wear my watch now that I am not involved in school life. That way I do not look at it every five minutes.

Schools not only require punctuality, but also they impose a structure on everyone's time. Whether one is a teacher or a headmaster, one's day is structured and one's year is structured. One can only take vacations at certain times of the year. Now I have the flexibility to use my time as I choose. We have been able to travel at times of the year when we never could before. It has been particularly good to be able to visit Cara, King, and our granddaughters Raina and Sophie in New York City during the school year. Martha and I were in Paris during some of the time that Kevin was a writer-in-residence at the legendary Shakespeare and Company. In an apartment where Allen Ginsberg and other great poets have stayed, he was awakened each morning by the bells of Notre Dame.

I have also allowed myself flexibility in what writing I do. While this book has been a goal since I left schoolwork, I have felt free to set it aside from time to time for other projects. For example, when I got interested in sonnets for the first time in my life, I took time off from this book to write a narrative poem consisting of forty-seven sonnets. Having spent so much of my life being highly focused on particular goals, I find the new flexibility quite refreshing.

I still enjoy the pleasure of moving by leg power. These days I run slowly and thoughtfully, but I very much enjoy doing five or six miles along the bank of the Rivanna River near our home in Charlottesville, upstream from where Thomas Jefferson was born. I also relish having time to read more books and to read more widely. I have joined a reading group, which I had never done before. Of the eleven members, three are university professors, representing very divergent academic disciplines: architectural history, astronomy, and psychiatry. The other members are also interesting. They include the president of the Virginia Foundation for the Humanities, an oriental rug merchant, a horticulturist, and a man who has appeared in ads for the local fitness and health club.

A mile from our Charlottesville home, there is a hundred-year-old Episcopal church. It is made entirely of stone and has the feel of a lovely English country parish church. The second Sunday I attended it, another retired priest recognized me and told the rector that I was a priest and former canon of Washington Cathedral. The rector graciously asked me if I would like to take any services. "We have enough clergy in the parish that we do not need help. But if you would like to take a service from time to time, I would be glad to fit you in."

I thanked him for his kindness but declined. "I just want to come and worship." All those years in schools, I had had to think about what I was going to say in my talks to students. And if I were not preaching, I kept an eye on how the kids were behaving. Now, I wanted to be able to focus on God when I was in church.

I have celebrated several weddings and baptisms for relatives and friends, but Sunday mornings I am just one more member of the congregation. I also appreciate that I have more time for private prayer now that I do not have administrative or pastoral responsibilities for a school community.

During our second year in Charlottesville, I was pleased to receive a call from Roger Bowen. He had been a very effective chaplain at St. Albans during the 1980s. He then went on to administrative work at other schools.

Roger believed in helping those in need. He served two separate terms in the Peace Corps. While he was at St. Albans he took students to help the poor of Haiti.

Roger called to ask if I would be the speaker at his first graduation as headmaster of St. Stephen's School, in Austin, Texas. I was thrilled to share that service with a former colleague who was a brother priest, headmaster, and friend.

I feel very blessed to have spent my professional life in schools. For twenty-five years, I loved the challenges and opportunities of leading a school. Now I find I also enjoy a new life away from schools. Best of all has been having more time with Martha. A young man does not get to spend enough time with the girl he loves. One of the rewards of reaching a certain age is to have that time.

GHOSTS

My parents left Mt. Carroll, Illinois, in 1968. I only returned to that small town twice after that. The first time was in 1983. By then Shimer College had closed, although it was resurrected later in a Chicago suburb. It was strange and sad to wander the Mt. Carroll campus of Shimer. Here I had lived for four years, those high school years that are so important. Now it was deserted, almost haunted.

Martha and I had come back to Mt. Carroll for my twenty-fifth high school reunion. My classmates were now about the same age their parents had been when we were in high school. Not surprisingly, many of my classmates now resembled their parents. Several said to me, "You seem just like your father."

It was not just genetics that produced that sense of continuity. Perhaps it is small town life. When I was in high school, Mr. Eaton was the wise old lawyer in town. Mr. Weismiller was the young go-getter lawyer. They had no blood relationship. The afternoon before my twenty-fifth reunion, Martha and I were walking down the main street of Mt. Carroll. Across the street I saw Mr. Eaton. I was surprised at how good he looked all these years later. I called to him, "Mr. Eaton. It's Mark Mullin. Great to see you."

We crossed the street to him, and he said, "I am not Ralph Eaton. I am Bob Weismiller." He had become the wise old lawyer in Mt. Carroll.

In 1992, we were driving back from California with fourteen-year-old Kevin and decided to take a short detour to show him the small town where I had gone to high school. We got a room in the only motel and had supper. Later that evening we decided that we wanted another snack. At that hour, the only places open were a bar and a small coffee shop. We chose the coffee shop. It had tables and a counter with stools. On one stool sat an unshaven, overweight, slovenly dressed man. Even a stranger could tell that he probably occupied that same stool every night, drinking his coffee. He turned around and looked at us. Kevin jumped when the man said, "Mark Mullin?" He had been a year ahead of me in high school, never left Mt. Carroll, and worked as a day laborer. We talked with him as we ate our ice cream. He spoke of people who had stayed in Mt. Carroll. Frank Tipton, my barber, had died. Now my classmate, Don Slick, was the town's barber. Judy McDearmon, the redhead with whom I broke the Prom date, had married another classmate, Gene Moshure. Their children had been good athletes at Mt. Carroll High School but had now all graduated. Randy Smith, a strong runner on the track team with me, was operating his father's lumberyard. Then the man on the stool said, "You know, the place hasn't changed much. It's still the same." As we drove out of Mt. Carroll the next morning, Kevin said he had gotten a sense of what life was like in a small Midwestern town in the 1950s.

Every time I have returned to St. Albans, it has been in my capacity as a priest. The first time was in 2004, when Fred Towers got married at St. Albans. Fred had been in the Class of 1951. His son had been in the Class of 1979. The son died in an automobile accident two months after he graduated. Fred served two years as chairman of the St. Albans Board. Martha and I were close to Fred and his wife Kay. Some years after Kay died, Fred was ready to marry a fine woman from Maine. We were invited to the wedding but had not yet decided if we would attend. Then Will Billow called us. "I'm doing Fred's wedding in the Little Sanctuary. It would mean a lot to Fred if you would take part in the service. And he would be thrilled if you would preach."

I felt a little nervous about returning but knew that this would be a wedding not a regular service. At the beginning of my sermon, I apologized that I could only tell Fred stories because I did not know the bride. I did tell a few stories about him but then spoke of what a good occasion this was. Both bride and groom had known the great pain of loss, but now they were proclaiming the triumph of love. It was good to be back in the Little Sanctuary again sharing a service with Will.

Months later, Will invited me to preach on a Sunday evening for the Epiphany series. At first I thought that I did not want to do it. I knew that going back for something other than a wedding would be painful. But then I thought, "I am a priest and a priest has asked me to preach. I should not refuse him."

I have rarely felt such conflicting emotions as I did just before that service. The pain of eight years before came back. Yet I felt good about preparing to preach in a place that had meant so much to me. As I walked to the altar, the pain was replaced with joy. I saw the faces of colleagues, friends, and people with whom my family and I had shared so much of our lives. The Little Sanctuary was full.

Assuming there would be many teachers there, I stressed the power of example to influence others. I spoke of our late colleague, Vaughn Keith, and the example he set when he contracted AIDS. After the service, I walked into the Common Room of the Lane-Johnston Building. It is in the center of St. Albans's oldest building. I looked up at my portrait that hung with the portraits of other former St. Albans headmasters. It was the first time I had seen it. The painting depicts me in my role as a teacher. I am standing in front of a blackboard, apparently listening to the answer being given by a student in class. There is a piece of chalk in my right hand. In my handwriting on the blackboard are the words "agape" and "hessed." They are the English transliterations of the Greek and Hebrew words for love. I thought it was a good likeness of me. Most of all, I was pleased that, of all the responsibilities a headmaster has, it was as an educator that I was portrayed.

The service also gave Martha and me a chance to visit with so many friends we had not seen in years. I was particularly glad to see Leonard and Carol Steuart. Leonard was the first chairman of the Governing Board who served a full two-year term while I was at St. Albans. Frank Jones had been halfway through his term as chairman when I came to Washington. Among other friends was Jed Lyons, president of the Rowman & Littlefield Publishing Group. When he asked Martha what I was doing with my time, she told him that I had been writing down stories from my years in schools. Sadly, four times in the first half of 2007, I returned to participate in memorial services for members of the St. Albans School family.

In the fall of 2005, we received an invitation to attend the rededication of the Seymour St. John Chapel at Choate. Seymour had given me my first job at an independent school. He had also set an example for me of a caring headmaster. Martha and I had not seen Seymour in many years and knew that this would probably be our last chance to see him, since he was well into his nineties. Moreover, the Choate Chapel was where I was ordained to the priesthood.

We arrived early at the chapel just as Seymour did. He was in a wheelchair but had the same old sparkle in his eyes. It was great to be able to greet him before all the activity began. During the service, we enjoyed hearing the many nice things said about Seymour. I was particularly touched by the moving statements from his adult children about what it was like to grow up as a headmaster's child.

When the service ended, we decided to skip the reception because we had already had a chance to talk with Seymour. Instead, we walked up to Hill House where we had lived our first year at Choate and where I had an office when I was a dean. Outside the deans' offices were two walls of photographs, each one eight by ten inches. They were of faculty members who had worked at Choate for twenty years or longer. We knew many of them because some part of their career had overlapped our time at Choate. Some were now dead, some retired, and some still teaching at Choate.

These were the men and women with whom I had taught, coached, and lived when I was a young man at the start of my teaching career. Now my school career was over. Thirty-seven years had passed since I first met them. Their faces, so familiar yet so distant, looked down at me from the wall.

They brought to mind other faces, students and teachers, from the schools I had attended and the schools where I had taught or been a headmaster. To my mind's eye came young faces and mature faces, faces I had not seen in years, faces that I still see from time to time, faces I will never see again, faces from all those years in schools.

As I stood in that Choate hallway looking at those faces, I remembered the last paragraph of *Mutiny on the Bounty*. After the mutiny, Midshipman Roger Byam is set ashore on Tahiti. He marries a Tahitian girl, and they have a daughter. Then a British ship arrives in Tahiti. Byam, but not his family, is forcefully taken back to England. Eventually, he rejoins the British navy and rises as an officer. Twenty years after the mutiny, a ship Byam is commanding puts in to Tahiti for food and water. He goes ashore and learns that his Tahitian wife is dead. Someone points out his grown daughter to him. He does not identify himself to her, knowing that he will soon have to sail away again. "The moon was bright overhead when I reembarked in the pinnace to return to my ship. A chill night breeze came whispering down from the depths of the valley, and suddenly the place was full of ghosts,—shadows of men alive and dead,—my own among them."

TORCHES

Being back at Choate in 2005 reminded me that a teacher never knows when or where his words or actions will reappear. Seymour St. John was headmaster of Choate from 1947 to 1973. He directly succeeded his father, George St. John, who served as headmaster for thirty-nine years. George was fond of saying, "Ask not what your school can do for you, but what you can do for your school." President John F. Kennedy (a 1935 graduate of Choate) reworked those words for the next to last paragraph of his inaugural address in 1960. George St. John lived long enough to know that "ask not what your country can do for you, but what you can do for your country" became the most famous and remembered words of John F. Kennedy.

Kennedy began his inaugural address with a theme of change. "Let the word go forth from this time and place, to friend and foe alike, that the torch has been passed to a new generation of Americans." Those words have always resonated with me. Any teacher should respond to the image of passing torches, for that is what teachers do. Perhaps the words mean even more to a schoolman who was once a serious runner. Every four years a torch is passed from runner to runner from Mt. Olympus to the new site of the Olympic games.

One of the great joys of being a teacher is watching the torch be picked up by succeeding generations. To see one's students become adults, assume positions of responsibility, contribute to the welfare of others, and start their own families is one of the great rewards of being a teacher. I have been proud of the accomplishments of so many of my students. Of course, it is nice when one of them gets national recognition, but I am even more pleased when one chooses to spend his life helping other people. There is a special personal thrill for me when one of them becomes a teacher or a clergyman. At least twelve of my former students have returned to teach or coach at St. Albans. Several of them stand out in my memory.

Wayne Williams came to St. Albans as a scholarship student. A couple of years after he graduated from college, he came to see me. "Mr. Grant suggested I talk with you. I am thinking about going into the ministry. But I am not certain. I am trying to figure out what I should do while I think about it."

"Well, Wayne. I think teaching is just as much a ministry as being a clergyman. After all, Jesus is frequently addressed in the Bible as 'Rabbi,' which means teacher."

"That might be a good thing to do for a few years while I think about the ministry. How would I go about looking for a teaching job?"

"Would you be interested in teaching in the St. Albans Lower School? I know we will have an opening there next year."

I was proud when Wayne began teaching at St. Albans and soon proved himself a worthy role model for his students. I was also delighted when he became the youngest person elected to the Governing Board of St. Albans. It is a rewarding passing of the torch when a headmaster has a board member who is his former student.

John Sharon was not an outstanding athlete at St. Albans. In fact, his varsity athletic career lasted less than ten minutes. John was born with severe physical limitations. In order to walk, he had to have metal braces on his legs. When he wanted to sit down, he had to reach down and unlock them, so that they would bend as his legs did. His hands were also deformed. Although he could perform some functions with them, he had trouble gripping objects of any size. He could not even hold a drinking glass. He drank by taking the edge of the glass in his teeth and tipping his head way back to let the liquid flow into his mouth. However, he liked athletics. He served as an announcer for varsity football games and as a manager for the varsity soccer team. Finally, in his senior year, he talked the coach into putting him into a varsity soccer game. It scared me. He had no way to protect himself if a hard kick sent the ball toward him. He could not move quickly out of the way because of the braces on his legs, and his withered arms would have provided little protection from a fast moving soccer ball. Yet the look of pride on John's face when he did leave the field made the risk worth it.

Playing in a varsity soccer game at St. Albans was typical of John. His attitude was, "I may not have the physical abilities of some other people. But I am not handicapped. I am going to try to do everything I can." Not surprisingly, he asked the headmaster's wife to dance with him at the spring Prom.

When John graduated from Connecticut College he returned to St. Albans as a teacher. His sense of humor and quick wit made him a success in the classroom. The example he set of courage in adversity was of inestimable value. After John had taught at St. Albans for several years he told me, "I am going to look at some other schools. I went to St. Albans for nine years and then returned to teach here. I've loved it, but if I am going to grow, I need to experience some other schools." It was typical of John's attitude toward life.

I last saw John at the National Association of Independent Schools meeting in Boston in 2001. He was married and was heading the Lower School division of a good independent school.

Two members of my first graduating class at St. Albans gave me a great thrill after we had moved to Charlottesville and I was no longer in schoolwork. Tom Goodrich was my first senior prefect. He did so much that year to help me when I was a new headmaster that I was immensely grateful. While he was a student at the University of Virginia he came up to the cabin we leased north of Charlottesville to spend a weekend with us. He brought with him a guitar that he was just learning to play. Some years later he became part of one of the most popular musical groups on East Coast campuses, Speidel, Goodrich, Goggin & Lille. Although its members all have other careers now, they still play annually at the Barns of Wolf Trap. Tom taught for some years in boarding schools and then entered the Presbyterian ministry.

Tom's St. Albans classmate, Jamie Evans had a book published while he was still in college. It was called *An Uncommon Gift* and tells of how his struggle with dyslexia in a school as demanding as St. Albans taught him the values of perseverance and hard work.

Jamie was ordained in the Presbyterian Church. Before he went to a parish, I persuaded him to return to St. Albans to teach. "So many people go into teaching because they found school easy and therefore they liked it. Those students who are struggling need someone like you as a role model to show them that if they work hard they can succeed."

Jamie taught in the Lower School. He became particularly famous for his chapel talks that were always popular and always began, "It was a dark and stormy night." Jamie taught at St. Albans for several years and then went to California to serve in a parish.

At the start of our second year in Charlottesville, Martha and I attended the installation of Tom Goodrich as pastor of Meadows Presbyterian Church, which is a couple of miles north of the University of Virginia campus. The preacher at the installation was his St. Albans classmate, Jamie Evans. All clergy present were invited to come forward and join in the laying on of hands. How thrilled I was to join Jamie in putting our hands on Tom's head.

Of course the most important torches any of us pass are to our children. Our daughter, Cara, used the coordinate relationship between National Cathedral School and St. Albans to take Paul Piazza's expository writing course. Paul was the chairman of the English Department and had learned the art of teaching writing from the St. Albans legend, Ferdinand Ruge. Paul carried on Ruge's tradition brilliantly. He showed his students how to write, and rewrite, and rewrite until their writing contained what he wanted: "clear, concise, grammatically correct, reasonably graceful sentences." Cara Mullin was the beneficiary of Paul's teaching, as were hundreds of St. Albans graduates.

When Cara was right out of college, she was doing an unpaid internship with a public relations firm. The firm did some work for a Ritz-Carlton Hotel. Her writing came to the attention of the Ritz-Carlton Hotel management, and she became the director of public relations at a Ritz-Carlton Hotel a month after her twenty-third birthday. I gave Paul Piazza a bottle of champagne in thanks.

When she and King Milling got married they moved to New Orleans, where he had grown up. Cara applied for a job with the Development Office of Tulane University Medical School. I reminded her that when she was twelve years old she was helping with the serving at a dinner party we were giving in our home for St. Albans people. I remember freezing as I watched in horror while Cara spilled a bowl of hot cream soup on the silk dress of a $100,000 donor. I told Cara to tell the people at Tulane that as a twelve-year-old she handled that situation so well that, years later, the donor gave a bridal shower for Cara. She got the job.

I realized the torch had been passed when, after she had worked at Tulane for a year, Cara asked me about the St. Albans Capital Campaign. "Oh, it's going well. We've just passed $10,000,000."

"That's good, Dad. We've just hit $85,000,000 toward our $100,000,000 goal."

That fund-raising torch appears to have been passed on to yet another generation. By selling lemonade on a street corner near their home in New York City, Cara's daughters, Raina and Sophie Milling, raised $1,800 for relief for New Orleans victims of Hurricane Katrina. They were nine and seven years old at the time.

Charlottesville is only two hours from Washington, and so Martha and I have made a number of trips there to see friends. We have gone to Washington for other reasons also. One day, we joined our sons, Sean and Kevin, on the Mall. With thousands of other Americans, we marched from the Washington Monument past the White House. We were asking our government not to start a preemptive war. Four days later, the United States invaded Iraq.

In 2005 Martha and I went to Arlington Cemetery outside of Washington to see the exhibit "Faces of the Fallen." Artists from around the United States contributed portraits of each of the more than thirteen hundred American service men and women who had died in the Afghanistan and Iraq wars before November 11, 2004. Our son Kevin was chosen to paint four of the portraits. While I was proud to march with our sons in opposition to our government's war policies, I was also proud that Kevin was a part of honoring those who had been killed.

On another trip to Washington, we sat in a classroom observing a teacher at Cesar Chavez Charter School at Thirteenth and R Streets in the Shaw section of the city. The parents of almost all the students had received no college education. Many of the parents were not high school graduates.

I always like to see good teaching. I was impressed by the way this teacher at Cesar Chavez engaged these young people in a vigorous discussion of literature. They were articulate and involved. The teacher was skilled at getting them to trade ideas and to challenge each other. I knew that earlier in his career the teacher had received an outstanding teacher award at an independent school. While teaching at another independent school he had been elected by the senior class to give the graduation address. It was wonderful to see that he was able to work the same magic in a classroom full of students from disadvantaged backgrounds. Of course, my great pride was that the teacher was our son Sean. He is the fourth generation of Mullins to be an educator.

What joy there is for Martha and me to see the torches being carried by the next generation. It makes the running all worthwhile.

Acknowledgments

$\mathscr{I}$t is important to note that when I use only a first name of a student, it may be a pseudonym.

Although track is often called an "individual sport," my coach Bill McCurdy always stressed that being part of a team is more important than individual success. Certainly, any great school is a community in which students, teachers, staff, alumni, and parents all contribute. While writing is in many ways a solitary activity, many people have helped make this a better book. I am particularly grateful to four of them. The professional expertise of James E. Lyons, Brendan V. Sullivan Jr., and Wayne C. Thompson greatly strengthened the text. The creativity and vision of Kev Mullin did so much to hone my writing.

I am also thankful to those who have read all or part of this manuscript and made thoughtful and perceptive suggestions: Will Billow, Nancy Frye, Catherine Lowe, Cara Milling, Martha Mullin, Sean Mullin, Bruce Sanford, and Susie Thompson. I found, as I did when I wrote *Educating for the 21st Century* fifteen years ago, that the editors at the Rowman & Littlefield Publishing Group are talented and thorough.

I am grateful to Donna Denize and Dennis Stiles for permission to use their poems. I have tried to locate Margaret Meyers to ask her permission to use the poem she wrote for me but have been unable to find her. I thank her for the poem. I also appreciate receiving permission from St. Albans School, Choate Rosemary Hall, and Harvard University to reproduce their photographs.

I am thankful that my children, Cara, Sean, and Kevin, survived the double whammy of being clergy kids and the headmaster's children to become fine adults. Most of all, I am thankful to Martha who has shared all my years of working in schools, given so much of herself to those schools, and filled my life with love. Finally, my thanks to all the people I have known in schools while I was a student, a teacher, and a headmaster. Many are mentioned in this book. Even more are not. I am sorry I could not write about them all. I am grateful to all those I have known for being part of what has been for me a priceless gift: the life I was called to run.